Robert Browning:
The Poems

ANALYSING TEXTS

General Editor: Nicholas Marsh

Published

Jane Austen: The Novels   *Nicholas Marsh*
Aphra Behn: The Comedies   *Kate Aughterson*
William Blake: The Poems   *Nicholas Marsh*
Charlotte Brontë: The Novels   *Mike Edwards*
Emily Brontë: Wuthering Heights   *Nicholas Marsh*
Robert Browning: The Poems   *John Blades*
Chaucer: The Canterbury Tales   *Gail Ashton*
Daniel Defoe: The Novels   *Nicholas Marsh*
Charles Dickens: David Copperfield/Great Expectations   *Nicolas Tredell*
Charles Dickens: Hard Times/Bleak House   *Nicholas Marsh*
John Donne: The Poems   *Joe Nutt*
George Eliot: The Novels   *Mike Edwards*
F. Scott Fitzgerald: The Great Gatsby/Tender is the Night   *Nicolas Tredell*
E. M. Forster: The Novels   *Mike Edwards*
Thomas Hardy: The Novels   *Norman Page*
Thomas Hardy: The Poems   *Gillian Steinberg*
John Keats: The Poems   *John Blades*
Charles Dickens: Hard Times/Bleak House   *Nicholas Marsh*
Philip Larkin: The Poems   *Nicholas Marsh*
D. H. Lawrence: The Novels   *Nicholas Marsh*
Marlowe: The Plays   *Stevie Simkin*
John Milton: Paradise Lost   *Mike Edwards*
Shakespeare: The Comedies   *R. P. Draper*
Shakespeare: The Histories   *John Blades*
Shakespeare: The Late Plays   *Kate Aughterson*
Shakespeare: The Sonnets   *John Blades*
Shakespeare: The Tragedies   *Nicholas Marsh*
Shakespeare: Three Problem Plays   *Nicholas Marsh*
Mary Shelley: Frankenstein   *Nicholas Marsh*
Webster: The Tragedies   *Kate Aughterson*
Virginia Woolf: The Novels   *Nicholas Marsh*
Wordsworth and Coleridge: Lyrical Ballads   *John Blades*

Analysing Texts
Series Standing Order ISBN 978-0-333-73260-1
(outside North America only)

You can receive future titles in this series as they are published by placing a standing order. Please contact your bookseller or, in the case of difficulty, write to us at the address below with your name and address, the title of the series and the ISBN quoted above.

Customer Services Department, Macmillan Distribution Ltd, Houndmills, Basingstoke, Hampshire. RG21 6XS, UK

Robert Browning: The Poems

JOHN BLADES

 palgrave

© John Blades 2018

All rights reserved. No reproduction, copy or transmission of this publication may be made without written permission.

No portion of this publication may be reproduced, copied or transmitted save with written permission or in accordance with the provisions of the Copyright, Designs and Patents Act 1988, or under the terms of any licence permitting limited copying issued by the Copyright Licensing Agency, Saffron House, 6–10 Kirby Street, London EC1N 8TS.

Any person who does any unauthorized act in relation to this publication may be liable to criminal prosecution and civil claims for damages.

The author has asserted his right to be identified as the author of this work in accordance with the Copyright, Designs and Patents Act 1988.

First published 2018 by
PALGRAVE

Palgrave in the UK is an imprint of Macmillan Publishers Limited, registered in England, company number 785998, of 4 Crinan Street, London, N1 9XW.

Palgrave® and Macmillan® are registered trademarks in the United States, the United Kingdom, Europe and other countries.

ISBN 978–1–137–41474–8 hardback
ISBN 978–1–137–41473–1 paperback

This book is printed on paper suitable for recycling and made from fully managed and sustained forest sources. Logging, pulping and manufacturing processes are expected to conform to the environmental regulations of the country of origin.

A catalogue record for this book is available from the British Library.

A catalog record for this book is available from the Library of Congress.

For
Giuseppe Cambise
di
Varagine

Contents

General Editor's Preface	x
Introduction	xi

PART 1 ANALYSING BROWNING'S POETRY   1

1 Sex, Murder and the Construction of Identity   3
    'My Last Duchess'   4
      Commentary   17
    'Porphyria's Lover'   23
      Commentary   34
    'The Laboratory'   37
      Commentary   45
    Conclusions   49
    Methods of analysis   50
    Suggested work   51

2 Missions, Silence and Exile   52
    'Childe Roland to the Dark Tower Came'   53
      Commentary   67
    'The Patriot'   70
      Commentary   79
    'The Lost Leader'   82
      Commentary   93
    Conclusions   94
    Methods of analysis   95
    Suggested work   96

3 Reach and Grasp: Two Artists   97
    'Andrea del Sarto (Called "The Faultless Painter")'   98
      Commentary   115
    'Fra Lippo Lippi'   117
      Commentary   137

	Conclusions	138
	Methods of analysis	139
	Suggested work	140
4	**Religion – Fears and Scruples**	**141**
	Introduction	141
	'The Bishop Orders His Tomb at Saint Praxed's Church' *Rome, 15—*	143
	Commentary	150
	'Bishop Blougram's Apology'	153
	Commentary	162
	'Caliban Upon Setebos; or, Natural Theology in the Island'	168
	Commentary	177
	Conclusions	184
	Methods of analysis	185
	Suggested work	186

PART 2 THE CONTEXT AND THE CRITICS   187

5	**Browning's Life and Work**	**189**
	1812–1832 Browning's early life	189
	1833–1844 Browning's early career	193
	1845–1846 Elizabeth Barrett	194
	1846–1855 Italy	196
	1856–1889 The death of Elizabeth, and Browning's later career	197
6	**The Context of Browning's Poetry**	**200**
	Romanticism	200
	The Victorian literary scene	202
	Three Victorian poets	204
	Browning's Views on poetry	210
7	**A Sample of Critical Views**	**214**
	G. K. Chesterton, *Robert Browning* (1903)	217
	Robert Langbaum, *The Poetry of Experience: The Dramatic Monologue in Modern Literary Tradition* (1957; second edition 1985)	223

Barbara Melchiori: *Browning's Poetry of Reticence* (1968)   227
E. Warwick Slinn, *Browning and the Fictions of
Identity* (1982)   230
Britta Martens, *Browning, Victorian Poets and the Romantic
Legacy: Challenging the Personal Voice* (2011)   234

Glossary of Literary Terms   238

Further Reading   241

Index   245

General Editor's Preface

This series is dedicated to one clear belief: that we can all enjoy, understand and analyse literature for ourselves, provided we know how to do it. How can we build on close understanding of a short passage, and develop our insight into the whole work? What features do we expect to find in a text? Why do we study style in so much detail? In demystifying the study of literature, these are only some of the questions the *Analysing Texts* series addresses and answers.

The books in this series will not do all the work for you, but will provide you with the tools, and show you how to use them. Here, you will find samples of close, detailed analysis, with an explanation of the analytical techniques utilised. At the end of each chapter there are useful suggestions for further work you can do to practise, develop and hone the skills demonstrated and build confidence in your own analytical ability.

An author's individuality shows in the way they write: every work they produce bears the hallmark of that writer's personal 'style'. In the main part of each book we concentrate therefore on analysing the particular flavour and concerns of one author's work, and explain the features of their writing in connection with major themes. In Part II there are chapters about the author's life and work, assessing their contribution to developments in literature; and a sample of critics' views are summarised and discussed in comparison with each other.

Some suggestions for further reading provide a bridge towards further critical research.

Analysing Texts is designed to stimulate and encourage your critical and analytic faculty, to develop your personal insight into the author's work and individual style, and to provide you with the skills and techniques to enjoy at first hand the excitement of discovering the richness of the text.

николай Marsh

NICHOLAS MARSH

Introduction

In a letter of 1883 to a female friend who had enquired about some of his poems, Robert Browning wrote in his typically self-effacing way:

> If you would - when you please to give them your attention ... I cannot but think you would find little difficulty ...

And it is true that Browning's poems are not, on the whole, difficult to get into, but it is also true that, once 'in', each one of them benefits immeasurably from detailed analysis, bringing them alive in exciting ways that perhaps their creator himself may not have been fully aware of.

The aim of this book is to introduce readers to some of the best poetry of Robert Browning. In each of the four chapters of Part 1 the approach is to study in detail extracts from a selection of poems, chosen according to their themes. Browning's popular poetry is already widely known through anthologies and poetry workshops in school, which often start with old favourites such as 'The Pied Piper of Hamelin', 'How they Brought the Good News from Ghent to Aix' and 'Home Thoughts from Abroad'.

With this in mind, the poems I have selected here are those which most frequently appear on examination papers. Not unnaturally, these turn out to be some of Browning's more challenging and stimulating verse, highly rewarding works in terms of technique and themes, dealing with sex, violence, personal quests, art and religion. The poems chosen are also those most likely to be included in popular editions of his work, such as those published by Penguin, Longman and Norton (details of which can be found in the 'Further Reading' section at the end). Your enjoyment and understanding of Browning will of course benefit immensely if, after studying the poems here, you read the poet's work more broadly, and there are suggestions for further analysis in each of Part 1's chapters.

The general approach adopted in this study is to select important extracts from Browning's poems in order to subject them to close, detailed examination employing a range of analytical methods. This investigation is then broadened by a 'Commentary' that explores the wider context of each extract, with the object of applying our textual analysis to the poem as a whole, to bring out connections with other relevant writings of Browning, or to locate the work in the relevant circumstances of its period.

The object of our textual analysis is to demonstrate how a reader can examine the details of a poem, but more importantly, to encourage a reader to develop his or her own individual readings or interpretations of the text. It is valuable to remember that literary texts are 'open' in the sense that they permit a variety of responses to them, even seemingly opposing ones. The crucial point is that interpretations should always be referenced carefully to the words as used in the text. After each analysis, it is always good practice to read the whole poem through again ... and again.

In addition to 'what' Browning writes, his poetic techniques are equally exciting and innovative, and it is these too that marked his work out from the vast body of Victorian verse. Our analysis will take full account of these, including the poet's daring use of what is called the 'dramatic monologue', a device in which the reader is placed inside the mind of a character so we directly experience their telling of their own story.

The dramatic monologue was not an entirely new device in the nineteenth century, but Browning developed it in his own, unique style to explore bold new areas of adult experience as well as psychology and as an experimental means of approaching traditional ideas and narratives.

Browning's verse began to appear shortly after the great Romantic period of Wordsworth, Coleridge, Keats and Byron, and he is the heir to their revolutionary poetics. He adopts the special vision and language of some of these poets yet puts his own unique twist on them through a special use of irony and satire. All of these elements are explored through deep analysis of the selected poems.

The poems discussed here cover a broad spectrum of human emotions, mental states, and relationships, and involve an exotic range of fascinating people: lovers, a couple of murderers, art collectors and art makers, philanderers, bishops, thieves, a poisoner, a man who awaits the gallows, and a man who dreams of witches, sorcerers and storm-gods. It is an amazing array of characters. The poems teem with impersonators, dreamers, schemers, and ventriloquists, nightmares, reveries, horrors, deceptions and cheats. It is most definitely a side of Browning that is not often recognised.

Part 2 of the book, 'The Context and the Critics', considers Browning in the context of his remarkable life and period. Even someone who has not yet read the poetry is still likely to have encountered the celebrated story of Browning's relationship, elopement and marriage to Elizabeth Barrett, herself a very successful poet in her own right and one who had a crucial impact on Robert's poetic career, not least as his deepest inspiration and sternest critic. Chapter 6 enlarges the context to give an impression of Victorian culture and verse, with a brief survey of Browning's contemporaries in poetry and ideas. If you are new to the study of Browning's work, then Chapters 5 and 6 are a good place to start by way of an introduction.

Chapter 7 outlines the critical reception of Browning's verse in his own day and discusses in detail a sample of writings from five important critics. The chapter discusses these in depth in order to suggest something of the broad range of different critical responses available to a reader.

As with any critical study, I have used a range of technical terms, most of which will be familiar to literary students but, just in case, a glossary of these is included at the end. Those whose appetite for technical terms is not satiated by the glossary may like to consult *The Penguin Dictionary of Literary Terms and Literary Theory*, edited by J. A. Cuddon and M. A. R. Habib (2014) or *Literary Terms and Criticism* (3rd Edition) by John Peck and Martin Coyle (Palgrave Macmillan, 2002). A good internet resource for such terms is the Cambridge University website www.english.cam.ac.uk.classroom/terms.

I would like to record my gratitude for the valuable support received from my editors, Rachel Bridgewater and Nicholas Marsh, and for generous assistance from Giuseppe Cambise, John Cule, George Wilson and Jessica Frew. However, I take exclusive responsibility for any errors or omissions that may have crept in.

PART 1

ANALYSING BROWNING'S POETRY

1
Sex, Murder and the Construction of Identity

In this chapter we will be examining extracts from three of Robert Browning's poems taken from different stages in his writing life, primarily in order to investigate how he develops the identities of his characters, especially in terms of their gender. These are

'My Last Duchess'
'Porphyria's Lover'
'The Laboratory'

The chapter also sets out to show different attitudes to sex in these poems and the part it plays in impelling the lives of the principal characters, each of whom is involved in some way in a murder. In particular we will try to bring out the ways in which Browning focuses on the psychology of his characters, what motivates them, how it drives them to extremes of action and how they respond to these actions.

Above all, the chapter will try to demonstrate the role of Browning's highly original techniques and approaches. Browning had failed in his early determination to write successful plays for the commercial theatre, but in dedicating himself to a career of poetry he applied some of the important methods of the stage to his new arena, methods that proved both revolutionary and controversial, and whose effects are still seminal in the literature of today.

'My Last Duchess'

Our first poem, 'My Last Duchess', is an important, highly sophisticated poem in which Browning's trademark irony plays a crucial part. At the centre of its sophistication lies a double perspective, the one standing inside the speech, narrating, and the other detached, observing and assessing. It is this double perspective that gives the poem its multiple ironies and much of its great appeal.

'My Last Duchess' is Browning's first stab at portraying characters of Renaissance Italy – which provides the setting for so many of the characters in the 1855 volume *Men and Women*. The poem first appeared in 1842 and seems to have grown out of sketches Browning had made fifteen years earlier for his long poetic narrative *Sordello*. 'My Last Duchess' marks Browning's radical departure from his old manner as he begins to achieve the critical success and popularity that had eluded his earlier work. At the heart of this success is the technique of the 'dramatic monologue' which Browning brought to perfection, and for many readers 'My Last Duchess' is the ultimate consummation of this form (we will discuss the many features of the dramatic monologue as we explore those poems embodying it, but you may like to check the Glossary for a summary of its key elements).

In this poem, as in so many of Browning's, we come to something like an understanding of the poem's circumstances only at the end of its monologue, and even then we are likely to feel that this is merely partial (in both senses of the word). Reading this breathtakingly enigmatic poem, we are located in the position of an outsider, an eavesdropper, come to the table late. We come by information piecemeal, obliquely, and the poem is riddled by many silences or lacunae, so that we are repeatedly constrained to join up the dots and make connections as we strive to see the situation from within (a striving which is repeatedly thwarted).

The poem's details are often understated or entirely omitted, with the result that the reader quickly becomes an active participant in a text which is very much concerned with reading and watching (the two men watch the duchess watching them, as the duke had watched her, and 'her looks went everywhere'). We watch the watchers.

For the reasons behind this, we need look no further than the nature of the monologue – the speaker of a monologue has no obligation to explain things to himself. Yet, on the other hand, the role of the Count's envoy is a superb technical device in the poem, working to situate us naturally inside the monologue: the duke simultaneously enrols both ourselves and the envoy into the circumstances concerning his previous wife.

In his dealings here with the envoy, the duke plainly has a number of identifiable aims ('my object') and equally clearly he wishes to impress for a good report to be transmitted to the Count. However, since marriage negotiations are already quite advanced the duke is now directing his strategy onto key details, among which is the fate of his previous duchess – and the reasons behind it. The portrait painted on or in the wall (probably a fresco, and so she is literally immured) presents the duke as well as Browning with the chance to expatiate on the woman and her fate.

Put bluntly, the situation compels the duke to reveal his values and expectations in a prospective marriage, especially those regarding his wife's conduct. His previous duchess, a spirited and highly cordial woman, treated everyone alike and gave no special reverence to an aristocrat with a lengthy pedigree:

> ... all and each
> Would draw from her alike the approving speech ...   (29–30)

With noticeable irony, the painting of the dead woman renders her 'as if she were alive' (lines 2 and 47), thereby setting up a dichotomy in the poem of art and life. His account of the duchess leaves us in no doubt about her vitality and her charm, which become, firstly, sources of frustration then objects of deep envy, ending in abhorrence. Personally and metaphorically she evades him utterly – living beyond his expectations. His shameful and uninspired remedy to this is murder: to put an end to those indiscriminate smiles, 'I gave commands'.

Life itself, in all its vitality, simply eludes the duke, while sophistication takes the possessive form of collecting and concealing, especially material articles: women, painting, statues. He has come to regulate his lacklustre existence through manageable items of luxury. Take his Neptune: a 'rarity', depicting a male 'taming' the life of the horse just as Neptune himself has been tamed, reduced to the form of a bronze. All 'for me' – his insipid world is organised by and wholly for himself.

We now need to start looking in more detail at this important poem by tackling an analysis of it in two parts; the first part I have selected is lines 1–34, the second from line 34 to the close.

Passage (i) lines 1–34

> That's my last Duchess painted on the wall,
> Looking as if she were alive; I call
> That piece a wonder, now: Frà Pandolf's hands
> Worked busily a day, and there she stands.
> Will't please you sit and look at her? I said   5
> 'Frà Pandolf' by design, for never read
> Strangers like you that pictured countenance,
> The depth and passion of its earnest glance,
> But to myself they turned (since none puts by
> The curtain I have drawn for you, but I)   10
> And seemed as they would ask me, if they durst,
> How such a glance came there; so, not the first
> Are you to turn and ask thus. Sir, 'twas not
> Her husband's presence only, called that spot
> Of joy into the Duchess' cheek: perhaps   15
> Frà Pandolf chanced to say 'Her mantle laps
> Over my lady's wrist too much,' or 'Paint
> Must never hope to reproduce the faint
> Half-flush that dies along her throat'; such stuff
> Was courtesy, she thought, and cause enough   20
> For calling up that spot of joy. She had
> A heart ... how shall I say? ... too soon made glad,
> Too easily impressed; she liked whate'er
> She looked on, and her looks went everywhere.
> Sir, 'twas all one! My favour at her breast,   25
> The dropping of the daylight in the West,
> The bough of cherries some officious fool
> Broke in the orchard for her, the white mule
> She rode with round the terrace - all and each
> Would draw from her alike the approving speech,   30
> Or blush, at least. She thanked men, - good! but thanked
> Somehow - I know not how - as if she ranked
> My gift of a nine-hundred-years-old name
> With anybody's gift.

To begin at the beginning, the opening word of the poem itself is of utmost significance, telling us such a lot about the rest of the poem.

That's ...   (1)

As deixis, the word points of course. And as such tells us that someone – the Duke of Ferrara as speaker – is doing the pointing. And so there must be a listener too, and this is a key feature of Browning's dramatic monologues. To summarise then. We have a speaker, a listener and the more distant 'that' pointed at. These are the three basic triangulation points of the whole poem, set up in that very short opening word, and this triangle is the governing principle of the poem.

In spite of the anonymity in the word 'That', we learn quickly it refers to a painting of the speaker's previous duchess. Yet, strictly speaking, she remains anonymous – she is the woman in his mind, an object to be dismissed as 'that'. The next line reveals she is dead but, in a real way, she continues to live, flourishes defiantly in the painting and most vividly in the duke's consciousness, as the rest of the poem will reveal. Art brings the dead back to life, imbuing a kind of immortality.

Escorting an envoy round his palace, the duke draws aside a curtain to reveal this hidden portrait. Her 'pictured countenance' may be in a frame painting or, perhaps, in the form of a fresco, painted directly into the plaster of the wall. The distinction is important because he now has her fixed, formulated, helpless on his wall.

Thus we learn early on that Browning's words are highly particular, often highly charged. For instance, the word, 'looking' in line 2 – does it mean simply the picture seems alive? Or does it mean the duchess herself is looking? Of course, it means both, and yet the latter implies that she persists as a haunting indictment of her putative owner. So she must remain, somewhat theatrically, confined behind a cloak, fixed onto the wall.

The opening lines are interesting too in setting a tone. Line 1 is a fairly cold, flat direct statement, blandly extended by line 2, seemingly an afterthought. The tone is disengaged, blasé, encouraging the idea that the duke is simply strolling around his palace, parading his material objects for effect. And yet this apparent composure appears wholly contrived for his prospective father-in-law.

The flat tone resembles that of an inventory, making the woman behind it a mere afterthought. The duke becomes only slightly more animated when he muses that it is a 'piece of wonder' (3). With no small irony, the word 'wonder' refers both to the woman and to the art object – but for different reasons in each case.

To be fair, the duke does admire the craftsmanship of Frà (i.e. 'Fratello' or brother) Pandolf, as he later admires that of the sculptor, Claus of Innsbruck (56). It is a wonder too how the artist managed to evoke the likeness of the remarkable former wife, so much so that the painting mordantly generates a painful recollection of her life. This device is a common theme in Browning's work, the way in which a work of imagination can itself set off the imagination, often through the memory (a feature of increasing interest to Victorian psychologists).

In the process of itemising his hoard of treasures, the Duke of Ferrara is suddenly halted by the portrait, inviting the Count's envoy to sit. She 'stands' while he sits. Overly courteous to the envoy, the duke even addresses this servant unctuously as 'Sir'! (25). Now beginning to enliven the portrait, his own emotions are becoming more stirred. However, the question is begged of why, if the Count's envoy comes to discuss arrangements for the daughter's marriage, does the duke dwell on his previous spouse? One answer lies in his exposition itself.

With the duke's deliberate reference to 'Frà Pandolf', we begin to get the impression of how calculating he is in almost his dealings. Manipulating the envoy's route, controlling his ex-wife's world, even deciding its end. He is a man for whom control, organisation and constraint represent his primary rationale. He anticipates how the envoy may respond to the portrait, because every previous viewer of it has prompted him to expand on

> The depth and passion of its earnest glance ... (8)

To the duke, the painting seems almost alive – so much so that he points to 'she' and 'her' once the poem is on its way, gradually conflating the woman and her image (both on the wall and in real life), until she comes vividly alive to him. Line 7's 'strangers' recalls those men with whom the duchess had played, flirted and 'thanked' in lines 27 on. Yet the sycophantic aristocrat tries to convince the envoy that the curtain is drawn back only for a select few (10).

Notice how the verb 'durst' or 'dares' in line 11, hinting at the duke's domineering nature, implies that the envoy has clearly dared to ask about the portrait, in the moment before the start of the poem (an example of how Browning fills out his scene by suggesting events outside of the monologue – see another example at lines 52–53). As the listener, the envoy functions as our agent in the poem – a common dramatic or filmic device – with the result that the duke is effectively addressing us, the reader.

We quickly discover there is something mysteriously elusive about this painting. In discussing our own response to works of art, words and verbal definition can take us only so far, and for the duke this painting has especial difficulties. It is a great realist painting in itself ('as if she were alive'), yet crucially it has poignant personal associations for him (after all, she is not just anybody). Not surprisingly, his exegesis of it/her is highly flavoured – as this monologue itself, very much a partial interpretation.

His exegesis dwells on what he terms his wife's 'glance' and, even more significantly, that 'spot of joy' (lines 14 and 21). Because of its moral dimension, the latter phrase is key: combining the words 'spot' and 'joy' makes it point unmistakeably at the sexual element in her relationships (and in the nineteenth century, 'blush' often stands for 'sexual arousal'; see line 31 too). With similar force, 'glance' and 'spot' both function metaphorically, signifying vitality or libido and perhaps promiscuity, at least in the duke's own reading.

Thus we gradually come to learn here just how much is unsaid, fizzing beneath the surface as subtext:

> ... Sir 'twas not
> Her husband's presence only, called that spot
> Of joy into the Duchess' cheek ...   (13–15)

It is his noticing of this 'spot of joy' that now calls to mind his wife's presumed infidelity. And in order to deflect the painful memory he resorts to the odd phrase 'Her husband' about himself, hoping to safely depersonalise that moment (although he does tend to live life at a distance, like a spectator). Yet another of the poem's many dualisms occurs in the opening and closing rhythms generated in the duke's re-enactment and repudiation of their relationship. Gradually nearing him, he swiftly dispels her memory, just as he had repelled her life.

In spite of this, the emotions of that period stream awkwardly back. Other men admired her and she was naive (or genuine) enough to accept this at face value – even the painter, a monk, might have lusted after her ('a courtesy, she thought'; line 20). But the duke's highly suggestive remarks here highlight one of the difficulties of the poem – as well as one of its brilliant strengths: the indefiniteness of received impressions.

Noting that the duchess believed she was simply being flattered by the painter, the duke is actually ignorant of what either she or the painter really felt or desired. As in life itself, we do not know for certain what the duke himself is thinking – though we can make a decent guess: he was unbearably jealous about her and the attentions she gave to other men. By the same token, we cannot be sure if her demeanour was innocent, sly, provocative or just offered as a 'courtesy'. Our constantly changing perceptions of the duchess, the painter and the other male visitors are all filtered through the strong partiality of the jealous, manipulative viewpoint of the duke-narrator.

Having said that, it is clear that the duke is alert to the precision of words, for example, in the way he deliberates over his diction, 'how shall I say ... '. This is, of course, all one with his precise, clinical nature, a counter to her spontaneity. However, this phrase is important too because it points to the poem's theme of interpretation, hinted in the word 'read' in line 6. Just as the duke struggled to interpret his wife's behaviour (was it flirting or just play?), so we have the difficulty of separating the facts from the forgeries of jealousy. In his case, there were only surfaces and actions available to him, while in ours solely the poetry.

As the duke embarks on a description of her, he assures us the duchess 'had a heart', inducing us perhaps to warm to this new positive note ... cordial, genial, sensitive? Then with a sly flourish he swipes this away: 'too soon made glad / Too easily impressed' (22–23). The abrupt cadence here is typical of the duke's dogmatic nature: his decisions are swift and absolute. The adverb 'too' is one strand of the poem's persistent imagery of excess; thus, the mantle laps too much and the duchess plays and smiles intemperately. The duke cannot tolerate any hint of excess to challenge his studied poise.

We observe the gathering strength of duke's intense passion, until eventually it too becomes excessive, peaking for the first time in line 25: 'Sir, 'twas all one!' But how shall *we* say? ... the memory has rudely undercut his poise, leaving him to replay its agonising reality. Its 'depth and passion' have become fixed in his psyche, causing that 'spot of joy' to gnaw incessantly away at his seeming composure.

"Twas all one' – she treated everything and everyone in the same way, with the same democratic congeniality:

> The dropping of the daylight in the West,
> The bough of cherries some officious fool
> Broke in the orchard for her, the white mule ...   (26–28)

These are a few of her favourite things, these beautifully striking images, suffusing the passage with brief insights on the vitality of the duchess.

As so often, we learn about the duke only obliquely. Nowhere does Browning intimate what kind of man the duke is but, one way or another, the duke himself betrays his nature and his values through his monologue – which is of course all we have. Here he arrogantly presumes that his listener (as well as his reader) share his own peculiar values.

One of those key values is implicit in the line 'My favour at her breast' (25). Perhaps the duke is glancing again at the painting's detail, and literally the phrase means she wears his family's crest or coat of arms. His favour symbolises trust and loyalty since he endows her with his own name (the 'gift' in line 33). Conversely, and metaphorically, it is a badge of ownership, he possesses her and in the Renaissance period this would be both total and absolute, body and soul. To be sure, she is '*My* Last Duchess'.

Moreover, the word 'favour' carries sexual connotations and thus the stern suspicion of *his* woman's duplicity. She sports *his* favour but she may have been bestowing *her* favours elsewhere. After all, one spirited admirer has plucked the very fruit from the duke's own orchard (and some have dared to ask how Pandolf captured her 'earnest glance' in the portrait; line 12).

In the middle area of the poem, other references too help to build up this image of sexual treachery, at least in the mind of the duke, yet without ever becoming explicit. Her smile, her looks and approval are promiscuous, they went 'everywhere', and then there occurs another 'blush' in line 31. She 'thanked men' but he does not know exactly how. Trifles, which to the rational mind are light as air, become to the jealous, irrefutable proofs of duplicity.

Yet, for all this, the duke himself strives (however briefly) to acknowledge that his jealousy is unwarranted:

> She thanked men, - good

hastily realising that no one should object to a wife's gratitude. Alas, this glimmer of charity is doused in his sour protest that she held the great duke on the same level as everyone else, ranking

> My gift of a nine-hundred-years-old name
> With anybody's gift. (33)

Lines once more heavy with connotation, they point first to his strident aristocratic pride in family pedigree: not just any old courtier, but the Duke of Ferrara, that even the merest whisper of this should invoke fear and deference. Regrettably, the duchess seems singularly to have displayed neither response.

Secondly, these lines point to the man's general sense of elitism. He is a rich collector, a connoisseur of art, commissioning works that must conform to his exacting instructions. As yet one more of his impounded possessions, she has failed to privilege his noble ancestry – not even above that bunch of cherries her rapacious admirer has so passionately looted from his orchard.

Failing to realise that the listener may not synchronise with his own lifeless values, the duke slowly unmasks his own curiously grotesque ethos. Detached from her life, he emerges in lines 25–29 as emasculated and lonely, self-deluded, desperately struggling to reassert his pride and authority.

Passage (ii) lines 34–56

> ... Who'd stoop to blame
> This sort of trifling? Even had you skill   35
> In speech - (which I have not) - to make your will
> Quite clear to such an one, and say, 'Just this
> Or that in you disgusts me; here you miss,
> Or there exceed the mark' - and if she let
> Herself be lessoned so, nor plainly set   40
> Her wits to yours, forsooth, and made excuse,
> - E'en then would be some stooping; and I choose
> Never to stoop. Oh sir, she smiled, no doubt,
> Whene'er I passed her; but who passed without
> Much the same smile? This grew; I gave commands;   45
> Then all smiles stopped together. There she stands
> As if alive. Will't please you rise? We'll meet
> The company below, then. I repeat,

> The Count your master's known munificence
> Is ample warrant that no just pretence   50
> Of mine for dowry will be disallowed;
> Though his fair daughter's self, as I avowed
> At starting, is my object. Nay, we'll go
> Together down, sir. Notice Neptune, though,
> Taming a sea-horse, thought a rarity,   55
> Which Claus of Innsbruck cast in bronze for me!

The second part of the poem is chiefly concerned with the duke's imperious response to the duchess's individual lapses – at least, as he sees them. His manner sways between false modesty and genuine conceit, alternately assuming a mask and striking an attitude. Having felt humiliated by his wife's public exuberance, the duke now endeavours to make himself seem permissive by way of a rhetorical question: 'who'd stoop to reprove this sort of trifling?' His lexical choices draw reader's attention here, particularly 'stoop' and 'trifling'. The former, 'stoop', ironically underlines his sense of superiority, while 'trifling' marks a clumsy effort to let his values appear temperate: in reality, he now laughs off as mere 'trifling' the behaviour that actually drove him to murder.

Wishing to project to the Count's envoy a figure both dignified and disciplined, he hopes at the same time to impress as a reasonable man, proportionate, modest in the face of a mere bagatelle, indeed a man not easily ruffled at all. By contrast, however, as readers, we can begin to discern the gap between what he declares and what he actually is, the mask and the man, a binary feature that is a mark of Browning's creative genius.

Through his next few lines the duke hopes to extend this gesture of false modesty:

> ... Even had you skill
> In speech - (which I have not) - to make your will
> Quite clear to such an one ...   (35–37)

The woman was below his dignity. Yet, aloof, he readopts a mask of self-deprecation, denying his obvious adroitness in language. This kind of device is called *occupatio* – a speaker repudiating his linguistic skill even while doing so most eloquently. The duke, as we have noted, is a manipulative man, and one quite adept at manipulating his own persona. As we proceed we will encounter Browning's use of mask as a very common feature in the poetry (and the life), especially in the dramatic monologues.

Of course, the duke may also be rationalising his inability to communicate meaningfully on her terms. And yet, his cool detachment, combining with a stubborn pride, has seemingly instilled an obstacle to communication, and his subsequent frustration over this will drive him to an extreme solution.

The word 'will' in line 36 focuses on a driving force quite evident in both the duke's character as well as in his past relationship. He sought to subject the duchess to his considerable willpower, having then discovered that she was far from the docile or timid creature that he had been expecting. While expressing his inability to impose his demands upon her, he crucially endeavours to lay a modicum of blame on her skittish obduracy,

> ... and if she let
> Herself be lessoned so, nor plainly set
> Her wits to yours ... (39–41)

Astonishingly, he confesses his ineffectualness with what he regards as a dangerously protean woman – perhaps with women as a whole. The duchess was a woman of exceptional mettle, defying his willpower, refusing to be 'lessoned' or tamed, as the 'white mule' or as the 'sea-horse'. In reality, it was she who had broken his spirit, setting her wits against his.

Painfully, the duke relives his decisive humiliation. His mind has been wrung through a complexity of emotions, compensating for what he understands as a failure in sexual politics, until once again he discovers resort in his pride:

> ... I choose
> Never to stoop. (42–43)

The words come to resonate as he soothes his beaten honour, the verb 'choose' pointing once more to the theme of the 'will'. It seems as if he is contorting his failure into an honourable success – grounded in a refusal to demean himself. But do we believe him? do we buy into any of this?

Finally, the word 'stoop' brings this short tumult of emotion to an unnerving climax. The duke gathers together his wounded nobility, letting out a deep sigh of despondency, 'Oh sir ... '. Remember that the duke is recounting all this highly personal minutiae to a servant, which gives us a measure of just how deeply he was wounded. The man of arch-control has become lost in the fierce, writhing anguish of memory.

'She smiled ... '. Yet she smiled thus at everyone. What does this signify? Was she a cheerful, unflagging, genial soul? Or resentful? How did she smile? – with innocent cheer, perhaps, or was it scoffing, taunting him? He seemed to believe it was the latter. Yet, there in her portrait in that 'spot of joy' her smile persists relentlessly, seared into his retinal frailty.

Momentously, three short, bald statements bring to a close the feverish middle movement in which the duke re-enacts his distress:

> ... This grew; I gave commands;
> Then all smiles stopped together. (45–46)

Perhaps more than anything else the chill asperity of these direct statements drives home to us the icy tyranny of this man. Like a poleaxe, these three utterances bring the sequence and the woman to a precipitous end at the same chilling instant, a grim epiphany, its mystery turning the reader back in a hasty search for an answer, until the horror dawns. A brilliant tour de force, we discover the awful truth for ourselves even at the instant that we hope to be mistaken.

The duke now steps back from the portrait with all its disconcerting memories. Gathering his control once again, he becomes typically objective. 'There she stands', repeats line 4; and 'as if alive', recalls line 2. His words invest the account with a drear circularity that mimics the paralysis of his life, paralysis being the second source of the poem's grotesque horror. Completing his narrative, he moves blithely on (note the flippant effect of the adverb 'then' in line 48). She is simply one more item in a catalogue of possessions. He had expected much of her; she failed him; he has disentangled himself and now she is behind him. It could be a dog he was discussing, or maybe that 'white mule' he had once given her.

The envoy rises and they walk nonchalantly away. Once again Browning *shows* us experience rather than *tells*, and he shows through a narrow aperture.

The phrase 'the company below' (48) suddenly broadens the perspective to the rest of the house, unsettling any assumptions that the two men were alone. Moreover, Browning subtly discloses that the portrait is hung upstairs, for his own private gratification. These shifts serve to remind us of Browning's very subtle deconstructions, keeping us guessing, almost revealing, then interrogating certainty.

The next item on the duke's agenda is the dowry for his next marriage. We are likely to realise that the backdrop to what has so far been happening is the duke's negotiations for a financial settlement with the Count, father of the next bride. Typically, the duke's thoughts turn to the materialism of the matrimonial arrangements – with a presumptuous touch of flattery to lubricate the haggling:

> The Count your master's known munificence
> Is ample warrant that no just pretence
> Of mine for dowry will be disallowed; (49–51)

'Pretence' here signifies 'claim'. With unintended irony, the duke affirms that the Count's 'fair daughter' is his fresh target:

> Though his fair daughter's self, as I avowed
> At starting, is my object. (52–53)

The pun in 'object', line 53, gathers together earlier threads of materialism and manipulation. The modifier 'my' helps us to make an easy connection with both the egoism in the poem's title and with the irony of the duke's utter failure to wholly possess the previous duchess.

Once again and with unctuous sycophancy, the duke addresses his social inferior as 'sir' (in line 54). Stressing the word 'together' in this line is another attempt to strike an affiliation, a common cause, but it makes the duke appear uncomfortable. By inverting their differing social levels, the duke actually looks to be hoping to recover his patrician values,

> ... Nay, we'll go
> Together down, sir. (53–54)

But then, as they amble past more precious objects, something catches his eye. The duke beckons the envoy's attention, 'Notice ...'. It reminds us how typically his lines teem with imperative deixis, controlling the attention: here, there, that, now, look, this, below.

Moving on, we discover that the new object of attention is a statue. It is of course a special object, a 'rarity' and struck in bronze '*for me*'. Objects have the value of reinforcing the duke's sense of worth (as he hopes his new duchess will too – if she knows what's good for her) and of privilege. With Browning's characteristic irony, the statue turns out to be a scene of one creature violently taming another, clearly a token of the duke's own urge to trap, tame and dominate and, if necessary, dispose of. Anyway, there the figure stands, frozen in action, like all the other pieces and objects redolent of the duke's own living paralysis.

These final ten lines are a real masterstroke by Browning. After focusing so much on the duchess, the turn at line 47 may seem at first merely to be introducing a coda, a postscript to wrap it all up. Yet, conversely, it plays a crucial structural role, requiring us refocus – and to almost redraft our interpretation of lines 1–46. To test the crucial importance of these final lines, imagine the effect of omitting them and decide what would be missing.

Reinforcing the poem's style of grotesquerie, these final lines present to us a series of jolts. After we witness the duke stooping to the envoy, grovelling for a dowry, his attention strolls on, happening next upon that gruesome seahorse figure, euphemism of cruelty. In one stroke the duchess, who had seemed once a woman of momentous attention, is rendered a non-person, a discard, a briefly diverting trifle in a sequence of amusing objects.

Commentary

Reviewing 'My Last Duchess' in 1864, the critic William Stigand recorded his surprise at the duke's behaviour in revealing so much of himself to a Count's envoy (an Italian duke would rank higher than even a count):

> ... in the piece called 'My Last Duchess', it is very unnatural that the duke should betray himself so entirely to the envoy who comes to negotiate a new marriage as to let him have the opportunity of knowing as we have ourselves that his cold austerity and pride had been the death of his late wife ...
> (*Edinburgh Review*, October 1864)

Put like this, and in a poem of so much intrigue, why does Ferrara unmask himself? Does he act out of pure folly in revealing the fate of his 'last Duchess', insensible to the consequences of his disclosure? or is it that his power is so absolute that he feels impervious of an avenging justice? Perhaps he is simply tendering an oblique warning via the Count's emissary?

Any of these may apply, but we can be confident that he is eager to get his hands on the Count's daughter (and her dowry). That said, the question of the duke's state of mind presents an irresistible point of departure for discussing this brilliant poem and in particular the duke himself.

In spite of his cold-bloodedness, one of the duke's many character traits that emerge unmistakably from the poem is his insecurity. This appears to stem from his strong need to control ('by design'; line 5). One way he does this is by manipulating people and situations – for instance the way he tries to manipulate the Count's envoy in his pitch for cash. Another demonstration of his psychosis is evident in the need to impress and be respected. Lofty and superior, he finds himself unable to 'stoop'.

This need to impress is apparent also in the gratifying of his wife – or what he takes to be gratifying: his 'favour at her breast', her freedom to socialise and, not forgetting, his 'gift of a nine-hundred-years-old name' (his gifts seem actually to be snares). His pride in family goes almost without saying, yet on *his* terms her lack of reverence amounts to impertinence. It seems to have been the final straw in his short-lived sufferance.

The duchess's failure to esteem his pedigree, the lifeblood of his pride, clearly undermines his selfhood. It is as though he is defined by others' regard for him, fitting him into the social pattern, which goes some long way to reinforcing his name and position. Thus, she was expected to complement his noble identity through her decorum. However, as far as the duke is concerned, her animated familiarity with visitors betrayed a lack of sangfroid and finesse.

His property too, the commodities about him and his palace, which are the trappings of power, also serve to secure his power identity. In fact, it could be argued that in a true sense they *are* him, his persona. Hence his decision to escort the envoy around his treasures as if to say – look how great I am, I not only recognise the finer values in life and art but I can also afford them. And these commodities fulfil him.

Collecting, whether in the form of paintings, statues or women, thus mollifies his paranoia (collecting is almost certainly a sublimation of his displaced sex drive). His objects are indelibly marked as an extension or endorsement of the self and its power. Indicative of this egoism is the recurrence of possessive pronouns from him: my lady, my favour, my object and, of course, my duchess. Practically everything is referenced through his ego (including the poem itself): the painting was made for him, and Claus of Innsbruck cast Neptune exclusively 'for me'. The word 'I' appears no less than twelve times ('we' only twice – and then with reference to the envoy). The interplay of such pronouns effectively enacts the contest of wills at work here.

Drawing things into himself like this can be seen as an expression of the duke's predilection for control, objects being much more redolent of manipulation than wives. Thus it comes as no surprise that in the second part of the poem we get an impression of the volatility of things, as they subvert his authority, intimidating the duke with hubristic chaos.

Everywhere there is evidence of the duchess's failure to submit to his will, and as such she embodies the values of 'carnival'. Key features of 'carnival' in the poem include play, jeopardy, subversion or disruption, spontaneity, and impending chaos. Challenging her husband's principle of decorum, hauteur and reaction, the duchess signifies the culture of insurgency, perturbation and mutability. Order and respect are juxtaposed against play, joy and love.

The moment of the poem should be for the duke one of relaxation as he guides the envoy round his treasures. In fact it exposes his turmoil and obsessions. Beneath the disciplined surface of the poem (with its regular metre and rhyme scheme), the duke's outlook feels fraught with anxiety – about the past, his place in the world, his future relationship with the count. So much so that control has become translated into a clear state of moral paralysis.

And despite his efforts at holding his precarious world and mind in check, the force of emotion – like life itself – continually breaks through. For example the narrator reports the vibrant feelings of the duchess ('she had a heart ... too soon made glad'; line 22), of Frà Pandolf's admiring portrayal, along with the 'officious fool' who impulsively set off scrumping for cherries. The duke backhands all of these contemptibly dissident spots of joy as 'trifling'.

Control implies supremacy over others and, in spite of his nervousness about esteem, the duke fully demonstrates this maxim in his local demesne. He personally embodies the themes of discipline, restraint and morality, all ultimately actualised into coldness, austerity and paralysis. Secure in his luxurious palazzo the Duke of Ferrara is an avatar of despotic masculine power (rendered meaningless without a female predicate). He dwells in the simulacrum of a doll's house and the one thing needful is a woman to venerate his esteem and his sovereignty.

Unchallenged strength has given rise to other apoplectic traits. Censoriousness is one, insecurity another. Conceit is also evident in his choice of pronouns, manifest too in those objects fashioned at his commission, equally obdurate, equally indisposed to stooping. The new wife is like an art 'object' commissioned by himself, a plaything, one more trophy to aggrandise himself (ironically, while he cannot stoop he expects his wife to be sculpted to his will like Pygmalion's Galatea). The poem opens with 'my' and closes with 'me' and, in spite of the title, the narration between these two nodes pointedly broods on himself.

Objects are, of course, usually much less troublesome and much easier to subdue. A collector, the duke's use of the word 'last' in the title indicates that his previous wife may be one of a series. The duke's tour of his palace is likewise routed through an insipid sequence: here a painting, now a statue, this duchess, that duchess, the next and so forth. Consistent with the poem's gnomic style it also feels highly metonymic, fleeting images and objects in which greater wealth is hinted at by few.

Curiously this point draws attention to two clear tendencies going on in the poem: one for stasis and the other for vigour. On the one hand, there is the duke's struggle to control, confine, restrain, in other words to keep things still, as they are. The duchess is fixed, immured in the wall – 'there she stands'. Along with imagery of inertness – 'sit', 'never read', 'never hope', 'smiles stopped', 'taming' – the palazzo exudes a general aura of confinement and torpor, stifling life and change, a real woman reduced to an immobile and permanent imprint. The mule that the duchess was given, seemingly a hope of diversion, merely runs 'round the terrace' (29), round and round, fixed inside its bounds, symbolising paralysis as a tractable beast of burden.

Paralysis dominates the poem in nightmare form. The melancholy vignettes of the duchess's life flicker unrelentingly on the duke's mind like a zoetrope. The duke himself is held in the vice of his nine-hundred-years-old-name that will never change, trapped inside a dead history. His narration too has a costive circularity about it – 'Will't please you' (5 and 47), 'as if alive' (2 and 47) – beginning and ending with a conversational art object.

Like Samuel Taylor Coleridge's Ancient Mariner, it seems he is damned to continually relate his woeful story, cursed by his murder of the innocent. This is the duchess's 'revenge', and her piercing 'earnest glance' is the equivalent of the mariner's albatross, hung about his neck for a 'hellish' sin. The 'curse' of her stare, a constant reminder, creates an indelible sting of memory.

Underpinning this tendency towards inertness are the poem's near-palpable negative cadences, such as dies, never hope, dropping, stoop, disgusts, taming and so on – and perhaps we should include 'lessoned' (40) as sound-pun on 'lessened'.

On the other hand, working as counterpoint to paralysis is imagery of an opposite tendency, relating to vigour, even exuberance; for example earnest, spot of joy, made glad, approving, fair, flush and blush. Equally important in this respect is the imagery of sequence – two figures processing through the house, a chain of events, 'first' and 'then', past tenses giving way to future tenses (and he measures out his life in duchesses). Nevertheless, these sequences ultimately become circular.

Paralysis wins out in the end as indeed it must here. The deathly chill hand of the duke asserts total control, allaying even hope of vitality. Gladness and joy are roped in, vitality is converted into mere trifling, then action is frozen altogether as finally the gloomy 'cast in bronze' transfixes the movement:

> This grew ... then stopped (45–46)

Something grew, but growth being anathema in this infertile realm, it choked. Conceivably, this refers in part to the duchess's own esteem, almost certainly to the duke's loathing of her amiability. The smiles stopped and there she still 'stands' while he moves (contrast lines 28–29 in which she moves as he stood aloof, fixedly observing).

If this is correct, that the cadences of gloom and paralysis win out inevitably, then we may ask what it is that actually motivates the duke. He appears to be spurred by two key forces, memory and desire.

Because of its interplay of silence and desire, 'My Last Duchess' implicitly draws attention to the question of interpretation. In 'My Last Duchess' the theme of desire is intricately fused with the matter of interpretation. The duke himself speaks for us in drawing attention to the difficulties of interpretation; he admits that he does not know how his wife thanked men (32). In the same way, visitors did not know how to read her portrait:

> ... for never read
> Strangers like you that pictured countenance,
> The depth and passion of its earnest glance,
> But to myself they turned ...   (6–9)

They 'seemed as they would ask' – but he is not certain. In line 5 the envoy is invited to sit and interpret the portrait – though in fact, the duke himself does the interpreting, the poem too being his version of her. Near the end, the duke tries to confirm his interpretation of the Count's dowry (line 50). Even the duchess herself undertakes interpretations – of Frà Pandolf's words and of the peculiar behaviour of men – yet she had a heart 'too soon made glad / Too easily impressed' (22–23). Emotions intervened to displace her unique unveiling of the context.

The difficulty of interpretation extends to us of course – but with less lethal stakes, one hopes. Critic Robert Langbaum believes that the brilliance of the poem lies in our suspending moral judgement of the duke in the great struggle to discover what it is we are actually trying to judge.

> The Duke reveals all this about himself, grows to his full stature, because we allow him to have his way with us; we subordinate all other considerations to the business of understanding him.
>
> (Langbaum 1957, p. 85)

And yet we are likely to realise that a full understanding is going to be a futile (and undesirable) endeavour. The nature of the dramatic monologue itself poses great difficulties, but also great riches. As we can appreciate, I hope, the totality of events that the duke describes is mediated by the filtering presence of the narrator. The whole thing is played out in the arena of the imagination. Browning locates the narrator between the apparent contents of the poem and the reader, continuously holding us at arm's length, rendering them uncertain. Mediating the account in this way makes the duke an unreliable narrator, and this urges us towards rereading.

'Porphyria's Lover'

In our second poem for consideration, 'Porphyria's Lover', we meet another powerful male figure and, like the Duke of Ferrara, he is harassed by his own disordered emotions into the desperate murder of a woman. The chief difference is that in this poem the murder is conducted before our eyes.

Like 'My Last Duchess', the setting of 'Porphyria's Lover' action is chiefly interior – both physically (inside a house) and personally: the poem is primarily a study-in-action of a disturbed, alienated mind – a study, viscerally intensified by its claustral setting. However, where the Duke of Ferrara's monologue addressed an external listener, here the speaker's audience may be himself (a point that intensifies the feeling of confinement and horror). The lyric form of this poem takes us away from the 'public' or external domain into the inner world of its macabre drama.

Most likely composed on a trip in 1834 to St Petersburg, 'Porphyria's Lover' was originally intended by Browning as a companion piece to 'Johannes Agricola in Meditation', and among many other things they share a similar rhyme pattern of ABABB, both written in iambic tetrameter (see Glossary under 'metre'). Both poems were originally published in the journal *Monthly Repository* in January 1836, and signed 'Z' – although the current poem was titled simply 'Porphyria'.

When the two poems were reprinted side by side in *Dramatic Lyrics* (1842) they were yoked under the indicative title '*Madhouse Cells*'. Browning appears to have based 'Porphyria's Lover' on two separate contemporary accounts in which psychotic murderers dispassionately contemplate the corpses of their victims. Strangely, the poem went by almost completely unnoticed by contemporary reviewers.

The poem is a little too long for detailed scrutiny, so for the purposes of close analysis I have decided to focus on the opening twenty-five lines and to take them in three phases: (i) lines 1–4, (ii) lines 5–15 and (iii) lines 15–25.

> The rain set early in to-night,
> The sullen wind was soon awake,
> It tore the elm-tops down for spite,
> And did its worst to vex the lake:
> I listened, with heart fit to break,   5

When glided in Porphyria: straight
She shut the cold out and the storm,
And kneeled and made the cheerless grate
Blaze up, and all the cottage warm;
Which done, she rose, and from her form   10
Withdrew the dripping cloak and shawl,
And laid her soiled gloves by; untied
Her hat and let the damp hair fall,
And, last, she sat down by my side
And called me. When no voice replied,   15
She put my arm about her waist,
And made her smooth white shoulder bare,
And all her yellow hair displaced,
And, stooping, made my cheek lie there
And spread o'er all her yellow hair,   20
Murmuring how she loved me—she
Too weak, for all her heart's endeavour,
To set its struggling passion free
From pride, and vainer ties dissever,
And give herself to me for ever.   25

It will help our analysis if we can first establish an overview of the whole poem. 'Porphyria's Lover' begins with strong discordant evocations, violent and vivid, presaging all of the chilling events to follow. The wild, non-human turbulence outside both contrasts with the quiet of the cottage and parallels the tumultuous emotions of the Lover awaiting Porphyria's arrival. The intense external scene introduces the tone of agonising tension that energises the first half of the poem. These ferocious natural elements contrast too with Porphyria's more gentle actions, as she glides in and promptly addresses the practical task of fire-lighting.

Before the transfixed gaze of her lover, Porphyria's actions of fire-lighting and disrobing seem wholly disconnected from the cerebral narrator. So emotionally disengaged is he, that even the act of insinuating herself beneath his inert arms could be seen as happening to someone else.

As she murmurs her love for him (21), the Lover appears not to respond directly, only to comment at a strange distance on the feelings stirred in himself by her devotion. She has sped through the wild tumult, of 'wind and rain', out of a sense of commitment to his palely waiting self (30).

Narcissistic contemplation deepens as he saturates his thoughts with pride in her affection for him.

Following the above passage, lines 26–37 bring about a reversal that contrasts, on the one hand, the mental disturbance of the Lover's pride and triumph against, on the other, the serene Porphyria, motionless in his possessive arms. His rising internal agitation becomes translated into external violence, wrapping her hair about her throat until life is strangled from her. Ironically, in death her cheeks and blue eyes seem vitally alluring again, under the Lover's uncompromising stranglehold. His 'burning kiss' takes up earlier references to fire and warmth, now heavily tinged with the numbing tone of awful futility.

Our reaction of shocked incredulity turns into horror when the Lover toys with the dead girl's body (49). He has reduced the spirited woman of part one to his own sullen state of inertia. Mixing self-satisfied explanation with joy, he rejoices in the belief that he has defied mortal time by making her his eternal sweetheart. With gruesome complacency the Lover nurses her corpse through the night, noting with ghastly ambivalence how God has not intervened.

(i) lines 1–4

These opening four lines clearly delineate a highly visual, naturalistic sketch, incorporating, on the one hand, a vivid depiction of stormy weather and, on the other, an unsettling foreboding.

> The rain set early in to-night,
> The sullen wind was soon awake,
> It tore the elm-tops down for spite,
> And did its worst to vex the lake ...   (lines 1–4)

Of course murders can – and do – occur on warm sunny days, with a similar sense of presentiment. Employing humanistic words – 'awake', 'spite' and 'did its worst', Browning satirises the Romantic device of naturalistic fallacy (much in vogue in Victorian verse – and beloved even today of Hollywood directors). He invokes a graphic texture in the natural topography of trees and lake and then challenges this with these human attributes, and yet since it is the Lover's story, it assigns motives and psychological causes to the insentient.

It is of course this idiosyncratic mix of familiar and disjoint that draws the reader forward. Browning achieves much in this impressionistic overture, balancing visual, mood, temporality and drama. Its prickly sensuality invites curiosity yet these opening four lines seem locked in a capsule, shut off from the cottage interior scene (in the same way that Porphyria shuts out the cold) yet grimly besieging.

The phrase 'set in early' signals immediately a warning of the extraordinary. The phrase anticipates the poem's note of prematurity, made real later in Porphyria's murder, while line 2's 'sullen' hints at the depressive mood of the narrator. On Porphyria's arrival, the words 'soon awake' are echoed in her rousing the fire to 'Blaze up' (9), the adverb 'soon' reinforcing this earlier note of prematurity or even rashness.

Likewise, other threads here anticipate later events; for example, the violence in 'tore ... down' and in 'vex' prepare for the violence to come. Both of these hint too at the tumult in the Lover's mind both now and at the moment of the murder. At the same time, the blind destruction here contrasts with the deliberative and calculated motives of the Lover. In the immediately ensuing lines the torment of the opening is only a little eased, remaining an undertone until the end of the poem (and even then not completely abated).

In line 1 the word 'to-night' is curious – the narrator does not say 'that night' or 'last night', as we may have expected. Clearly it points to the narrative present and is a first suggestion of the poem's interconnected themes of time and mortality (the moment is reiterated in line 27). Imagery of time abounds, including 'soon' (2), 'still' (34 and 51), 'all night long' (59), plus the prescient adverb 'yet' in the final line. Related to this is an awareness of change and movement running through the poem, bolstering an awareness of temporality, mortality.

The word 'to-night' (1) invokes too an idea of a continuous moment, its events constantly and searingly present in the psychopathic mind of the murderer/lover. Ironically, then, Browning cultivates a feeling of change (both through nature imagery and human conduct) yet also an awareness of constancy, in the enduring epiphany of the moment that continues in the mind of the narrator. Thus there are at least three clear narrative instants within the poem: the murder itself, the time later when the Lover clasps the dead girl (from line 51 – implicit in the word 'still') and the cold, dispassionate recollection before us (in the final three lines).

The word 'to-night' may also suggest that the events are being narrated on the night of the killing to an externalised listener, possibly in a police statement or confession to a cleric. The sentence structure of the first four lines is pertly simple and employing predominantly monosyllabic words – each statement complete within a line, suggesting a mind carefully trying to sift the facts straight. Browning's earlier strap-line of *Madhouse Cells* supports this conjecture or indeed a view that the murderer is trapped within the memory of that night – just as he had sought to transfix time and preserve for eternity the moment of Porphyria's affection.

(ii) lines 5–15

The opening lines establish the poem's emphatic rhythm as well as its rhyme scheme, each of which are, on the whole, surprisingly regular. Composed in iambic tetrameter throughout, with occasional irregular lines, this simple form recalls that of English ballad verse and song, lending a mythic tenor to the reported events. The rhyme scheme of ABABB is equally simple, its couplets emphasising a repeated tendency to finish that is never quite final until the last line.

After the first four lines of the exterior sketch, the next line surprises by its sudden change of view to interior setting and onto the speaker/observer himself:

> I listened, with heart fit to break ...   (5)

The violence and lacunae of the beginning sets up reader expectations, at the same time contrasting the storm outside with feelings of security and hospitality within the cottage. The active violence of the storm contrasts too with the seeming passivity of the narrator, yet also prepares for the outrage to follow. As we enter the cottage there is at once a release of tension in its seeming safety – but one likely to deepen the horror.

> ... When glided in Porphyria: straight
> She shut the cold out and the storm,
> And kneeled and made the cheerless grate
> Blaze up, and all the cottage warm ...   (6–9)

Conventionally, the cottage suggests a cosy haven of safety, shelter from the treacherous exterior, while it is in reality a cave-like deathtrap. Porphyria herself carries in a cosiness in her caring touch and in the gift of fire. It is she who arrives to liberate her Lover, only to become ensnared by his fanatical possessiveness.

What do these few lines tell us of the Lover's view of Porphyria? The verb phrase 'glided in' suggests something softly ephemeral, with easy graceful movement. Another point that seems clear is that she is a woman of action, direct and practical. Contrasting with the Lover who has been languishing in the cold (and probably shadowy) house, her first actions are not to embrace him but to make a change to the house. Frankly, the contrast makes him seem a withdrawn, sullen and ineffectual mentality.

Her directness of mind is echoed in the verbs of these and later lines – 'glided', 'shut', 'kneeled' and 'made' – these are all in active mood and emanate from Porphyria. We also find transferred epithet, thus her shutting out the cold and storm implies her vital spiritual effect as well as the physical. Likewise, 'cheerless grate' refers to the whole chill, deadly atmosphere of the cottage (with obvious ominous overtones) while 'blaze up' speaks of her power to rouse her Lover, sexually too (though 'kneeled' hints too at an inferior social and menial status – compare line 19). 'Blaze up' parallels a movement similar to that of 'soon awake' in line 3.

She closes out the warring elements and this action is part of a peristaltic rhythm of binary imageryhere: rising and falling (lines 8, 9, 10, etc.), against constraint and release (lines 12, 13, 16, etc.).

This rhythm of constraint and release is mirrored too in the poem's themes. The events of the text clearly reveal that the Lover is himself trapped in the cottage, while her arrival and then the murder liberate him – first, from a cold austerity and loneliness, then from an anxiety implicit in her uncertain love, and finally from the impermanence of love and companionship. For her, containment is conveyed in the obligation to leave the 'gay feast' to return to him, and confinement comes in

> putting my arm about her waist ... (16)

At the same time, release is symbolised in Porphyria's untying her hat, disrobing and the loosening of her yellow hair. The Lover himself recognises this idea of release in Porphyria's murder, yielding to his power over her will and its future:

> So glad it has its utmost will
> That all it scorned at once is fled ...　　　　　　　　(53–54)

These lines all linger on the visual aspects of the woman's busy caring actions – all filtered through the man's point of view. Such are the points he discerned, making him appear disengaged yet intense. Just as in 'My Last Duchess', what *we* receive is a view that is partial in both senses of the word (limited and coloured), thus any judgements about Porphyria are likely also to be judgements that actually reflect on the *voyeur* himself.

So, with only a few studied details, Browning configures some key fragments regarding the external actions of Porphyria (one of the limitations of this monologue is that neither he nor the Lover can reveal the thoughts or feelings of the woman – so she remains detached from us too). We do not see or hear her but the few details allow us to think we know her, by what she does.

In effect each character is defined by the other – either literally, through narration, or metaphorically in the contrasts: Porphyria is defined by what the Lover is not. And this air of balance lies at the heart of the whole poem – in movement and theme, in the reciprocity of the two characters, and in the way for the whole of the poem each character is focused intensely on the other by way of the narrator's voice.

She comes to him. She is active, instrumental, a motivator, associated with warmth, both in her promethean provision of fire and in the way she enlivens the Lover. Her dynamism and the fact that *she* visits him make her emerge free, possibly even impulsive. Leaving and returning, she appears to the Lover elusive, chimerical, the whirlpool to his rock and she symbolises change, perhaps time itself, the natural element that he abhors and seeks to deny (compare the duke of Ferrara). In killing Porphyria he does of course attempt the folly of transfixing the moment, holding back time (holding or restraining being a key strand of the poem). By contrast he is correlated with paralysis, inert in his cottage, at least until the later fatal reversal, associated with coldness, isolation and death.

In terms of their relationship, the description 'Lover' implies that she is neither his wife nor partner. But her actions point to a relaxed intimacy with him and the house – gliding in, lighting fire and removing clothes in one familiar action.

Her lover claims she is proud and vain but there is no evidence either way. We can guess he resents her social ties and exploits this to nourish his own brooding jealousy. She is assertive ('straight'), addressing the cold, then slipping beneath his chill enfolded arms and against his cheek.

> Murmuring how she loved me ... (21)

In another of the poem's reversals, Porphyria becomes the Lover's servant. She has hastened through a stormy night from her 'gay feast' to his humble cottage. Although the 'gay feast' can imply she is his social superior Porphyria acts as his menial, a servant, kneeling, 'stooping' and lighting the fire, a grimy messy task (recall that the Duchess of Ferrara was a kind of menial, a decorative ancillary).

The word 'gloves' (line 12) lends support to the theory of her higher social class. In which case, what can we make of the modifier 'soiled' there too? It clearly represents her care for the Lover and symbolises the sacrifice she has made in this morganatic relationship – if our assumptions about him are accurate. This would be a bar to their marriage – a point which gives extra motive to the Lover's wish to marry her through death.

Another way in which we can track Porphyria's character is by what the narrator tells us explicitly (with our obvious reservations). For example, he believes she is very proud:

> Be sure I looked up at her eyes
> Proud – very proud ... (31–32)

And in line 24 he regards this as the chief reason she has not given herself over exclusively to him. The upshot of the one-sided account is we can only fumble towards an interpretation of her character by the metaphorical effect of the narrator's details.

Glancing back at line 5 of the poem, the Lover/narrator listens to the night 'with heart fit to break'. While most readers do not read even their favourite authors with heart fit to break, the Lover's pursuit here and especially in the first half of the poem emulates the role of a reader, striving towards understanding. The Lover too tries to discern or ascribe meanings based on a few scant details, trying to discover in the text of the landscape which elements are significant.

Adopting this monologue kind of narrative, Browning brings us in close viewpoint to that of the Lover as reader. Close but not quite, since we learn less than the narrator. The opening four lines are already a schema of the speaker's mind, his interpretation of an ambiguous situation. Lines 5–21 are by and large a selective description of Porphyria's actions. Then, from line 22 on, the narrator offers us and himself a reading of the meaning and motives behind these silent actions, based on a belief in her passion and pride.

In the face of her silence his reading concludes that 'she felt no pain' (41) and supposes she is 'glad' to be dead in his arms (53). Porphyria herself is subject to this kind of readerly activity, at line 56: 'she guessed not' – she was unable to extract meaning or truth from the exterior surfaces. Likewise, once engaged on the poem's silences and ambiguities, the reader's imagination sets about an interpretation to navigate them. The poem's silences are a trigger to the reader's desire to know and interpret in the face of the text's evasions, denial and absences. And the poem does have a plethora of silences (explicitly in lines 15 and 60) and these incite the Lover as himself a reader.

Much of our guessing focuses, of course, on Porphyria. We are told a few descriptive facts and the rest is, if not silence, then guesswork. Chief among her attributes seems that of caring, an important theme in the poem. What her motives are we cannot know, yet she seems dedicated, perhaps out of affection for her Lover, perhaps even remorse (due to 'pride' or possibly social class). She abases herself before him and the result is his peculiar inference:

> ... at last I knew
> Porphyria worshipped me ...   (32–33)

We cannot guess the truth of this but the point is he now subjectively becomes convinced of her devotion.

On the theme of care, the opening four lines of the poem enact the antithesis of care. The poem's title is clearly ironic when seen from within this perspective, and its ironic significance gradually becomes more clear in the latter half of the poem when the murder of Porphyria is presented as an act of care, extinguishing worldly anxieties:

> So glad it has its utmost will,
> That all it scorned at once is fled ... (53–54)

In point of fact this is of course redolent of care for oneself, a conspicuous facet of the speaker's narcissism that is a main driver of the poem. His cool visualisation of the murder (and its aftermath) in terms of protection look like a grotesque perversion of care, and for the reader it is the clinching evidence of insanity.

His 'care' is a grotesque inversion of hers for him. Where she attends to him in terms of warmth, touch and affection, his 'care' is warped into ownership, fixing her beneath his superior controlling strength.

(iii) lines 15–25

Almost every line in this first section of the poem has a caesura, measuring out the calm, studied tempo of Porphyria's smooth unruffled movements. Not until lines 22 and 24–25 is this evenness agitated, when the speaker describes Porphyria's 'struggling passion' – and then here the syntax too becomes convoluted. The words themselves speak of Porphyria, but the turmoil in the syntax and rhythm confirm that it is the speaker's own turbulence which is his real subject (a similar disruption of syntax and rhythm occurs in lines 32–37, the narrator's thoughts reeling in passion).

After some simple, loose clauses describing Porphyria's fire-lighting skills, the narrator signals a change of tone and focus with the suspended sentence in line 15:

> When no voice replied ...

Suspending the clause like this actually mimics the silence in the room and the delicate air of uncertainty between the lovers. This phrase 'no voice replied' evokes the thick pregnant air of the scene; it casts back to the straining ear in line 5 while anticipating the final line of the poem, a different kind of silence in each case. The brief hiatus is not dispelled until she once again takes the initiative with a series of actions, each introduced by the word 'And ...'.

Clearly, this series operates as a catalogue of small, cumulative actions building around the taciturn narrator. As in the rest of the poem they are highly visual, reinforced by the rich abundance of subjective colour imagery. However, the scene quickly becomes more intimate, even erotic with sensual body detail: arm, waist, bare shoulder, cheek and yellow hair. It is an instance of demasking, the mask being a recurring motif in Browning: not only is she patently the more active but also the more daring in her striptease before the paralysed onlooker.

Porphyria takes a chance in a love situation, and few things in personal life are so risky; words such as 'bare', 'stooping' and 'weak' point to her adopting a vulnerable attitude, a gambit directed at provoking her unresponsive 'lover' from the moody brooding.

Conversely, an alternative scenario is that she may have something to atone for. Her attending the 'gay feast' without him has irked, and there may even be stirring in his melancholy a jealous suspicion of a rival. This possibility of jealousy finds some faint support in his ambiguous words at line 27 on:

> Nor could tonight's gay feast restrain
> A sudden thought of one so pale
> For love of her – and all in vain ... (27–29)

While the limitations of the monologue mean we cannot be certain of Porphyria's character, we do understand the narrator's subjective states, both by his thoughts and, importantly, by the nature of the poem itself. He comes across as passionate in his love for her (for example in lines 33 and 48), and this passion eventually overpowers his strong predilection for control, one of his abiding principles (the strong regularity of the verse form and metre seem in sympathy with this trait). Sensitive to her, he responds feelingly to her overtures but he is actually self-possessed and calculating. In another of Browning's macabre touches, the Lover is hypersensitive about not causing her pain.

> No pain felt she;
> I am quite sure she felt no pain. (41–42)

(in Bishop Blougram's Apology, the prelate speaks of 'the tender murderer ...'; line 396.)

Given his solicitousness and compassion, what then is his motivation? On the one hand he justifies the murder as a kind of catharsis for Porphyria, purging her of immorality (implied in the 'soiled' of her gloves, line 12 – but see also lines 37 and 45). His perverse rationale convinces him that he kills for the victim's own benefit (lines 53 and 57).

The Lover understands her death in terms of liberation (the copious imagery of 'release' underpins this idea). It is liberation for *her* in terms of release from the pains of life, while it represents liberation for himself in terms of the turbulent feelings of jealous ownership. Moreover, for the Lover it is release from uncertainty and ignorance, from ambivalence about her feelings for him:

> So glad it has its utmost will,
> That all it scorned at once is fled ... (53–54)

We have noted the high regularity of the verse as analogous with the Lover's urge to control. Throughout the early part of the poem this is almost thwarted by Porphyria's dominant activeness, her will to love and her superior emotional strength, both in itself and its power over his spiritual weakness (a point of contact with Andrea del Sarto; see Chapter 3). He is forced to resort to brute masculine strength in order to overcome her emotional strength and finally to demonstrate his darkly commanding will-to-possess.

Commentary

In the final line, the Lover refers to the apparent absence of God, and we are left to speculate how God figures in his scheme of thinking. The Lover's single-minded power over life and death leads him to a repugnant murder that he has rationalised to himself. However, close to the end something new emerges in his thoughts, something perhaps present even from the outset:

> And yet God has not said a word! (60)

God is the missing element of the poem's triumvirate. Is God's silence taken as tacit approval of the murder or as implicit evidence of his non-existence?

(In Bishop Blougram's Apology, the Bishop himself haughtily pronounces that God's continued silence should be taken as tacit approval of his decadent lifestyle; lines 801–805). Certainly the Lover images himself as a kind of demigod in his power over life and death, and the poem testifies to his self-validation of this.

Accordingly, should we regard the Lover as amoral or immoral? There is here a contrast with the Duke of Ferrara who seems to me to be amoral, since his power prevents the question of morality from entering the mind. The duke is a clear-thinking individual who acts out of clinically logical conclusions however abhorrent we find them. His judgement is not impaired. This is not quite the case with Porphyria's Lover. He kills on the basis of his own subjective logic – but it is a logic profoundly impaired.

His reason unbalanced by emotional intensity, the Lover comes across as psychotic. While the duke's homicide is the result of cold, extended deliberation, the Lover's appears more like an almost spontaneous impulse, a decision taken at a pivotal moment:

> While I debated what to do
> That moment she was mine, - mine, fair,
> Perfectly pure and good: I found
> A thing to do ... (35–38)

It is a 'surprise' remedy that spurs his emotions to the killing act.

Her apparent devotion, his rising passion together with a psychotic tendency, all converge on the critical decision to preserve Porphyria's love at its quintessential moment. Is he mad? Iain Finlayson in his biography of Robert Browning finds a 'grim amorality' in the poem and that the Lover is mad, a fantasist 'to whom reality is a mirage' (Finlayson 2004, p. 138). However, Stefan Hawlin views the Lover as not mad in any simple sense on the grounds that Browning has imbued him with 'an exaggeration of feelings or tendencies that we may all have experienced' (Hawlin 2002, p. 74) and Hawlin goes on to depict the speaker as a 'tender murderer', the poem a study of a 'disturbed, alienated mindset' (155).

Browning himself pointed to this kind of conclusion by pairing this poem with 'Johannes Agricola in Meditation' and adopting the 1842 banner title 'Madhouse Cells'. We do not really need this clue to arrive at the impression that the speakers of these two companion poems have aberrant mindsets.

Johannes Agricola is a religious obsessive who prospers under the delusion that, singled out by 'God's warrant', he is incapable of sin and impervious to hell's temptations, a special case guaranteed a place on God's heavenly right hand. Both Agricola and Porphyria's lover suffer from paranoid hallucinations and may, at the present point of their respective narrations, be inmates of such cells.

Roy E. Gridley describes this a 'sick and twisted mind' (Gridley 1972, p. 113) but its argument seems coherent, with its own plausible interior logic. Gridley reductively dismisses the Lover as an 'evil and criminal character' (p. 158). Most critics accept the possibility of the murderer as rational, even intellectual, and he is rational in the sense that the thoughts are not chaotic or suffering from delusion about itself, however deluded the motivation may be.

In fact Michael Mason has tracked down two possible sources for Browning's study of this 'alien state of mind'. Mason describes 'Porphyria's Lover' as 'surprisingly sympathetic', the murder proceeding from 'motives we actually approve', that is to encapsulate and prolong the moment of love.

One source is the verse 'Marcian Colonna' of 1820, a third-person description of a murderer contemplating his dead lover. The other is John Wilson's 'Extracts from Gosschen's Diary' (1818), a first-person 'confession' of the stabbing of his golden-haired, blue-eyed mistress by a self-righteous killer who sets out to minimise her pain (in Armstrong 1974, pp. 255–256; and see Woolford et al. 2010, *Selected Poems*, pp. 70–71). Browning's poem, like these two texts, identifies a subtle change in contemporary psychiatric attitudes towards the 'lunatic' by disentangling an analysis of mind from our loathing of the shocking act and its consequences.

The decorum of Browning's dramatic style here is itself expressive, cleverly matching the style of his monologue to the mind of the speaker. Accordingly, we understand the Lover's mind almost as much by the way he speaks as by his thoughts, actions and inaction, as we are drawn into sharing the strange sadistic fantasy.

Before leaving this disturbing poem we should consider its title, the only explicit input from Browning (if we suspend our disbelief about its form, metre, lexis and so on). This is the poet's master ploy, standing as it does outside the poem and therefore unlikely to derive from the murderer. The title focuses on both main characters but chiefly on the 'Lover' (though it does faintly whisper the possibility of a rival for Porphyria's attention). At one time the title of the poem was simply 'Porphyria', and Browning's alteration clearly marks an important shift in the emphasis, demonstrating the possibility of heavy irony in the notion of 'love'.

Curiously, the new title sets up from the start the theme and focus on love, and what we witness is the gradual warping of our expectations by way of the narrative consciousness. In effect, the Lover tries to manipulate us too until 'love' and the 'murder' are made to appear synonymous. This process begins with the notion of care, embodied in the attentive Porphyria, then works through various shadings until it flips over in the Lover's transmutive psyche. In this progression Browning's irony leads us to become detached from the earlier, conventional meaning of love or care before the Lover submits his own, proprietorial, version.

> Only, this time *my* shoulder bore
> Her head, which droops upon it still:
> The smiling rosy little head,
> So glad it has its utmost will ...   (50–53)

The final poem for analysis in this chapter, 'The Laboratory', is yet another variation on Browning's fascination with eccentric states of mind, in a particularly atmospheric setting.

'The Laboratory'

When Browning showed an early draft of 'The Laboratory' to Elizabeth Barrett her first reaction was, 'the Laboratory is hideous as you meant to make it' (21 July 1845; *The Love Letters of Robert Browning and Elizabeth Barrett Browning*, I.135). She was lighting on the fact that once again we are in the realm of the disturbed or alien mind or, in literary terms, the grotesque. It is a mind that savours the delight not only of murdering but also of making the victim suffer.

Almost certainly composed in March 1844, it appeared in *Hood's Magazine* in June that year. The poem later underwent significant revision following Elizabeth Barrett's criticism of its earlier manifestation, on the grounds of its metre being likely too difficult for the average reader (though she heartily approved of its 'hideous' scenario). 'The Laboratory' was republished in 1845, one of a clutch of twenty poems collected as *Dramatic Romances and Lyrics*.

For analysis and discussion I would like to begin with a look at the second half of the poem (from line 25 to the end), but first a brief summary of the whole poem.

Set, more than likely, in seventeenth-century France, a fiercely jealous woman describes how her chemist prepares a poison to murder her rivals. Peering excitedly through a protective glass mask she becomes exhilarated by the combination of gothic laboratory setting, the painstaking scientific procedure and, eventually, by the lethal potency of the poison. She exults on the various chemicals, their exotic provenance, and on science's great power over life and death. Her mind switches frenziedly to past and future, reminding herself of the necessity of the poison, and of her loathing of Pauline, Elise, among others. When at last the admixture is complete she marvels at its minuteness in contrast with its power. Addressing the deadly phial she urges it to maximum efficacy, in merciless pain and death, before she pays off the mighty chemist with gold and a kiss.

Clearly this anonymous woman is both the poem's narrator and its central character, and as a result the onus is, once again, on the reader to work hard to join the dots, work out what is exactly happening. A complexity of hints, guesses and suspicion on our part parallels the complexity of the woman's relationships – both with other characters and with her reader here. For example in line 7, two lovers are reportedly laughing at her: they know that she knows where they are. They believe and she believes that they believe. The woman's narrative enacts in its intricacy the challenges with which the reader is confronted – we not knowing fully why she is preparing the poison or her relationship with those her victims.

Here is the passage for analysis:

VII
Quick - is it finished? The colour's too grim!   25
Why not soft like the phial's, enticing and dim?
Let it brighten her drink, let her turn it and stir,
And try it and taste, ere she fix and prefer!

VIII

What a drop! She's not little, no minion like me!
That's why she ensnared him: this never will free   30
The soul from those masculine eyes: say, 'No!'
To that pulse's magnificent come-and-go.

IX

For only last night, as they whispered, I brought
My own eyes to bear on her so, that I thought
Could I keep them one half minute fixed, she would fall   35
Shrivelled; she fell not; yet this does it all!

X

Not that I bid you spare her the pain;
Let death be felt and the proof remain;
Brand, burn up, bite into its grace -
He is sure to remember her dying face!   40

XI

Is it done? Take my mask off! Nay, be not morose!
It kills her, and this prevents seeing it close;
The delicate droplet, my whole fortune's fee!
If it hurts her, beside, can it ever hurt me?

XII

Now, take all my jewels, gorge gold to your fill,   45
You may kiss me, old man, on my mouth if you will!
But brush this dust off me, lest horror it brings
Ere I know it - next moment I dance at the King's!

As in the first part of the poem, the anonymous narrator dots between different moments: stanzas VII and VIII refer mostly to the present, XI to the previous night, X to the future, XI and XII the present. Her mind feverishly links the causes in the past with the 'remedy' currently in preparation, and also with the putative outcomes of the future. These flashes merge in an ecstatic climax in line 43 when she reverently and triumphantly holds the poison aloft:

> The delicate droplet, my whole fortune's fee!

This poem extends some of the key themes of other poems in this chapter, particularly Browning's forensic scrutiny of disparate kinds neurotic behaviour, and linking it with sexual feeling. Each of the three poems in this chapter uncovers a psyche which comes to regard the living existence of a lover or rival as unbearable and deranging. Once again the grotesque and the dramatic are key ingredients.

The opening word of stanza VII, 'Quick ...' has already forgotten line 10's 'I am not in haste'. But the earlier reference looks more like a note to herself – to relax her impatient urge and to defer to the chemist. The narrator's exhilaration soars as the chemical process reaches its apotheosis, her excitement reflected in the punctuation, with a glut of exclamations and questions that repeatedly confront herself as well as the chemist.

She complains about the poison's colour – 'too grim', not seductively blue 'like the phial's' (see line 15). In a poem in which a greenish-blue darkness seems to suffuse the whole atmosphere, the poison takes on a luminous radiance.

What is more, she muses on the sexual entrapment ('enticing') that will lure the victim via the poison's sensuality. Other sensual thoughts follow, 'brighten' and 'taste' in order to seduce ('fix and prefer'). Combined with these thoughts of predation are the mild commands 'Let it' and 'let her' that, along with rhyming couplets, intone like a spell over the mixture, or like a macabre blessing. This is an idea which develops further on in the poem ('Let death be felt ... '; line 38).

Naively, she equates size with power, hence her astonishment in stanza VIII that this deadly tincture is so miniature, 'What a drop' (a point re-emphasised in line 43). Or perhaps she holds it aloft to revere its potency. Unlike herself, Pauline – her adversary – is no 'minion'. Attractively petite, it is Pauline's stature that originally 'ensnared' their unwitting male victim (note again the predatory imagery). As a constituent of her intense hatred, the narrator is acutely aware of her own inferiority, and the poison is to compensate for it.

In lines 31–32 the speaker turns to address the poison phial directly. The poison will:

> ... say, 'No!'
> To that pulse's magnificent come-and-go.

This is a complex statement and there are several possible interpretations. One is that the poison will curtail the victim's pulse, which is 'magnificent' in the sense of powerful or mighty (life being difficult to stub out, especially with something so tiny). Another possibility is that the 'magnificent pulse' is that of the man's, object of her desire, and thus the poisoner means to separate the two happy lovers. The pulse would be 'magnificent' either because it belongs to him, or perhaps because life itself is so marvellous or, again, her future life will be so.

The natural pulse is magnificent in the sense of its mysterious origin, delicate in its fragility, yet obdurately resilient in terms of the persistence of life, and line 32 focuses – perhaps inadvertently – on what is magnificent about nature. This evokes yet another dichotomy in this superbly complex poem: that between nature and science. Nature is evident not only in the 'pulse' but also in the intensity of human love and hate, in jealousy and anger, in the climax of ecstasy, the reflexes of hope and fear, and even the dark ironic humour at the end.

Nature and life contrast markedly with the eminence of science as a theme here. By the same token, science, the new opiate, is juxtaposed against religion: stanza II portentously refers to the 'Empty church' (8), and rather than pray to God, the narrator looks to the scientist's practical skill for solutions, declaring 'I am here' (the poem as a whole resembles a black mass that proceeds to the hushed consubstantiation of the poison, that is then held aloft priest-like for adulation – more on this theme follows below).

Science is crucial in the poem, instilling important tensions, while embracing two of the poem's important themes: knowledge and materialism, each central to the Victorian paradigm and each encapsulated in the poem's concept of power. These are all centred on the figure of the chemist in his laboratory, manufactory of the lethal admixture.

The poison is the direct product of science, presumably expressed in a formula, the outcome of empirical research. The narrator is evidently in awe of the apparent power of the poison, especially its power over life and death, the ultimate expression of the power theme of this chapter. Moreover, in stanza V the woman venerates the skill and knowledge of the chemist ('thee and thy treasures'), fascinated by the arcane mechanics of the science of concoction.

> Better sit thus, and observe thy strange things ...   (11)

She is enthralled by the materialism as much by the mystery. Not surprisingly the poem teems with imagery of the corporeal: for instance, mask, powder casket and basket, lozenge and pulse. There is a myriad of items relating to the senses, including taste, burn, bite, kiss, moist and mash. Words relating to material wealth also have a strong showing: gold, treasures, jewels. And yet the speaker does not appear to act out of motives of cupidity, being more than ready to surrender 'all my jewels' to reward this erudite master.

As we might expect, the poem incorporates a number of allusions to knowledge: she marvels at the chemist for his specialised scientific learning (see lines 17–18); she refers to the limits of her rival's knowledge about herself (see lines 5 and 6), while she is denied the knowledge of the esoteric method on account of her gender or culture.

It is easy to see that for her, the chemical process is illicit knowledge, both in the sense that it is esoteric and that it represents power over life and death, forbidden by her Christian religion. To her the chemist represents a sorcerer or magician, and as his acolyte she vicariously indulges in the frisson of his power in the dark arts. She characterises his laboratory as 'this devil's-smithy' (3), implying perhaps that his practices lie on the margins of proscribed wisdom.

If all this is viable then what we have here is something of a black mass, involving the transubstantiation of natural elements into an alchemical essence of death. This in itself produces a thrill akin to that erotic charge which lethal poison imparts to the narrator.

This inference is made all the more feasible when we remember Browning's hint that she is a nun or religious votary – in stanza II her enemies believe she is in the 'drear empty church' praying for them. By resorting to the 'devil's-smithy' she makes a pact of alliance with the devil, sealed by an erotic kiss with her shaman of science.

The church, 'drear' and 'empty', displaced by the laboratory, becomes the new focus of miracles in Browning's century. The laboratory symbolises empirical science, rational and humanist progress (of a sort), manipulating as it does both life and death. Where in 'Porphyria's Lover' God is referred to as an immanent power (albeit by a lunatic), here – and in 'My Last Duchess' – God is noticeably and significantly absent. Science supplies a swift and decisive resolution, putting might in the hands of a disempowered female.

In passing, it is worth noting that young Browning himself was captivated by science – perhaps under the influence of his readings in Shelley, himself an early explorer in the new disciplines (as a teenager young Percy Shelley delighted in electrocuting servants and family members, all in the cause of science, of course). Science fuses knowledge and materialism, which in turn forges a new power base. Yet, conversely, perhaps mature Browning is also warning about science – the pre-eminent driving force in nineteenth-century England. Like its portrayal in Mary Shelley's *Frankenstein* (1818), science here has 'gone wrong', exploited for corrupt aims.

In a period in which literature and especially poetry acclaimed both nature and the positive in humanity, Browning's poem is conspicuous as highly polemical. By revealing an alien mind that throws into doubt the great contemporary optimism in science as a force exclusively for good, the poet attracted accusations of subversion.

However, returning to our analysis, this may not be the narrator's first dabbling in secret wisdom, for in stanza IX there is a strong hint that she has previously resorted to the occult for dominance:

> For only last night, as they whispered, I brought
> My own eyes to bear on her so, that I thought
> Could I keep them one half minute fixed, she would fall
> Shrivelled; she fell not; yet this does it all!

Deictic 'they' situates us intimately in her thought waves, pointing to the lovers through her eyes. By assuming the role of a witch last night she had desperately tried to fix and shrivel her rival by a stare. The phrase 'brought ... to bear' vividly depicts how she summoned all her resources of fluence and hex to focus, like a laser of bitter hatred onto her victim (note again how many of her utterances resemble spells: 'Let it brighten ... let her turn it ... Let death be felt ...').

Taking up the word 'fix' from line 28, 'fixed' (35) implies paralysis, her stupefied enemy petrified beneath her mercy. Nevertheless, witchcraft, like religion, ultimately fails – while mundane science 'does it all'. The indicative pronoun 'this' gives the poison an exalted status, while 'does it all' implies both science's thorough efficiency and a finality regarding its mortal effect. In contrast to the contingent merits of religion and sorcery, it does exactly what it says on the tin.

The technician cooks up one poison, while the narrator herself is poisoned by a different, systemic toxin: jealousy. In stanza X her invocation transfers the object of hatred to the object of solution, the phial or potion. She 'prays' that her victim not merely die but die in ghastly pain:

> Let death be felt and the proof remain ... (38)

The word 'felt' suggests a protracted agony but perhaps also that her loss be felt by those around her, stinging friends as well as lover. The proof should 'remain' in the sense that no one should forget this: let it stand as a warning of her new invincibility.

Her alliterative plea for the poison to:

> Brand, burn up, bite into its grace (39)

represents a direct curse as well as a witch's incantation (with echoes of *Macbeth's* witches).

The plosive /b/ sound here marvellously conveys her bitter sense of spite, and this, more than any of the other gruesome lines of the poem, evokes her pernicious nature: her victim should not merely die, and die in anguish, but be utterly disfigured in the process.

The word 'grace' in the same line refers in part to the rival's face, its purity and elegance – both of which are presumably a source of attraction to her lover. Browning sometimes likes to use words in their Elizabethan or Shakespearean sense ('brave' in line 14 is an example) and 'grace' here includes its older, religious sense of honour, virtue and propriety. However, both of its meanings apply to the moral realm, suggesting that the witch fiercely resents not only the rival's beauty or charm but her moral state as well, of virtue and decorum. As the alienated outsider, the witch desires too the intense mortification of the rival's lover, implying that, consumed by hatred and the new power, she has lost sight of her original rationale.

In this bitter line (39) can also be traced all the angry impotence of the woman in this society. The power vested in the toxic chemicals compensates for the absence of political power – her role in society has been degraded to praying for others and performing well at the King's dance. Knowledge equals power, and she must rely on the chemist-man, still the reserve of knowledge-power, and she defers to his monopoly. Science is the domain of man, so she pays with her treasure and possibly also sexual favour (see stanza XII).

As a consequence of this relative impotence she appears to make a pact with the devil, then accuses her rival of something of the same kind of thing, using unfair means, possibly including witchcraft:

> That's why she ensnared him ... (30)

Commentary

The source of the narrator's own real power resides in her seductive mastery of poetic, incantatory sound, evidenced in the poem's assonantal opening line and extended through countless alliterative lines:

> Sure to taste sweetly ... (16)
> And her breast and her arms and her hands ... (24)
> If it hurts her, beside, can it ever hurt me ... (44)

Each of these lines show a mastery too of the poem's mesmeric dactylic metre (see Glossary under 'metre'). While this obviously emanates from Browning, it is all one with a view of the character creating an aura of spells and sorcery. Other aural tricks include 'poison to poison' (4), 'moisten and mash' (9) and 'gorge gold' (45). The narrator's penchant for musical sounds is conspicuous in her orthodox coinages, for example 'whitely', 'devil's-smithy' (3) and 'come-and-go' (32). She has a curiosity and rapture in the technology of words: 'you call it a gum?' (13), foregrounding language as a theme in its own right.

After becoming distracted by thoughts of venom, in stanzas IX and X, she returns to the reality of the present in XI, pondering once more on the lethal droplet:

> Is it done? Take my mask off! Nay, be not morose!
> It kills her, and this prevents seeing it close;
> The delicate droplet, my whole fortune's fee!
> If it hurts her, beside, can it ever hurt me?

Her opening sentence in this stanza has the aura of finality about it, possibly anticipating the murder itself. The removal of her mask connects with a phrase in the following line, 'this prevents seeing it close', all suggesting her former preference to live at a little distance from events. An observer, she seems in this laboratory to be detached while others appear more active: dancing, laughing, ensnaring, mixing and mashing. Using poison to kill maintains anonymity (as the poem itself does), precludes her having to risk close engagement ('... can it ever hurt me?').

Nevertheless the poison dose is tiny in terms of its consequences for herself. 'My whole fortune's fee' (line 43) may refer to the material charge of the chemist, paid out of her fortune – which thus connects this line with line 45. Or it may hint at her hopes for the future and this bolsters the tumultuous climax that arises in line 41. With no small irony, murder is the medicine, the cure for her own life and she pins all her future, 'her fortune', on this as a fix for her problems, namely the awkward, unbearable presence of the other woman or women.

Line 45 picks up and extends this theme of fortune:

> Now, take all my jewels, gorge gold to your fill,
> You may kiss me, old man, on my mouth if you will!
> But brush this dust off me, lest horror it brings
> Ere I know it – next moment I dance at the King's! (45–48)

She is willing to pay an enormous fee for this power to kill. Moreover, line 45 amply demonstrates the enormous depth of her jealous loathing, in her readiness to cast at the phlegmatic chemist all her own 'treasure', in one enormous paroxysm of abandon.

The opening word of this final stanza, 'Now', echoes that word at the start of the poem, yet with differing inferences. Where the opening 'Now' popped out of her impatient eagerness to observe the mysterious alchemical cocktail process, the 'Now' of line 45 mixes relief with an intense resolution to murder. Where line 1 turns the reader's eye into the poem, line 45 begins to look beyond it, the smiling advance towards the dance.

'All my jewels, gorge gold' – the sensuality of this phrase encapsulates well the narrator's feeling of relief as well as triumph, and 'to your fill' blithely expresses her resolute abandonment of everything to her single-minded goal (in a figurative sense this alchemist has managed to succeed in converting base elements into gold).

Her thrill of danger transmutes into one of sexual delight, inviting the old chemist to kiss her 'on my mouth if you will', to 'gorge' on her, the alliterative /m/ beautifully catching the osculant sensuality. It is as though erotic excitement has suddenly released her inhibition towards what is, in fact, a servant.

Typically, Browning himself cannot restrain the urge for macabre irony. In almost the same breath of a kiss the narrator becomes coldly realistic, a shudder of fear snapping her from the erotic trance induced by her bliss:

> But brush this dust off ...

The blatant alliteration underpins the poet's joke that she could even kill herself – at her very eureka moment. And the poem ends with defiance, boldly urging herself to the very ball that in stanza III she had spurned. Tension and expectation have both been swelling and long held in check until, in the final line, there erupts a dramatic sense of release, epitomised by the final exclamation mark.

This is truly a dramatic monologue, in a way that 'Porphyria's Lover' is not. Here we apprehend a great intensity of the dramatic moment, and in the interplay with the silent chemist, we have the other major trait of the dramatic monologue, the listener. We also get a great sense of growing excitement as the chemical process passes expertly through its macabre stages of production.

The laboratory as central setting is associated with danger, chemical jeopardy but, above all for Victorian readers, modernity. Yet the title of the poem, 'The Laboratory', can be extended to the woman's own devious experiments with the people around her, her human elements so intensely present in mind: Pauline, Elise, the men 'at the King's' as well as herself and the chemist.

She is thrilled by the magic of the laboratory because she is the outsider in terms of understanding the recondite process of chemical transformation (which by extension she hopes will transform her own situation). Hence her astonishment at the power of a mere droplet. In line 17 she refers to the chemist's dark materials as 'treasures' while in line 18 they are seductively 'invisible'. As a result of her ignorance she must resort to describing appearances, their aesthetics, with a sense of awe.

Within the confines of her society – or at least her consciousness of it – there is a great sense of the 'other', the shadowy presence of a threat, rivalry, danger etc. This can take many forms – other women, the law, society, possibly even a projection or construct of herself. The prospect of the removal of this shadowy 'other' holds out the possibility of relief or freedom, helping to impel the poem.

In each case the character and her narration are very much defined by the 'other', the core of irritation and jealousy and bitter odium. By the same token, this is an extremely economical device of Browning's himself in delineating the woman's character, by letting her give herself away at the same time maintaining the semblance of naturalism. Although, in line 1, she dons a lab mask (the Brownian motif of the mask once again) we do actually begin to glimpse the woman behind the mask, behind the deceit.

While we learn much about the 'other' women, we discover little about the men. She prefers the company of the old magus-like chemist:

>Than go where men wait me and dance at the King's.   (12)

The 'masculine eyes' in line 31 seem equally persistent in their probing watchful desire as her own. The female speaker of the poem may be regarded by others as quite passive, a simple sexual object, and in the poem these elements are used to contrast with the other received view of the woman as a strongly active and potent force of destiny.

Regarding the woman as a 'force of destiny' inevitably raises questions of ethics. Again we ask the question, is she immoral, or amoral (or perhaps she somehow transcends the question)? The chemist comes across as generally amoral, an instrument in her hands, but when in line 41 she directs the chemist to 'be not morose', she may have detected a glimmer of moral reproof in his frown. But, if so, she swiftly dismisses it with a pragmatic shrug: 'It kills her ...', and that is ample.

Without doubt, the driving force of the poem lies in the woman herself, incorporating her nuanced character through tense, rapidly fluctuating moods. As in 'My Last Duchess' and 'Porphyria's Lover', the shock of the poem's grotesquerie, in theme as well as people, goes a long way to account for the appeal of this gruesome yarn.

The character as narrator carries with it immediacy and tension, suspense being generated by a slow release of information through the character's point of view. Once again, to exert a moral dimension in the poem, Browning relies on the horror of the proposed murders to provoke the reader's abhorrence.

One consequence of this emotional immediacy is that we are likely to feel more engaged because the form shifts the onus onto the reader to discover and fill the gaps, reading the inferences and subtext. The poem itself has all this readerliness about it: through the mediating glass and smoke, the narrator watches the enigmatic scientific process, seeking to interpret what is unfolding. She speculates what others are doing (and what they think *she* is doing; stanza II), while hazarding conjectural guesses concerning the effect of the poison on her rival. Adopting the woman's point of view naturally deepens the intrigue by way of her silences and the drip-feed of information, all of these helping to sharpen the emotional intensity of the poem.

Certainly a strength of this approach – as well as a weakness – is that we hear the narrator's words directly and we are thus placed in immediate proximity to the woman. We almost see through her eyes, through that mask and the smoke. Her diction is deceptively simple and there is a spareness of figurative material too. This may imply her own simplicity, her lack of education or merely her overpowering excitement.

Conclusions

Each of the three core poems we have examined in this chapter deal with a murder, although each deals with a different stage in a murder: 'My Last Duchess' reflects on the aftermath, 'The Laboratory' focuses passionately on the preparation, while 'Porphyria's Lover' presents a commentary on the gruesome act itself.

Yet in many ways the murders are of secondary interest since Browning uses them as a starting point to explore a range of diverse subjects, including character and motivation, questions of morality, the nature of gender and the status of woman (all the victims being women), themes of art and science, the significance or otherwise of religion in their lives.

As a narrative device death is utilised to energise the themes, by intensifying the role that these themes play in the threatened lives of the characters and in society as a whole. Death also gives increased meaning to the lives of the living, especially in terms of the intensely engaged consciousness of the perpetrators.

Because of the crucial role that Browning gives to consciousness, we have seen how he uses to full effect two key devices: the grotesque, in setting and style, and the dramatic monologue.

Methods of analysis

Overall, the method I have adopted is one of close textual analysis, selecting what I believe are important passages, important in revealing, among other things, character, themes, key turning points, verbal textures or technical elements of Browning's writing. To achieve a fuller analysis I have tried to show how a passage relates to the poem as a whole, and this approach will be the basis of our strategy in this book as a whole. The features highlighted by analysis in this chapter include the following:

1. *Language.* My approach has been to centre as closely as possible on Browning's choice and use of words, how they carry individual meanings and how these meanings work within the fluid context of other words. I have attempted to indicate how these verbal interactions produce highly sophisticated texts that yield a raft of different interpretations, which themselves are affected by the contexts of other poems.
2. *Figures of speech.* By the same token, I have tried to draw out the important role of the poet's figurative devices, imagery and symbol especially, and to see their role in the creation of meanings and character.
3. *Rhythm and verse form.* We have made a useful start in noting the function that poetic metre plays and also the effect of different verse forms and patterns in the overall tone of a poem.
4. *Sentences.* The discussion has given attention to the structure and length of sentences in terms of Browning's aim of creating naturalistic conver-

sations, while working within the constraints of poetic form. We have noted too how different structures can affect tone and perceived attributes of character.
5. *Narrator*. We have given strong emphasis to the nature of Browning's narrators, to reveal and discuss the following literary points: the implications of different points of view, the creation of suspense by the control and flow of information, the generation of character and theme, and, above all, the crucial role of the dramatic monologue.

Suggested work

(a) Take another look at the three poems we have examined and consider the dramatic image of women Browning presents in them. How far would you agree with the view that the women are important only because they reveal the characters of the men in these poems? Give reasons for your conclusions.

(b) For further practice in the techniques of textual analysis, choose other interesting passages from 'Porphyria's Lover' or 'The Laboratory'; or perhaps try some of Browning's love poetry, for instance 'Love Among the Ruins' and 'A Lover's Quarrel'.

2
Missions, Silence and Exile

'Childe Roland to the Dark Tower Came'
'The Patriot'
'The Lost Leader'

The three poems that I have selected as the core of our discussion in this chapter all focus intensely on the inner states of their characters. I have chosen these titles as a starting point here because each concerns a form of mission in the way their characters respond to the travels, vocations or crusades that they undertake.

We have already encountered this interface of inner and outer realms in two of the poems of Chapter 1, namely 'Porphyria's Lover' and 'The Laboratory', and it can be argued that this concern forms one of the key interests of Browning's work as a whole. In the context of abstract states we will develop further an understanding of the complex operations of Browning's innovative developments in the dramatic monologue and the grotesque.

As well as offering a very convenient narrative form, the principal value of the mission as a poetic scenario is that it enables the intimate investigation of minds under duress, duress caused by the interplay of assorted limitations, coercions and incitements to action. In the poems of this chapter these motivational factors are invariably linked with traumatic moral and social forces or values (for example duty, loyalty, trust, idealism) – so each poem probes the acute psychological and emotional states that come to dominate a character's consciousness as a direct result of their mission or journey.

'Childe Roland to the Dark Tower Came'

Browning claimed to have composed 'Childe Roland to the Dark Tower Came' in a single day. In Paris on New Year's Day 1852 he announced his determination to write a poem every day and, over the next three days, he diligently composed three poems: 'Women and Roses', 'Childe Roland' and 'Love Among the Ruins'. However, like most New Year's resolutions Browning's soon petered away, and yet the chief outcome was the creation of one of his most astonishing poems.

This exceptional spurt of creativity appeared at a time when Browning's poetic output and critical reputation were in the doldrums. 'Childe Roland' is roughly contemporary with one of the most important statement of his poetic philosophy at this time – his so-called 'Essay on Shelley'. Browning had been approached to draft an introduction to an anthology of what its editor claimed to be some newly discovered letters of Shelley. Although these were later shown to be forgeries, Browning's introduction has survived as a valuable source for his aesthetic ideas and these are discussed below and in Chapter 6. We should thus expect some of the concerns of the 'Essay' to permeate the creativity behind 'Childe Roland'.

The tale of a man seemingly cursed to follow a nightmare journey gives the poem some fascinating points of contact with other cursed voyagers, most notably S. T. Coleridge's *The Rime of the Ancient Mariner*. Asked in 1887 if he had intended the poem as an allegory Browning was typically equivocal:

> Oh, no, not at all. Understand, I don't repudiate it either. I only mean I was conscious of no allegorical intention in writing it ... 'Childe Roland' came upon me as a kind of dream. I had to write it then and there.
> (see DeVane 1955, p. 229; Woolford et al. 2010, p. 349)

This dream – or nightmare, really – strengthens its resemblances with *Ancient Mariner* and also with Coleridge's *Kubla Khan*.

As the poem's byline indicates, the title of the poem originates in Shakespeare's *King Lear* and particularly Edgar's song in act 3, scene 4, line 182 on. This quote seems to have been a useful touchstone for Browning rather than any substantial influence (though the wilderness on the heath and the ever-present threat of madness are strong links between the play and the poem). Echoes and precursors abound in other literature, including the *New Testament,* Dante's *Inferno,* Edmund Spenser's *The Faerie Queene,* and John Bunyan's allegorical *The Pilgrim's Progress* as well as several fairy tales involving archetypal quests (including *Jack and the Beanstalk*). Interesting parallels can be traced too with other Browning poems, notably 'The Lost Leader' and *Paracelsus* (the latter wanders Europe, Asia and Africa in pursuit of hidden knowledge).

For this narrative poem I have decided to examine two short passages as a launch pad for a discussion of the whole poem. The first passage is taken from the beginning of the poem.

Passage (i) lines 1–24

I

My first thought was, he lied in every word
That hoary cripple, with malicious eye
Askance to watch the working of his lie
On mine, and mouth scarce able to afford
Suppression of the glee, that pursed and scored   5
Its edge, at one more victim gained thereby.

II

What else should he be set for, with his staff?
What, save to waylay with his lies, ensnare
All travellers who might find him posted there,
And ask the road? I guessed what skull-like laugh   10
Would break, what crutch 'gin write my epitaph
For pastime in the dusty thoroughfare.

III

If at his counsel I should turn aside
Into that ominous tract which, all agree,
Hides the Dark Tower. Yet acquiescingly   15
I did turn as he pointed: neither pride
Nor hope rekindling at the end descried,
So much as gladness that some end might be.

>   IV
> For, what with my whole world-wide wandering,
> What with my search drawn out through years, my hope   20
> Dwindled into a ghost not fit to cope
> With that obstreperous joy success would bring, -
> I hardly tried now to rebuke the spring
> My heart made, finding failure in its scope.

With regard to the poem's unusual title, we shall return later for a fuller discussion of its importance to the poem but we can note here that a 'childe' is a male youth, of noble birth. In medieval romances and ballads the word usually referred to a young man in training for a knighthood, for which they could be expected to undertake some ordeal of strength or endurance. The idea of a quest-ordeal has classical origins and in ancient religions there are similar circumstances in which a figure is thrust into the wilderness for reasons of catharsis or meditation: Jesus Christ, Mohammed and the Buddha spring to mind, among many others.

These opening verses, like the title, actually betray the ending to the narrative and clearly Roland is not narrating while on the journey itself, although some time after its finish. It is a first-person monologue so we know that, whatever else happened, he managed to survive. The obvious conclusion of this is, of course, that the narrator-character is at least as interested in the journey itself as in the successful arrival at the Tower – and the ending seems to confirm this view.

As we notice repeatedly while reading the poem, Roland's cadences tend to deflate even the slightest hints of optimism that arise during his ordeal. Relativism quickly dominates the rider's tone and outlook, with the effect that the landscape is unremittingly desolate, its function seemingly to puncture any suggestion of epic heroism.

Let us now turn to a detailed analysis.

Stanza I

The opening line of the poem is highly indicative of the content and attitude of what is to follow:

> My first thought was, he lied in every word ...

Although the title hints at action, this is a poem very much concerned with thought and re-action. The whole of its 'external' experience is mediated through the consciousness of its narrator, in fact it is this consciousness that is effectively the subject matter of the poem. As in so much of Browning's verse, the inner life is all we have, and the first word of the poem 'my' points us there – it is '*my*' version, Childe Roland's.

This recognition of versions of reality (rather than absolute truths) is also evident in the uncertainty underlying the opening line. Roland's 'first thought' is one he may revise later in the light of his suspicion that this mysterious 'he' is possibly lying. Deception and doubt are strong themes of the poem and here they are at the start, both in Roland's warning to us that things may not be as they seem, and in the prospect of outright deception (in fact, Browning's own style here and elsewhere can be described as 'askance'; see line 2). The narrative information is so oblique and evasive, making us work hard in our own quest, Browning himself may therefore seem to be the 'hoary cripple'? (There are many possibilities.)

This is a marvellously enigmatic opening, dropping us directly, *in medias res*, into a journey long ago already begun. The deictic pronouns ('My' and 'he') imply that Roland is narrating to someone already in the know, perhaps a previous traveller.

The opening line is typical of the poem's continual air of disappointment, deception being yet one more impediment to the progress of Roland's quest. It also shows us that, although essentially a loner, Roland depends on the service and advice of others. He cannot complete his life task without a complex of others, even if he comes to mistrust them.

As in the poems of Chapter 1, there is here the slow release of information. 'Hoary cripple' is pejorative, negative too, and so too his 'malicious eye', all intended as intrigues to draw us into the traveller's yarn. Negative metaphors like these signify Roland's own feelings of frustration and vulnerability since at this stage he has no idea of the cripple's veracity (but as it turns out the advice is probably true). Likewise, extending this theme of interpretation, the 'cripple' himself looks sideways to try to read how his words affect his listener. Each man is trying to read the face of the other, as we too are hoping to read for clues, but at second hand.

The opening stanza is important in introducing most of the poem's key elements: threat and deception, the proximity of death or disaster, and uncertainty amid cadences of disappointment. Equally, set out here are the poem's themes, of alienation, of being driven by mysterious anonymous causes, confusion and deprivation – with the nagging possibility of a complete loss of identity. These are all evidenced in the many negative-sounding words here, redolent of the dismal prospects for the whole odyssey: lied, hoary, malicious, suppression. Further, the first stanza gives an excellent clue to as the pivotal role that the senses (eye and mouth) will play in 'Childe Roland', intensifying the privations facing this acutely sensitive traveller ahead.

Stanza II

This almost relentless mood of pessimism is extended into the next stanza where its opening interrogation, suddenly and directly draws the reader into Roland's perplexity.

> What else should he be set for, with his staff?

It is of course a rhetorical question, one whose lack of answer perfectly communicates Roland's desperate conundrum. This is one of the poem's numerous paradoxes that repeatedly raise the question of why he perseveres with something that gives him so much pain and mental torture. One answer is that he seems to have no choice. However, this only leads to another paradox: these opening stanzas appear to present the appearance of choice with all its archetypal complexities (which road?), yet Roland never really has freedom of choice.

Browning brilliantly utilises this dilemma to confront the reader with the great torment in the hero's mind, the pressure to make an irreversible life-changing decision, with its concomitant dangers (here, it is the ultimate risk of death). Now, at the very start of the poem (actually in mid-journey) he expresses the awful angst of the existential condition: the inescapable duty of choice.

Employing a question in line 7 also helps introduce another elemental theme of the poem: archetypal desire. What desire was it that first caused Roland to embark on this quest? (though we do not yet know if it is a quest as such). It seems to be a model form of curiosity, an interrogation: he searches because he needs to search. On a simplistic level it may be the same intrinsic motivation that causes a reader to finish a book, even one in which he or she has no great interest or even hates. The reader here is placed in a direct parallel course of desire with the character. The inherent human drive to discover, to join up the dots and complete, lies behind reading itself. Browning knows and exploits this.

On a symbolic level, questions work to exacerbate the poem's texture of uncertainty. The second sentence of stanza II does not supply an answer, only another highly speculative question:

> What, save to waylay with his lies, ensnare
> All travellers who might find him posted there,
> And ask the road? (8–10)

This is a third reference to 'lies', and a claim that the 'cripple' consciously traps all enquiring travellers and waylays them. Ensnaring (line 8) is a recurrent theme in Browning's verse (see for example, 'The Laboratory', line 30, and all three poems of Chapter 1 involve some degree of trapping). This dovetails with the idea of the betrayed victim.

Convergent with this idea of deliberative action are the phrases 'be set for' and 'posted there'. These passive verbs seem to imply that the 'cripple' is a minion of some superior, anonymous and sinister force. But this for now can only be a suspicion, 'I guessed'. The word 'guessed' reiterates the theme of interpretation as well re-emphasising the hero's perplexity in the face of it. Roland's paranoia opens more explicitly when he visualises himself as a laughing stock of the 'cripple's' machinations. 'Skull-like' and 'epitaph' are of course early instalments in the narrative's imagery of death, while the word 'crutch' briefly underpins the idea of Roland's state of dependency.

In line 12 the modifier 'dusty' is a topographical pointer, implying desert or redundancy, the road less travelled. Throughout the poem the speaker is at pains to keep us informed of the terrain in which we travel. Given the asperity of the conditions and the paucity of description, ordinary lexical terms are likely to take on symbolic gravity – so we are on alert to the likelihood of 'dusty' implying a spiritual condition, 'dry' as a lack of faith (compare Christ's forty days in the wilderness and, for an interesting treatment of spiritual dryness, see T.S. Eliot's *The Wasteland*).

And what can we make of the word 'pastime' in line 12? It seems anathema to think of a pastime in this context but the word strengthens the idea of some entity toying with Roland as victim through torment and torture, that Roland's feelings of persecution force him constantly to suspect he is the unwitting object of an enormous deception. We ourselves may quite easily suspect the same.

And so we too progress with eagerness, a few qualms maybe, and a little hesitation. However, in stanza III, in place of the certainty we desire, we hear

> If at his counsel I should turn aside
> Into that ominous tract which, all agree,
> Hides the Dark Tower. (13–15)

Once again Roland is in the paradoxical dilemma of choice.

Whereas in the poems of Chapter 1 Browning preferred to *show* rather than to *tell*, here he goes a step further by making us directly share the experience of perplexity felt by Roland in the face of the enigmas of his journey in the wilderness. This technique plays on the same vacillations of desire and mistrust, the sceptical suspicion that we are trapped in a ghastly practical joke perpetuated by that inscrutable 'hoary cripple' and his kind.

Passage (ii) lines 73–96

The close of stanza IV sees Roland maundering in a state of demoralisation even in the same moment as he envisaged a triumphant end. Over the ensuing stanzas the focus of his tormented psyche flickers between thoughts of despair and uncertainty, suspicions of betrayal and entrapment. As the sun sets he moves forward deeper into the indeterminate terrain signposted by the 'hoary cripple', Roland himself crippled by the nihilism of self-doubt.

In stanza X he describes the wasteland of scrub as somewhere that operates outside of the normal laws of nature ('according to their law'; 58). While Roland is terrified of the threat of some hidden, yet indeterminate, force of malice, the actual threat seems to be an internal concoction of his own failure and despair, alienation and doubt, mixed in with the prospects of sickness and 'disgrace', and the almost certain prospect of failure. Endurance is less in terms of the brutal, hostile landscape that of the resources of his imagination to cope with it.

In stanza XI nature looms as an insouciant deity that Roland repudiates, so he is once more repelled by the grossly inhospitable vegetation threatening to 'baulk all hope'. Then he stumbles on the immobile form of a blind horse. The second passage I have chosen for discussion focuses on stanzas XIII to XVI, where the blind horse galvanises Roland's consciousness into memories of his precursors on this quest.

XIII

As for the grass, it grew as scant as hair
In leprosy; thin dry blades pricked the mud
Which underneath looked kneaded up with blood.   75
One stiff blind horse, his every bone a-stare,
Stood stupefied, however he came there:
Thrust out past service from the devil's stud!

XIV

Alive? he might be dead for aught I know,
With that red, gaunt and colloped neck a-strain,   80
And shut eyes underneath the rusty mane;
Seldom went such grotesqueness with such woe;
I never saw a brute I hated so;
He must be wicked to deserve such pain.

XV

I shut my eyes and turned them on my heart.   85
As a man calls for wine before he fights,
I asked one draught of earlier, happier sights,
Ere fitly I could hope to play my part.
Think first, fight afterwards - the soldier's art:
One taste of the old time sets all to rights.   90

XVI

Not it! I fancied Cuthbert's reddening face
Beneath its garniture of curly gold,
Dear fellow, till I almost felt him fold
An arm in mine to fix me to the place,
That way he used. Alas, one night's disgrace!   95
Out went my heart's new fire and left it cold.

Even a rudimentary glance at this reveals many of the themes in the poem as a whole: time, nature, duty, alienation, the fear of failure. In stanza XIII

Roland begins by describing his new stark location, the by-now familiar sparse, denuded vegetation; and standing in this blood-red scrub is the gaunt figure of the horse. Like himself, the beast seems abandoned, his existence pointless – in fact the viewer is unsure whether it is even alive. Its grotesqueness turns Roland's thoughts to duty and the prospect of failure, recalling the failure and disgrace of his former champion, Cuthbert.

Let us look in closer detail at the passage. Although individual scenes may vary in the poem, the whole ordeal presents an idea of Roland traversing an unremittingly hostile and barren wilderness, a wasteland in both natural and spiritual dimensions. The antagonistic terrain seems interminable, until the end, but even the finale is not an unqualified triumph.

Although the bleakness of the natural and spiritual topographies is ostensibly unrelenting, there is still variety and change within the anguish. Most clearly, the poem presents a rhythm of internal and external focuses, past, present and future moments, together with intervals of optimism and despondency. In stanza XI Roland passionately contemplates a future apocalyptic destruction of the land about him. Here, in stanza XII, there develops a kind of cadence of despair as his attention returns to the desolate prospect of external reality and the 'now' that he must deal with.

The tone also alters here: from the faint, contorted hope of destruction elsewhere to the melancholy acceptance of existence ahead. There seems to be again something of the existential curse of the conscience, Roland's recognition of intentionality, that the mind is always outward and attentive: to the cripple, some thistles, a horse – everything impending but without hope of closure. The silence of his exile seems to exacerbate the pain and intensity of consciousness.

> As for the grass, it grew as scant as hair
> In leprosy; thin dry blades pricked the mud ...   (73–74)

'Leprosy' is such a fine word here, like a cicatrice on the imagination, paralysed and diseased.

The poem's familiar imagery persists into stanza XIII: sickness, poverty and the grotesque. Nature here is far from the Romantic conception of a healthy regenerative force. It has transmuted into a sort of death-in-life, a parody of itself, and pursues Roland like an indictment. In this, nature appears all one with the malicious-eyed 'cripple' who like his landscape is 'pursed and scored' (line 5). The landscape actually resembles the 'cripple' in its 'ominous' antipathy, the Childe being assailed by threats of leprosy.

Its meagreness and aridity perhaps hint at spiritual sterility, a projection of incipient despair. Yet, curiously, this awful place never ceases to hold Roland's fascination, as if he were continually alert to the prospect of betrayal or death. This lurking possibility finds its appalling symbolic manifestation in the 'dry blades' that sprout from a mud underpinned by 'kneaded up' blood.

Line 75's reference to 'blood' is the sole mention in the poem of a substance normally associated with life and vitality, but here metamorphosed into something, by turns, lugubrious, contaminated and deathly. Nature is altogether brutish and, like the sole human resident, crippled and stunted, bereft of true growth.

The reader too is repeatedly surprised by the grotesque ugliness of the natural landscape, which is intensified, as J. Hillis Miller points out, through the 'fact that the reader is continually coaxed by the language to experience this ghastly scene as if it were his own body which had got into this sad state' (Miller 1963, p. 123). Elsewhere, the ground is blotchy, and grim, 'like boils'. Anything normally life-enhancing has become here a malevolent putrefaction.

Critic Betty S. Flowers compares the poem's nature landscapes to those in dreams – 'charged with undeniable significance, but a significance which is felt rather than understood' (Flowers 1976, p. 25). This is due in no small degree to the poem's striking and sensuous imagery. To a great extent it is possible to say that the poem's meaning is not be found in its narrative but in its imagery. Certainly Roland himself is both the product and source of his own imagery, uniting the external with its observer or deviser. In a real sense Roland's view of nature here is anthropomorphic since it often appears to originate in his own delicate self-abhorrence. Its modes – of sickness, death, deformation and hopelessness – cluster-in suicidal narcissism.

One further aspect of Roland's curse-of-conscience is his tendency for animating things as he encounters them. He does not just *see* phenomena but inevitably *interprets* them, inventing narrative explanations (which mimics the reader's own speculative response).

>One stiff blind horse, his every bone a-stare,
>Stood stupefied, however he came there ...

'Stupefied' runs the risk of making horses of us, the reader, too.

Once again resembling a reader, Roland actively concocts a story within a story: the wretched horse has been exploited, in service, to be abandoned as spent, impotent, formerly of the devil's 'wicked' host. Now it stands as some defiant parody of horse.

Like Rosinante, Don Quixote's sorry charger, the horse is a wretched bag of bones, discovered among sterile vegetation, pashing its life out in silent despair. However, any hints of movement are clearly out of place since the horse simply stands, stiff, blind, stupefied. Lifeless, it seems that for this animal existence is a cursed burden to be endured, eyelids closed, and thus Roland feels an odd affinity with the hopeless wretch.

When Browning prefaces stanza XIV with the question 'Alive?' he is actually confronting us, the reader, with the question, a question that is in effect unanswerable. We may be the ones who are 'stupefied'. In what meaningful sense could something be understood to be alive? The answer seems to be, simply and discouragingly, 'by the fact of its not being defunct'. It exists by dint of its impact on the subjective viewer, the horse by its obdurate standing. And perhaps this is the reason Roland despises the horse:

>I never saw a brute I hated so ...   (83)

I suggested above that the poem is to a great extent its imagery. One function of the poem's imagery is to help construct the strong moral landscape and the moral texture underpinning the poem.

At the same time, and because of its foregrounded role, the imagery does a lot of hinting at meaning without ever coalescing into even a shadow of meaning. In this sense (as in others) we are once more located in something of a similar quandary as Roland himself. Our reading of the poem is much like his epic quest, so much meaning is simply adumbrated; Roland himself does not understand meanings and we, at one stage removed, are left to grasp at things dimly understood by the narrator.

So, in stanza XIV, after starting on a positive high note with the word 'Alive?' the tone trickles away through 'hate', and wickedness, culminating in pain. The following couple of stanzas becomes more introverted and turns to the past for escape and revival of spirit, referring to 'happier sights' and setting 'all to rights'. But this is swiftly scuppered by line 91's 'Not it!', atrophying away to close in the dismal cadence, 'and left it cold' (line 96).

These inflections often have moral or didactic objectives. Accordingly, each of the above four stanzas finishes up in a moralising tenor: 'devil's stud' (78), 'He must be wicked' (84), 'sets all to rights' (90) and

> Alas one night's disgrace!
> Out went my heart's new fire and left it cold.   (95–96)

This melding of stark moral tone and spiritual cadence casts a divisive pall over the mood. Roland is further alienated, not only from his sorry landscape but also from his own sense of self-worth – the single element with any hope of sustaining him. The only talisman that compels him forward appears to be essentially the same reflex that urges a reader to continue with a book, film or play: a hazy moral instinct for completion.

Repeatedly we are drawn to wonder why Roland persists in this journey having suffered with such grotesque outward persecution and inner torment. And he does not yet appear to have become insane. The answer must be that there probably is no way on but forward since if the journey has been filled with the same suffering, there is no advantage to retracing his steps.

The knightly virtues of honour, fortitude and disinterested duty may imply some overarching but *internal* faculty of order in this alien terrain. Equally, the word 'deserve' (84), in discussing the horse's painful ugliness, seems to epitomise a faith in something, whether spirit, deity or possibility of redress. Perhaps this faith in universal order, the thing that disheartens him so much, is the very thing that motivates him to complete.

At the start of stanza XV, Roland turns his attention away from the outer scene, closing his eyes ('think first'), in order to find some inner moral resources:

> Ere fitly I could hope to play my part.   (87)

That small word 'fitly' is one feature of the important moral imagery of the poem (see line 42 as well). It refers in fact to his physical and martial readiness. As a knight presumptive, he feels acutely the moral imperative to act in a proper way, and to 'perform his *devoir*'. This latter phrase derives from old French for 'to owe' and refers to the duty of a knight, his selfless, courtly obligation and the notion of performing service for its own sake, rather than from instrumental or ulterior motives.

This duty, more than anything, seems to explain why Roland loyally perseveres with his quest. In this sense of *devoir*, the question 'why not?' does not realistically occur to him. This operates both to his glory and to his scorn because it could imply the absence of free will, slavish conformity. Browning's poem is chiefly the exploration of Roland through his dogged determination, his trudging interaction with the dark, ultimately unknowable universe where others, like Cuthbert and Giles, had fitly failed.

As a 'childe', a youth of noble birth, the quest-ordeal is intended as a moral test of the aspirant knight, his virtue and forbearance. But it is an absolute test – he either succeeds or fails since it is a test of absolute grace – there are no resits or intermediate pass grades. The ordeal does not make the knight, it selects him.

In literature and mythology as a whole, the 'quest' is a much-used plot device instilling naturalistic structure to a narrative, implicitly entailing suspense, while embodying a useful form on which to hang picaresque adventures and mini-quests. The hero's efforts are normally a test of virtue and fortitude, moral and physical, during which he undergoes epiphanies about himself and his life In this way, the form is consistent too with the rites of passage, or *Bildungsroman*, genre (see Glossary).

Typically, the quest genre is one that involves false turns and deceptions contrived by those who despatch the hero, or by those encountered en route, and the successful questor frequently faces an uncertain return home. Because of its perilous nature as a trial of heroic status, the quest form also incorporates the potential for literary tragedy, and 'Childe Roland' repeatedly teeters on the brink of a tragic outcome.

Everything about Roland's journey seems uncertain or ambiguous and the faintly out-of-focus landscape is for practical purposes a symbolic character in itself. Sometimes it appears that Roland is less on a quest for something specific than merely drifting around (for example line 20 refers to a search but the previous line talks of his 'wandering' – it seems that he has been so long on this mission he has forgotten why or for what).

While stanza IV talks of Roland's journey in terms both of 'wandering' and a 'search', the poem's title talks of him simply as 'came' rather than 'reached' – the former implying that he merely stumbles on the Tower. That said, the mysterious 'cripple' appears to be part of the validating fabric of the journey – at the crossroads, whichever direction is indicated by him implies that his role is teleologically embedded in the narrative (though we are doomed never to know whether his 'counsel' was itself just an arbitrary guess).

Even if Roland is victim of the cripple's malice, the notion of free will implicit in his choices seems to become a blight rather than a liberation. He appears to travel in the passive hope that whatever forces and factors threaten to beset him, they will turn out to be more benign than the ones behind (see lines 10–13).

If this journey is literally a 'quest' then this may imply some degree of free will, but if it is simply a 'wandering' this is less so. And he does come across as a passive traveller, seeking the path of least resistance instead of heroic confrontation. We do not get much of an impression of Roland imposing himself on the outer forces so much as a readiness to submit to them as their victim, which he may rationalise unthinkingly as 'duty'. For this reason we are unlikely to be convinced by line 89 (and compare line 86):

> Think first, fight afterwards - the soldier's art ...

For the most part passive, Roland responds to threat or stimulus affectively, that is through the feelings. Accordingly, 'heart' is the keyword of stanza XV (line 85), a stanza in which Roland escapes from the present ordeal into the sanctuary of his 'heart' and inner deliberation. In stanza XVI he escapes into the imagination and via this through to the past – hence the keyword 'fancied' which introduces it.

> I fancied Cuthbert's reddening face
> Beneath its garniture of curly gold ...   (91–92)

To a large extent the imagination is the root of all the poem's other themes since Roland projects the events and impressions through this. This stanza traces a typical pattern in the poem by which Browning uses Roland's creative imagination to fill out wider contextual detail and then fixing the importance of those details for him. In this way, the poem moves from the particular to more general perspectives of interpretation.

Thus in stanza II he tries to imagine the cripple's laugh, then in stanza V he drifts off into a reverie of sick men, in IX the safe road vanishes, in XI Roland dreams up Nature's words, in XVII he fantasises Giles, and in XXII the landscape is animated by imaginary toads and wild cats. In stanza XXIII Roland muses that a 'mad brewage' sets to work in the brains of these creatures, but clearly the same 'mad brewage' has been at work in his own. Is any of it true? What does 'true' mean here? even if there were truth it would, of course, be Roland's subjective truth.

Among other phenomena he imagines boils, a harrow, a dragon, bulls and giants, all operating for him as signs. At the root of his rich imagery, his metaphors and similes are as dazzling as they are profuse (the preposition 'like' appears at least ten times and the preposition 'as' eight times). Ironically Roland appears to have the sensitivity and imaginative brio of an artist. His imaginative dynamics – as expressed in visceral symbolism – reveal a viewpoint continually striving to penetrate to the substrate of his actual situation.

And at the centre of this supposed presence existing beneath the immediate surface, Roland appears constantly aware of an Otherness. This may be in the form of paranoid suspicions of a scheming 'cripple', or the supposed wickedness of a blind horse, or even a spiteful stream. As said before, the quest is inward too (perhaps it always was), fired by a desire to know that leads him to the heart of darkness and its horror within himself.

Commentary

As with the other Browning figures we have already examined, Roland's journey is really about himself – he himself is really the Other that always walks beside him. Beneath the mask of a conventionally dramatic journey we can observe how he is half in love with a danger that becomes eroticised through fear and risk, exciting himself with its ticklish hazards. As we read we are likely to suspend our disbelief in the melodrama of Roland's adversity while we consent to go along with this whole search enterprise. True, it is a wretched journey, but it is not a horrifying one, not in the same way of the haunting terror of, say, John Keats's *La Belle Dame Sans Merci*.

Perhaps the real horror is that, like Coleridge's 'Ancient Mariner', Roland is doomed for a certain time to relive, and thus briefly *relieve*, the events of the journey:

> And till my ghastly tale is told,
> This heart within me burns.
> (*The Rime of the Ancient Mariner*, lines 584–585)

Roland's curse constrains him too into experiencing again and again his journey in the sting of memory. Browning expects this of the reader as well, the ghastliness of the reader's journey being almost as unremitting.

For Roland an intense desire exists to be clear of this bodily confinement and to take refuge in the imagination. His hope is to evade the impoverishing constraints of the body, root of his malady, by way of the liberating power of the imagination, and the two are seen as in constant conflict throughout the poem. As we have seen, the latter is relentlessly at work attempting to neutralise the power of the physical and its shocks (river, horse, cripple, scrub and so on) to enable the consciousness to strive towards epiphany, in the form of knowledge about himself – which is the true goal of the quest (some critics, for example Harold Bloom, interpret the landscape as basically a total projection of his own nature; Bloom 1971, p. 168).

Like Roland's fertile imagery, his adjectives represent vivid subjective responses to his situation (for instance, in the second extract above, stiff, gaunt, rusty, wicked, happier, reddening and cold). This strong interiority of the first-person narration emphasises of course the mental, spiritual and subjective spheres plus a kind of dream logic that administers Roland's introspection.

The poem's alternation between outer and inner, and between hope and despair, gives rise to rhythms that are emphasised by the poem's stanza form. I have already mentioned the rhythm of cadences within each stanza, a feature that reinforces a boxing-off effect, each stanza inclining to be episodic. While each stanza is constructed of runner-over lines (iambic pentameter, in regular six line rhyming pattern ABBAAB), each invariably closes in a full stop, which tends to emphasise Roland's interior turmoil, his thought pattern repeatedly halting.

We too come to understand that the quest – or at least the journey – is really about Roland coming to define or be defined by that adversity caused by others. The ordeal is in fact created or intensified by each step towards self-knowledge: each step has the effect both of closing and opening his horizon. Cuthbert represents failure in moral force and thus a failure to 'fix me to the place' (94); Roland is not Cuthbert and so he moves on. Furthermore, each step of the way brings the likelihood that while there are more trials, the time will come when such ordeals will cease, and that what remains will be Roland himself, the dark tower of his own identity.

In this, Roland transcends that question of motives we raised earlier – the question is as absurd as trying to deny the ever-presence of consciousness itself. The journey and the goal are in fact one and the same. The reference to Cuthbert reiterates the moral aspect of suffering and, in making the past a source of perspective, reveals it to be a false exemplar, one further false lead:

> Better this present than a past like that ... (103)

The poem flows from Roland himself, of course – but, on the general terms we discussed in Chapter 1, is this a dramatic monologue? In his groundbreaking study of the dramatic monologue, Robert Langbaum rates 'Childe Roland' alongside Caliban Upon Setebos as among the best of Browning's dramatic monologues (Langbaum 1957, p. 76, and see Chapter 7). That it emulates speech is apparent – especially in the way Browning evokes non-fluency features (lines 79, 91 and 95), discourse markers (lines 73, 91 and 95) and exclamations. It is clearly a monologue and, while there is no implied listener within the poem, the fact that Roland has already survived implies narration *to* someone. Line 79 seems to imply too that Roland himself is conscious of himself as a narrator and of an exacting audience.

What then does it all finally add up to? Obviously, the Tower is nominally the archetypal endpoint, the explicit *raison d'être* of the quest, and as such it fulfils the aesthetic demand for closure, within the terms of the journey's suspense. The quest, well the part we see anyway, takes place largely at night but Roland's discovery of the Tower is like a daylight epiphany:

> Why, day
> Came back again for that! (187–188)

The awakening from nightmare is accompanied by a bell-like clarion sound, echoed in Roland's blasts from his mysterious 'slughorn'.

Yet there is no denying that the finish is somewhat melodramatic. Following Roland's arrival his feelings are less of triumph and of achievement than of relief – that he did not fail. To be sure, until he is suddenly standing in front of the Dark Tower, it does not dawn on him that this is his end point. His achievement actualises as the cessation of searching, the end of anguish, rather than in reaching a goal. His prolonged loneliness continues to point at the quest's singular absence of love and the deforming effect of this.

It dawns on Roland 'all at once' that this is the end, and the emptiness there comments rearwards on the search as somewhat illusory. The word 'trap' in line 174 is a likely hint again that Roland is the casualty of an elaborate trick. Lines 169–170 likewise:

> Yet half I seemed to recognise some trick
> Of mischief happened to me.

He had suspected fraud from the outset: 'My first thought was, he lied in every word'. But the lie was one of omission. Yet if a trick has been engineered then he will have learned and become a wiser man for that. However, like most phenomena in 'Childe Roland to the Dark Tower Came', the end is ambivalent. As we read we are likely to feel that while meaning is always impending, it never quite crystallises (that, after all, maybe he did follow the wrong path). It is a tale with certain elements absent, and a fuller meaning ultimately evades us since it also evades the incomplete narrator. There are lacunae and silences in plenty, with the necessary connectives having been deliberately and playfully omitted. Even Roland himself never quite comes into wholly sharp focus. Like Kafka's Joseph K., he struggles to make sense of his exile, and Roland may not yet understand that tomorrow he will arise and go to face again the journey's silences.

'The Patriot'

Extending the Missions and Journeys theme, 'The Patriot' may seem an odd choice to include here, but the poem covers a number of journeys and in his commitment to a cause the patriot of the title is or was convinced of a mission of sorts. As in 'Childe Roland', we find a lonely figure, alone in a 'wilderness', driven by dedication to an archetypal calling. On the other hand, the patriot more resembles Giles in stanza XVII of that poem in his ignominious disappointment:

> ... what hangman-hands
> Pin to his breast a parchment? His own bands read it.
> Poor traitor, spit upon and curst!
> ('Childe Roland to the Dark Tower Came', lines 100–102)

In composing 'The Patriot' in the early 1850s, Browning did not have in mind a particular patriot but was conflating several disparate people and moments. One of these featured a rising of the Florentine populace against the local Austrian governor during the early stages of the Italian Risorgimento. The Brownings were passionately sympathetic to the Italian republican cause and observed the cheering Tuscan patriots plant a 'tree of liberty' in the piazza opposite their apartment windows. However, after the republicans' defeat at the battle of Novara in 1849 the Italian spirit faded and the returning Austrians briskly rounded up the usual suspects.

Another possible moment in Browning's mind was Louis-Napoleon's triumphant coup of December 1851 witnessed at close hand by the Brownings in Paris. In addition, stanza VI of 'The Patriot' formerly contained a reference to Brescia in northern Italy and Browning may have had in mind the medieval figure Arnold of Brescia, executed for heading a popular rebellion against Church dogma and whose inspiration became one of the Italian icons of the nineteenth-century Risorgimento.

Browning's poem is none of these and yet it is all of them in its broadly universal treatment of apostasy and perfidy. Because it is a short lyric, I have decided to examine the poem in full.

'The Patriot'
An Old Story

I
It was roses, roses, all the way,
With myrtle mixed in my path like mad:
The house-roofs seemed to heave and sway,

The church-spires flamed, such flags they had,
A year ago on this very day.   5

II

The air broke into a mist with bells,
The old walls rocked with the crowd and cries.
Had I said, 'Good folk, mere noise repels -
But give me your sun from yonder skies!'
They had answered, 'And afterward, what else?'   10

III

Alack, it was I who leaped at the sun
To give it my loving friends to keep!
Naught man could do, have I left undone:
And you see my harvest, what I reap
This very day, now a year is run.   15

IV

There's nobody on the house-tops now -
Just a palsied few at the windows set;
For the best of the sight is, all allow,
At the Shambles' Gate - or, better yet,
By the very scaffold's foot, I trow.   20

V

I go in the rain, and, more than needs,
A rope cuts both my wrists behind;
And I think, by the feel, my forehead bleeds,
For they fling, whoever has a mind,
Stones at me for my year's misdeeds.   25

VI

Thus I entered, and thus I go!
In triumphs, people have dropped down dead.
'Paid by the world, what dost thou owe
Me?' - God might question; now instead,
'Tis God shall repay: I am safer so.   30

'The Patriot' is composed in six stanzas constructed as enclosed quintets (that is the stanzas do not run on, one to the next). Once again Browning favours a tight, constricting rhyme scheme of ABABA, suggesting a graphic equivalent of the hero's own incarceration. We saw how the poet favoured the closed type of stanza form in 'Childe Roland', and here too it underlines a general falling cadence. Also like 'Childe Roland', we find here this highly formal template is in acute tension with the seemingly free, naturalistic style of speech patterns, one of the poem's multiple ironies.

The poem has a deceptively simple look about it, but if we delve deeper we will discern some interesting complexities. One of these is the form of the poem, and our discussion should naturally take account of this.

Its six stanzas, narrated by the patriot himself, are constructed in pairs, suggesting a three-part form. Stanzas I and II are a memory of the past and its frenzied acclaim of the man as hero; the middle two stanzas are a vivid contrast, feeling more like melancholy reflections; and the final two look to the future and the dire prospect ahead. Yet, uniting this seeming fragmentation are two key factors: the central voice and consciousness of the narrator, and the strong chronological sequencing of the poem (time being a conspicuous thematic feature of the poem).

The general sense of the poem is not difficult to sum up: a disconsolate leader meditates on the traumatic collapse of his former immense popularity – that he had once revelled amidst cheering supporters whom, he felt, would have done or given him their everything. As he dejectedly awaits his short journey to the scaffold, this fallen Icarus glimpses another journey, the epiphany by which he grasps that he himself was alone in the commitment and idealism aspiring to a new order. He is a one-time messiah transforming into the crowd's scapegoat. Let us now set out to trace the course of the two journeys.

Stanzas I and II

The poem opens with a startlingly elated expression of triumph as the leader recalls his joyous entry to the anonymous town. The entire place seems intoxicated with the frenzied welcome:

> It was roses, roses, all the way,
> With myrtle mixed in my path like mad ...   (1–2)

Ecstasy is clearly evident in the colloquial repetition of 'roses, roses' and the phrase 'like mad'.

The whole stanza bubbles and tumbles forwards in an explosion of excitement accompanied by vivid imagery of flowers, flags, roofs and spires. These are literally the high points from which he will be toppled, but they also figuratively mimic his ambition, borne along in feeling.

In this opening part, the poem's language emulates the billowing flags and boisterous euphoria of the crowd scene. Lists of action words, the use of strong alliterative consonants, and mounting imagery of noise together generate a sense of boisterous festival teetering on chaos. Clearly, this prepares the poem for the great contrast with melancholy solitude in later stanzas. Out of a tumultuous chaos of emotion and life eventually comes a muted contemplation of failure and death.

The poem teems with acutely sardonic ironies and already in the opening diction there are hints of the man's demise. For instance, 'like mad' reflects the patriot's complete immersion in the feelings of that day, implying that his reason or perspective became clouded by the strong feelings generated. The high points of roof and spire contrast with the later metaphors, of 'foot' (20) and 'dropped down' (27).

By the same token, 'sway' in line 3 relates both to the exuberant motion of the loyal crowd and to the ironic idea of the leader's judgement being swayed by his followers. The opening lines sparkle with movement and sound (note all the alliteration on /m/ and /s/) and again this contrasts with the dull stillness later in the poem.

The anticlimax to come is prefigured slightly in line 5 since its consciousness steps out of the frenzy to reflect on time. A further irony is manifest in the poignancy of this, the day of his execution, being the 'very' anniversary of his late exultation. Furthermore, it has taken his followers only one year to turn their fierce loyalties around into even fiercer contempt, such that he will later demote this to 'my year's misdeeds' (25).

The patriot revisits these earlier elements in stanza II where clamour takes over in 'bells', 'cries' and 'noise'. The earlier 'sways' is mirrored now in 'rocked'. Perhaps 'mist' (6) reinforces his new feeling of having been deceived or misguided, while 'old' (7) suggests the preceding regime whose overthrow is now so joyously celebrated. It is a beautifully evocative reflection:

> The air broke into a mist with bells ... (6)

However, from line 8 on the ironies begin to thicken; for example '*Good folk*', 'repels', and in lines 9 and 10, a sense of the people's absolute dedication to him (or so he trusted). The word 'Had' at the start of line 8 alludes to the patriot's ponderous feeling of regret, regret that he could not spot that the 'Good folk' were 'mere noise'. They would have done anything for him, given him the lot, even the sun. The latter hints at the poem's Icarus theme – that his misguided ambition, buoyed along by their raucous backing, caused him fondly to commit himself too highly. They would have given their life itself – or so he understood – ironically as he is now to lose his.

In addition to implying the Icarus idea, references to 'sun' and 'skies' are instances of the 'high' imagery, establishing the patriot's lofty stature before the fall. All of these, plus the noise, along with elated embrace of his leadership, possibly hint too at Christ's triumphant entry into Jerusalem, prologue to his betrayal and victimisation, an analogy that gathers more credence in the light of the final two lines of the poem.

So, what have the opening stanzas established then? For one, they have set up an impression of a key moment in the past ready for its contrast to the present. Although we do not yet have an understanding of the narrator himself, he has given us something of that other 'character' in the poem, the people or mob. The poem's brilliantly rich imagery has evoked a vivid impression of an ecstatic crowd joyful in its support and loyalty. On the other hand, the slight hyperbole in this account of the crowd's joyfulness reservations nurtures a suspicion of the volte-face to come.

At the close of line 10, the rhetorical question 'what else?', hangs ominously in the air like a leaden expectation, before the tension is shattered by the next stanza's opening word, 'Alack'. The rhythm of the poem swings the reader between the poem's binary contrasts; for example high versus low, hope and despair, loyalty and betrayal, ecstasy and regret. Despite all this, Browning subtly holds us in suspense; until we arrive at stanza III we remain in the dark about what exactly is happening.

Stanzas III and IV

The dazzling carnival of the first part swiftly dissolves into a dull, solitary plod for the next two parts. The word 'Alack' also points neatly to new regret, that the leader's vision had been overwhelmed during the delirious festivities, subsuming his rationality.

The intensity of the opening lines subsides, reflected in the new short and simple clauses. Stanza III marks the beginning of the patriot-leader's epiphany, that where once he believed he was the spearhead of a popular movement with shared objectives, he now regards himself as delusional, in the vanguard only of folly. 'Leaped at the sun' (11) reiterates the Icarus ambition theme but also, if line 9 refers to the crowd's giving their 'everything', then it denotes that he too hazarded *his* everything.

Negative diction in line 13 underlines the slump to despondency (naught, undone, nobody), underlining the speaker's mood of restive disappointment. Tellingly, in the following line (14), the pronoun 'you' draws attention to the dramatic monologue format of the poem:

> you see my harvest, what I reap ...

The agricultural imagery here conveys the idea of a season having run its inevitable course, while also laying bare the bitter self-recrimination at his foolhardiness. In the same way, line 12's 'my loving friends' reveals his utter disdain for the crowd's timidity, his tone of exasperation reinforced by the closing exclamation mark at the end of the line.

The poem is acutely conscious of time frames; for example the reference in lines 14 and 15 to harvest, day and year. The patriot reaps the figurative harvest of his blindness, hence the deeply ironic reference to 'my loving friends' in line 12. Line 14 reiterates the idea of line 5, that a year is such a short time in politics. The verbs change to present tense, as the speaker turns to thoughts of incarceration. The imagery of height in the opening of the poem also modulates:

> There's nobody on the house-tops now (16)

And yet the apparently throwaway word 'loving' (12) touches on a deeper thread at work here. The rose and above all the myrtle are symbols of love, linked to the goddess Venus, implying that the patriot suffers a shock like that of amorous rejection, sharing the same pangs as the jilted lover.

In a marked naturalistic contrast to the opening jubilation, the only ones now on high are a 'palsied few' at the windows. The sick ones look down, perhaps only because they could not descend to street level and gloat on his via dolorosa to the scaffold (as in 'Childe Roland', sickness is identified with moral criticism).

Ironies continue to season his acquiescent malaise. The medieval 'Shambles' (line 19) was the animal slaughterhouse – and has come to mean a 'chaotic state'. In line 18 his former disciples are satirised as a muttering pack, flocked together to exult on his degradation. From the cheering host of stanzas I and II the people have metamorphosed into a savage mob obsessed with ghoulish spectacle. In this respect too, perhaps they are all 'palsied', or sick. However, the most poignant irony lies in the phrase 'the best of the sight' since it refers to the patriot. His insight at this moment allows the patriot to see more clearly his illusion about his ex-followers – whom he now views with new clarity, sharpened by his imminent death.

In lines 18 and 19, the qualifiers 'better' and 'best' are both part of the broad moral texture here. The 'best' is not now for the speaker but for the mob itself, and this word's satirical appearance here suggests the crowd's eager, selfish zeal in baying for a scapegoat, a zeal that we assume had always been present, masked, but now evident in their angry clamour.

How would you imagine that the patriot speaks these lines of stanza IV, especially 18–20? Is he resigned, stoical or does he spit his lines out derisively? Placing the phrase 'I trow' at the end of this stanza gives the whole a much stronger feeling of sardonic contempt. 'Trow' is an archaic form of 'believe' or 'trust' which lends yet one further, mordant twist to his innocent misreading of the people.

Stanzas V and VI

> I go in the rain, and, more than needs,
> A rope cuts both my wrists behind ...

Once again, Browning resorts to a naturalistic sympathy between the weather and the mood: the joyous tumult of earlier stanzas is linked to the sun, while bad luck is now equated with miserable weather (but of course it is a fallacy to suppose our fortunes are necessarily linked with meteorological conditions – we are just as likely to be executed in warm sunshine). Trussed like a captive animal for effect, the patriot is poignantly now unable even to check his body for injuries. All of this points up his utter degradation since he is entirely at the mercy of his former disciples; in his struggle to bring them freedom he has forfeited his own.

The moral ironies begin to thicken:

> For they fling, whoever has a mind,
> Stones at me for my year's misdeeds.   (24–25)

The phrase, 'whoever has a mind' (24) catches the eye since, as well as suggesting the idea of 'whoever wishes', it incriminates the dull-witted crowd, lacking a mind. In the following line, the heavily scornful 'my year's misdeeds' has a dual purpose, pointing both at the fickleness of the turncoat crowd and at his own failure to carry through his 'deeds', or political manifesto. It epitomises too the relativism and evanescence of the political (along with the moral) life. There is no sense that his earlier 'success' was either absolutely good or bad as it can be later relabelled as 'misdeeds' – and may very well come to be regarded as heroic when public opinion shifts back again. Moral and political judgements depend very much on individual point of view. Like the landscape in 'Childe Roland', the crowd is an amorphous, hostile and ultimately incomprehensible swamp.

A note on the reading of lines 24–25 (cited above) is called for since their syntax is patently awkward, even clumsy. The word 'stones' would, of course, normally appear after 'fling' and the phrase is couched in this way to make the metre more regular. The metre of the poem consists of three more-or-less regular anapaestic feet (see Glossary under 'metre'), and while Browning is fairly relaxed about rhythm, he is unusually determined here to subject the syntax of these lines to the demands of the metre (for a good example of an anapaestic line see line 9: 'But give me/ your sun from/ yonder skies').

Browning generally shuns strict regularity, having more interest in evoking the rhythms of speech rather than slavishly obeying orthodox poeticism. Having said that, his syntax commonly reflects the naturalism of the moment. The majority of the poem's sentences are quite loosely constructed – of its thirty or so sentences only three could be described as anything like complex (in lines 8–10, 13, 28), and for the most part they are simple direct or extended sentences.

The stripped-down approach of so much of Browning's verse is evident here too; for instance, in the whole poem there is a total of only six adjectives.

The rich metaphors and imagery of stanzas I and II eventually give out to a generally monosyllabic catalogue of actions. Together with the mundane syntax, this economy successfully strengthens the anonymous patriot's feeling of a fait accompli, of matters having fallen completely out of the leader's acquiescent hands. Silences draw the reader forward in the expectation of a 'deathbed' public confession on the scaffold, perhaps an expression of regret or an outburst of recrimination (though, ironically, the poem as a whole represents exactly this).

There are of course many precursors and archetypes of the betrayed leader. To the fore among Victorian readers would be the example of Jesus Christ, fallen leader, betrayed by Judas Iscariot, at first lauded and lorded by crowds until eventually he becomes the sacrificial victim. The final stanza lends some credence to this kind of interpretation with its religious nuances, suggesting that the patriot will eventually be redeemed by God:

> 'Paid by the world, what dost thou owe
> Me?' - God might question; now instead,
> 'Tis God shall repay: I am safer so.   (28–30)

Shakespeare too has many examples of political reversal – most notably in the case of Coriolanus (in a play with close moral affinities to 'The Patriot'), a Roman general who, in a fitful career of shifting allegiances, is first feted by Roman crowds (the 'mutable rank-scented many'; 3.1.65) then by their Volscian enemies who eventually murder him, mistrusting his popularity!

Commentary

(a) The People

Why, we should reasonably enquire, do the people turn against their patriot-leader?

The silence between lines 10 and 11, the poem's turning point, means that the narrator does not account for their strange and dramatic volte-face. During a local uprising in Browning's own Florence, the turn-around of local animus was caused by the arrival of Austrian troops, to arrest and punish rebel leaders. By omitting a reason or cause in the poem, the narrator implicitly attacks the populace, his own countrymen, as merely fickle and vindictive; they do not simply remain indoors for the execution but actively revel in the patriot's demise.

In yet one more irony, the patriot appears to be undergoing punishment for treason, as a result of others' treachery and betrayal. The narrator satirises them as a single, cohesive character: inconstant, not to be trusted, but above all, ineffectual and craven. If we view the patriot as idealistic and radical then they emerge as tractable, self-seeking pragmatists, and it is a sad quality of his bitter epiphany that he had failed to notice or penetrate his 'Good folk', his 'loving friends', for what they are. The poem's idealism and materialism denote another of the poem's binary elements that coexist in powerful tension; for instance, standing against the patriot's utopianism, the crowd is unmistakeably identified with bleak materialism.

Like 'My Last Duchess', 'The Patriot' focuses on two moments and two points of view in order to express the process of change. Imagery of time is apparent here (year, day, harvest, reap, now) and Browning signals change through the adjustment of his verb tenses. In stanza IV the rhythm too changes: opening with predominantly anapaestic lines, the rhythm later sinks to a more irregular metre. At the same time, the sentence-forms parallel this momentous change, modulating from loose, tumbling structures into more ordered prosaic statements.

Given the patriot's clear sense of resignation there is thus a feeling too of the inevitability of change – that the ecstasies of 'My Last Duchess' and 'The Patriot' are inescapably subject to the will not of God but of a capricious mankind. In the opening stanzas of 'The Patriot', Browning brilliantly evokes the triumphant ecstasy of a split second in time in which destiny appears to holds its breath. And yet it seems intrinsic to the nature of ecstasy that it entails its own doom.

(b) The Scapegoat

> ... a man's reach should exceed his grasp ...

These lines are spoken by the eponymous narrator of 'Andre del Sarto' (line 97; and see Chapter 3) but they could equally apply as a motto of the speaker of 'The Patriot'. Like Icarus, son of Daedalus the flier, in the ancient Greek myth, he reaches beyond his grasp and either by folly or miscalculation he pays a price exacted by the faint-hearted. The patriot-leader is a victim of many things – of time's cyclical conspiracy ('this very day'), of the vagary of the people and of his own imagination, his short-sighted estimate of their support.

The patriot's condemnation starts with their lack of moral support but deepens by the fact that he is to be sacrificed as a scapegoat. By his own (ironic) admission, he is to be punished for his idealism as the spearheading pioneer, and the over-reacher. His anonymity lends the man an archetypal quality: he symbolises the loner and all those who mark themselves apart from popular approbation, the risk-taker, rebel and radical, but above all the artist. In this respect the patriot stands typically alongside other familiar Browning figures, Childe Roland, the duchess, Fra Lippo Lippi, the Pied Piper of Hamelin, and Caliban. These loners (especially those with a sense of mission) and victims are the poet's true heroes.

In the light of his own early 'failures' in theatre (see Chapter 5), Browning himself was extremely sensitive to the caprice of popularity, and of public taste in particular as it was manipulated by critics in the contemporary press. Then as now, the wretched popular press regarded itself as the arbiters of social taste and, then as now, were notoriously treacherous, perfidious and, for Browning, not to be relied upon. So much so that he came to regard the literary press as the principal cause of his failure as a dramatist.

Returning again to the poem, as he shuffles along to the scaffold at the Shambles Gate, the patriot recognises himself to be a moral scapegoat on two counts: he is a convenient target for the crowd's rancour as well as its missiles but also, with his hands tied, he is literally trussed up like an animal on its way to the slaughterhouse. Both of these emphasise his ignominious helplessness in the face of its perfidy.

It is difficult not to conclude that Browning believes any enterprise or 'mission', especially when combined with a yearning for success, is necessarily fraught with a risk of alienation. In this and other poems he appears to argue that alienation is inherent in the act of becoming any kind of leader, inherent in that archetypal and existential stepping-out from the safety of conformity, habit or convention. The consequent feeling of angst is accompanied first by tumult and then by a dangerous-sounding silence, as 'mere noise repels' (8).

Is the patriot a tragic hero or just a pathetic victim of his own folly? Is the poem a tragedy or a farce, or somehow both? If we measure the poem and its central figure against, say, Aristotle's ideas on classical tragedy, we can establish a useful basis for further understanding the patriot. To the extent that the patriot's fate complies with classical ideas of a man in high position, whose fall is great and to a large extent beyond his control, one who is motivated by noble ideals, we may be inclined to designate him 'tragic hero'. And yet we cannot be sure of his motives; lines 11 and 12 hint at love or altruism:

> Alack, it was I who leaped at the sun
> To give it my loving friends to keep!

In less expansive eras such as our own, we have come to be deeply apprehensive about political motives and so perhaps it is difficult to recognise one who acts from altruism or a moral commitment to principle and is prepared to sacrifice himself for these.

By contrast with Aristotle's world of absolutes, that of Browning's verse is invariably marked by its relativism. For this reason we may be able to judge tragic heroism from a different angle: as much by outcome as by motive. In 'The Patriot' it is the crowd that inadvertently fixes the moral benchmark and so it is on their terms that the central character, as enemy of the people, can be assessed: it is in the contrast with the self-serving, capricious and duplicitous nature of his judge, jury and executioners that the leader emerges as martyr. By way of yet one more irony, it is their own perfidy that transmutes their villain into the tragic hero.

'The Lost Leader'

> Let a man contend to the uttermost
> For his life's set prize, be what it will!
> (Robert Browning, '*The Statue and the Bust*', lines 242–243)

Whilst twenty-first-century readers may prickle at the idea of 'life's set prize', the notion of one's life having a destiny or mission would to Victorian readers have seemed perfectly reasonable. In '*The Statue and the Bust*', Browning censures those who fail to act on their desires or conviction, the two 'lovers' of the lyric merely gazing on each other, procrastinating in 'idleness which aspires to strive' (212–213).

Many of Browning's poems satirise figures who lack conviction or who, recognising their duty, their mission, 'life's set prize', flunk it. Another example is Andrea del Sarto who takes the safe line to avoid contention while all the time is aware of his infirmity of will. In contrast there are those dedicated individuals like Childe Roland who doggedly see their destiny through even though at times it seems pointless or even misguided.

Reading 'The Lost Leader', one is likely to be struck immediately by at least two points, both of which mark off this poem from the greater body of Browning's output. First, the poem draws a great deal of its interest from the intensity of the speaker's idealism, and second is the highly rhetorical tenor of his voice. It can even be argued that the tone and the style are the actual subject matter of the poem.

Published 1845, 'The Lost Leader' is unusual in being set in the poet's own time and place. Virtually all critics concur that the 'Leader' in the poem is the ageing figure of William Wordsworth, the pre-eminent figure (the 'van') of the first generation of Romantic poets that in the late eighteenth century led the rebellion against the prevailing neoclassical style of English poetry. Together with Coleridge, Southey and Blake, Wordsworth urged a break from a restrictive literary establishment with its stale inflated forms of verse, heavily influenced by classical authors.

In their groundbreaking collection *Lyrical Ballads*, of 1798, Wordsworth and his friend Coleridge trumpeted a fresh approach to poetry, freeing itself of staid and restrictive conventions of objectivity. Instead they sought to centre their work on subjective perceptions of ordinary experience and the natural wilderness, expressed through simple verse forms and everyday diction. Their polemical approach sprang from the same intellectual roots as their radical politics (typified by trenchant support for the French Revolution and for egalitarian movements at home).

In his celebrated Preface to the 1802 edition of *Lyrical Ballads*, Wordsworth affirmed the community of human spirit behind his work, closely identifying himself with the labourer and the shepherd, common man and woman. A poet is defined as 'a man speaking to other men':

> ... the Poet, singing a song in which all human beings join with him, rejoices in the presence of truth as our visible friend and hourly companion.
>
> (*Lyrical Ballads*, p. 259)

The 'truth' of which Wordsworth writes is a moral truth, evident in nature, and thus true to oneself.

In his prefaces to *Lyrical Ballads*, Wordsworth – then in his early 30s – documents his own personal mission, delimiting himself as poet and man. And while no one likes to find his youthful proclamations thrown back in his face forty years on, Browning considered his ideals to be profoundly inspiring and, so he thought, deeply felt. Hence our current poem's sense of shock at the later desertion, the loss of their spiritual leader head.

For analysis of this poem I would like to look in detail at its second part but, to begin with, let us get a general feel for the first sixteen lines, beginning with:

> Just for a handful of silver he left us,
> Just for a riband to stick in his coat ...

These opening lines clearly introduce the 'first-person' point of view of the monologue. The symmetry in the syntax of these lines establishes the poem's strongly rhetorical tone of voice, with its many repetitions in its metaphorical diction. The adverb 'just' is strategically important in suggesting both the meanness of the Leader's betrayal and the speaker's satirical manner. There are unmistakeable biblical overtones in the 'handful of silver' with echoes of Judas Iscariot.

The accusative stance is unmistakeable ('he left us') and prepares for the feeling of disgrace that the poem aims at. Likewise, the infinitive 'to stick' (like 'handful' in line 2) encapsulates in its simple vernacular both the triviality of the Leader's materialism and the orator's dismissive contempt for this ('silver' too is inferior to the gold that might have been 'doled' to him; line 5).

To understand the force and sense of the speaker's thrust here we need just a little more background. The 'handful of silver' represents Wordsworth's acceptance of the Tory government's Civil List pension in 1842, and the 'riband to stick in his coat' symbolises his elevation to the Poet Laureateship in April 1843. For Browning these two events were probably not in themselves decisively critical moments but simply the outward and material demonstration of his Leader's apostasy. Other writers like Shelley, Byron and Hazlitt had long rumoured of the backsliding of the former champion of liberal values or action. Here at last was the proof.

The highly emotional first-person speaker of 'The Lost Leader' denounces Wordsworth's defection, and his material success at the cost of his spiritual degradation. The Leader has been seduced by wealth and celebrity, and the speaker acknowledges that his devoted followers were too poor to offer him similar ('our copper'), though they had venerated his earnest idealistic principles ('Learned his great language ...'). Formerly allied with a host of radical and republican poets (for instance Shakespeare, and Milton) the Leader's 'mild' reputation is now debased by its reproachful contrast with them. Where his vibrant social ideals once liberated him, now his surrender to bourgeois ambition has made him a slave to decadence.

'The Lost Leader' is another poem employing sets of binary contrasts to drive it forwards, together with a flurry of quickly alternating points of view. Other thematic contrasts in the poem include: time (part I past and present, part II the future); silver and gold; freemen and slaves; the rear and the van; twilight and morning. There are many thematic antitheses too, often in alternate lines: self versus group; principles versus opportunism; duty and desire. Antithesis is a fundamental stock-in-trade of classical rhetoric, of course, but Browning utilises this to create a pacy, gritty tension, both nervous and intense.

Part II extends the dense texture of confrontation, in a tightly wrought, highly disciplined performance. However, the tone now attempts to become more actively provocative:

> II
> We shall march prospering, - not through his presence;
> Songs may inspirit us, - not from his lyre;
> Deeds will be done, - while he boasts his quiescence,
> Still bidding crouch whom the rest bade aspire: 20
> Blot out his name, then, record one lost soul more,
> One task more declined, one more footpath untrod,
> One more devils'-triumph and sorrow for angels,
> One wrong more to man, one more insult to God!
> Life's night begins: let him never come back to us!   25
> There would be doubt, hesitation and pain,
> Forced praise on our part - the glimmer of twilight,
> Never glad confident morning again!
> Best fight on well, for we taught him - strike gallantly,

> Menace our heart ere we master his own: 30
> Then let him receive the new knowledge and wait us,
> Pardoned in heaven, the first by the throne!

Each of the poem's two sections consists of sixteen lines, composed in four quatrains usually rhyming ABCB – this ballad form of rhyme is tight, tidy and sharp; the metre of each line is commonly three dactylic feet, ending in either an iambic (line 22) or trochaic (line 17) foot. This is a loose prosody and once again the effect is of a spontaneous or conversational tone. At the same time, this looseness assists the sense of earnestness – though the conspicuous rhetorical devices sometimes conspire against this. Browning makes this an ideal vehicle for the theme of change.

The poem as a whole begins in an angry tirade against change as catalyst of betrayal. In contrast, part II stoically embraces the idea of change by moving forward, or at least onward:

> Deeds will be done ... (19)

Beneath this a mild tone of menace operates, yet this represents more of a rhetorical censure than a specific programme of action. We get a tremendous sense of the speaker's explosive energy – intensified by the poem's complexities and many ironies – though without our becoming aware of any particular direction for this energy.

However, while the poem's bursting energy tends to obscure any precise manifesto, its strength really lies in communication: of the speaker's driving anger at betrayal and of his acute feelings about the crucial role and responsibility of the poet in society. Moreover, it does give a strong hint of Browning's own political and poetic attitude at this time (behind the mask of an anonymous speaker). Additionally, the speaker sets down a strong idea of a community's own role concerning poetry (all of these draw out and expand on ideas evident in 'The Patriot').

While part I tends to focus on 'he', the burden of part II is on 'we' and on 'our' possible response to the Leader. The auxiliary verb 'shall' in line 17 announces the change in point of view and mood, with a new sense of resolve, and the next couple of lines tries to strengthen this feeling of one marshalling resources in the vacuum left by their former messiah. A large dose of self-condolence is manifest here and although the speaker does talk of 'we', what actually comes across is his own very strong sense of personal indignation at betrayal. It is as though he is squirming under the realisation of personal folly at his misplaced love, his trust in the Leader.

(i) Lines 17–20

So, part II outlines the struggle of the speaker to distance himself and his comrades from the former leader. Each of its first three lines visibly asserts the new antagonism, each line pivoting on the caesura, with the message: progress will be effected without him or his verse (symbolised by the word 'lyre'). Let us look at the first quatrain, lines 17–20:

> We shall march prospering, - not through his presence;
> Songs may inspirit us, - not from his lyre;
> Deeds will be done, - while he boasts his quiescence,
> Still bidding crouch whom the rest bade aspire ...

After the victim attitude of part I with its mood of dereliction and desertion, line 17 starts the second half with a strong sense of resolve. 'Prospering' would speak directly to the Victorian ear with its connotations of positivism, assurance and progress. While it runs the risk of colliding with Wordsworth's supposed materialism, the word has a cheering optimism about it. It speaks of enterprise and growth yet remains judiciously vague about action.

The poem has two chief modes: on the one hand a fierce attack on the Leader's betrayal, and this is strong and precise, while the other, the speaker's remedy, is quite ambiguous. Like much of the rhetoric in this part, what we hear is a great sense of intense feeling, rancour and lamentation, rather than detailed specifics; for example in line 19, what exactly are these 'deeds' to be done?

Symptomatic of this affective quality is the poem's diction: part II's emotive verbs, primarily in future tense, are on the whole vaguer in meaning than part I's verbs, being chiefly of action. Nouns too differ acutely, part I's being more concrete (silver, riband, rags, graves), part II's having a more figurative flair (lyre, heaven, throne).

Line 19 takes a particular swipe at Wordsworth on at least two counts, first satirising his famous view of poetry as a contemplative process:

> ... emotion recollected in tranquillity ...
> (*Lyrical Ballads*, 1798, p. 266)

The second is that in contrast to the radical polemicism of his youth, the elder Wordsworth had become somewhat inert, baggy both in poetic output and in progressive thinking. The verb 'boasts', in line 19, unmistakably depicts the old man as obdurately pompous and phlegmatic.

The following line 20 gives a political spin on the speaker's dynamic, that where the younger poet had spent his time in political vigour and revolutionary poetics, he now merely basked in the sedate platitudes of gentlemen's clubs and dinner parties.

> Still bidding crouch whom the rest bade aspire ...   (20)

Where once Wordsworth strove to stir the nation's conscience, he now is resigned to appease and to counsel orthodoxy (the word 'still' here nicely takes up and reinforces that notion of passivity in 'quiescence' from the preceding line).

In addition to compromising his principles by signing up for materialism, the ex-leader sins against the speaker and others in the theme of love. His sin of omission resides in abandoning his friends, something quite apparent in part I ('he left us', line 1 and 'we that had loved him', line 9). This theme goes some way to clarifying why in part II there is such an air of the slighted lover (the theme of love as counter to materialism is apparent in much of Browning's verse, especially in the *Men and Women* collection; see for example 'Love Among the Ruins', which gently concludes, 'Love is best').

Love is best too in the moral sense of 'justice'. This is equally apt here because the poem is energised by themes of duty and morality. Like 'The Patriot', 'The Lost Leader' implicitly prizes individual integrity and loyalty and, because individualism lies at the heart of both poems, there is a clear sense that the community derives its moral strength from duty, at the root of which is love. The leader offends this ethic partly by coldly abandoning his disciples but also by abandoning them for an elite (symbolised by the term 'riband').

(ii) Lines 21–24

Where the clauses of part I were mostly indicative, statements of fact, those of part II are predominantly imperative, the subject of them changing from 'he' to 'we'.

> Blot out his name, then, record one lost soul more,
> One task more declined, one more footpath untrod,
> One more devils'-triumph and sorrow for angels,
> One wrong more to man, one more insult to God!

The remedy that the speaker favours – blotting out identity – attempts to seize the moral high ground and the diction now resonates with a more biblical timbre – 'lost soul', 'footpath untrod', 'triumph and sorrow'.

Ironically, although the whole poem – and lines 21 and 17 in particular – seeks to 'blot out' or expunge 'his presence', the Leader's presence is in fact almost palpable: in vigorously denying the man, the speaker induces the opposite effect, of fixing him in the reader's eye. In a real and continuing way, and despite the explicit message behind the terse phrase 'good riddance', the speaker himself is in point of fact defined by the ever-present image of the lost leader. This is a point we must return in discussing some other unexpected ironies of the poem.

The allusion to the 'footpath untrod' may put us on the trail of Childe Roland, while the pietistic reference 'insult to God' connects this part both to this poem's opening line (Christ and silver) and to its closing, even Judas Iscariot being forgiven for his sin. Conversely, line 24 talks of the 'wrong ... to man' as well, and the speaker thinks of the offences as degrading, not just to himself and fellow disciples but also to the Leader himself, since he exists at two points in time – Wordsworth the great leader of the past, and the apostate of the present, almost in fact two separate individuals.

(iii) Lines 25–28

> Life's night begins: let him never come back to us!
> There would be doubt, hesitation and pain,
> Forced praise on our part - the glimmer of twilight,
> Never glad confident morning again!

This quatrain adopts imagery of light to propose the theme of ostracism and even of damnation, referred to in line 21's 'Blot out his name ... '. But what can we make of line 25 here? It seems ambivalent yet heavy with meaning.

'Life's night' in line 25 is indecisive; perhaps it refers to the speaker's consciousness, the idea of coping with life without their 'former pattern' to live by. Or it may equally refer to the Leader's prospective life of social darkness as a pariah ('blot'). And yet again, the final lines of the poem keep open the possibility of a redemption, of sorts.

If the Leader, Wordsworth, was allowed to return, this could be divisive, splitting opinions and allegiances, ending in renewed anguish over his loyalty and relationship. As a false friend he could provoke disciples into making polite tributes (a false 'glimmer of twilight'), in other words, into honouring someone who had, after all, deserted his principles as well as his loyal followers. After making a clean break from the man, any act of forgiveness on 'our' part could result in interrupting our fresh start, dashing the 'confident morning'.

Cutting through the lofty rhetorical language, the speaker's reference to 'glimmer of twilight' could equally be a smear aimed at Wordsworth's later verse, generally regarded as faded in comparison to the dazzling splendour of the early Romantic renaissance.

In more general terms the rhetoric of the poem is derived chiefly from three strands: the imagery, word sounds and the syntax. One of the most conspicuous threads of imagery here is what we may term belligerency, the use of sententious militant-sounding words so it resonates as a political or social anthem (march, triumph, strike, gallantly). Another thread is religion: devil, angels, God and throne. The poem has a rich musicality of consonant sounds (note again Browning's partiality for alliterative doubles: deeds done, more to man, gold give) while, among vowels, the /o/ assonance predominates (see lines 5–6, 11 and 23).

With regard to the sentence structure of the poem, two features in particular show up. One is Browning's use of formal rhetorical features: for instance *isomorphism* or parallel syntax (see especially lines 1 and 2, 'Just for a ...'; lines 14 and 15, 'He alone ...'; and lines 22–24, repeating 'one more'). The second important feature is the contrast in sentence types between the two parts. Part I's lines figure as a list of statements, often using parallel constructions (see lines 1–2, and 15–16); on the other hand, each of part II's lines more often has a feeling of symmetry within the line, pivoting on the caesura, as we noted above. The two halves of a line do usually have a connection, either by contrast (line 21: 'blot out' and 'record'; line 23: devils versus angels) or concord (line 18 has songs and lyre; line 20, bidding and bade).

At the heart of all this stands Browning's strategic use of caesurae. *Parataxis*, a rhetorical device using repetition of short, loosely connected clauses, and the poet uses these in part II either side of the caesura; so in the above quatrain lines 25–27 follow this pattern, and there are many examples throughout the poem. Used in conjunction with portentous diction and metaphor, the speaker seeks to impart a measured feeling of strength to the argument, manipulating the listener/reader by sound.

(iv) Lines 29–32

> Best fight on well, for we taught him - strike gallantly,
> Menace our heart ere we master his own:
> Then let him receive the new knowledge and wait us,
> Pardoned in heaven, the first by the throne!

Another rallying cry, more hectoring rhetoric, more confrontational diction: 'fight', 'strike', 'menace'. 'Menace' here, however, may carry the religious connotation of 'to rigorously interrogate' the soul or conscience, that is, to put our own house in order before we try to 'master his own'.

Lines 30 and 31 reverse the thrust of line 11 where it was 'we' who 'learned his great language' and in line 9 we who 'followed him'. Now the theme is that the Leader needs to be re-educated, re-formed so as to recover his former state of grace, 'the knowledge' – in Wordsworth's case this is a return to the simple language learned from communion with ordinary, everyday people, treated as equals.

Browning's references to 'knowledge' and 'pardoned' suggest that he has in mind the hope of an epiphany for the Leader, possibly religious (like St Paul's on the road to Damascus) and certainly moral. And this would hold out another chance of the 'confident morning' dismissed in line 28. The moral weight and conceit in the word 'Pardoned' reveals the thinking that the wayward Leader has not simply lapsed as a poet but also has sinned, and as such this portentous word is the climax of the moral and religious cluster of imagery in the poem. Moreover, the poem ends positively, in a glimmer of hope.

Although the word 'lost' in the title normally entails the notion of finality (note the word 'never' in line 25), the poem's final lines hold out a surprising possibility of hope and of redemption and return ('surprising' given the intensity of the invective that has preceded it). There remains the hope, proffered to the Leader, that he will be contrite, relent and then resume his former, pre-eminent position in the pantheon.

'Pardoned' in the final line, together with the other religious imagery, is important in another sense, that of drawing attention to the nineteenth century's special view of the role of the poet in society. The idea of the priest-poet as both a mouthpiece of society and as a semi-divine figure harks back to classical times and is one that was tenaciously embraced by Shelley, an early influence on Browning's philosophy. The Romantic poets as a whole recognised the role and responsibilities of the poet as a bardic figure, part-human, part-divine, a seer with a special faculty for apprehending and interpreting the truth of human reality. While for Browning and the Victorians this role had become somewhat secularised, a vestige of the privileged position of the poet lingered. 'The Lost Leader' has hints of this, for example in line 9, in the notion of following a leader with a 'magnificent eye', that is, a special genius. Line 17 speaks of 'Songs may inspirit us', implying the gift of the poet to interpret and infuse the soul with truth ('lyre' casts back to the classical origins of this ancient bardic function). The poem's religious imagery also helps to make explicit the hieratic strand in poeticism.

Browning defends this view of the poet as a semi-divine in his 1852 'Introductory Essay', a prose work that has become known as the 'Essay on Shelley' (see below, Chapter 6 for a brief discussion of this). Expounding his idea of two types of poet (the subjective and the objective), he visualises Shelley as the epitome of the semi-divine, thus assimilating the two:

> The [objective] poet's double faculty of seeing objects more clearly, widely, and deeply, than is possible to the average mind ...

and

> [The subjective poet] gifted like the objective poet with the fuller perception of nature and man, is impelled to embody the thing he perceives, not so much with reference to the many below as to the One above him, the supreme Intelligence.
> (Woolford et al. 2010, pp. 856, 858)

The poet sees 'Not what man sees, but what God sees' (Woolford et al. 2010, p. 858), and Browning uses the word 'seer' for this capacity.

The poet then is a kind of high priest, the followers being disciples or acolytes, novitiates in an arcane art. On these grounds Browning's poem condemns the Leader/Wordsworth for abjuring this noble responsibility all for a slavish quest of materialism, anathema of the divine ideal, 'Just for a handful of silver ...'.

Commentary

Confirmation that Wordsworth is clearly the object of the poem comes from Browning's letters; for example:

> Don't tell that I thought of - who else but Wordsworth ...
> (letter to Ruskin, 1 February 1856)

And in the same year, to novelist Vernon Lee he wrote with regret of the 'great poet's abandonment of liberalism' (DeVane 1955, p. 160). Nevertheless, some thirty years after the poem, in February 1875, a mellower Browning did ultimately regret the corrosive effect that his assault later had on Wordsworth's reputation. With some humility, Browning admitted:

> 'I *did* in my hasty youth presume to use the great and venerable personality of Wordsworth ...' [adding that his defection was 'an event to deplore']
> (Woolford et al. 2010, p. 207)

Elizabeth Barrett Browning, who did not share Robert's animosity, enjoyed 'The Lost Leader' 'supremely' and thought it 'worth all the journalising and pamphleteering in the world!', drawing attention to Robert's sense of mission in his poem (*Love Letters*, Volume I, p. 253).

Of course all this only works successfully if everyone understands the oblique allusion to Wordsworth, and the ironies and general laconic manner of the poem run the risk of it going over the head of the reader. Would that matter? Yes, because the very elements of silence and satire that make the poem less obvious enrich it with tension and hazard.

Line 23 talks of the 'devil's triumph' but also of the 'sorrow for angels'. 'The Lost Leader' is not wholly about apostasy, turncoats and recidivists, but by implication also about its obverse: admiration for those who remain loyal even in acute adversity, and Browning's verse has examples of both. He is hostile in denouncing hypocrites and moral fraudsters such as the bishop at Saint Praxed and Mr Sludge the Medium, as well as the ineffectual timorousness of Andrea del Sarto, swayed by mercenariness, and, as we have seen, the vacillating crowd in 'The Patriot' (by subtitling the latter 'The Old Story', Browning seems to charge this weakness as endemic in the human psyche).

Obverse figures, of integrity, include the Patriot, who retains his sense of a mission, and Childe Roland, who perseveres in the face of immense personal risk. Other interesting examples in Browning of steadfast protagonists appear in 'The Italian in England' and 'Count Gismond'. In the former an Italian patriot on the run from Austrian oppressors rebukes those former allies who have succumbed and switched allegiance (see lines 125–127). The eponymous figure of 'Count Gismond' too steps forward from the crowd to defend a woman slandered by Count Gauthier, and it is this perilous act of stepping forward that characterises the essential nobility of the hero-leader.

Conclusions

In the group of three poems of this chapter we have noted the different ways in which Browning expresses themes such as commitment, integrity, trust and idealism as well as the relationship between the individual psyche and the pressures of its environment, social, physical and psychological.

Each of the three poems has focused on a relatively isolated individual to explore situations of loneliness and betrayal and to discuss how issues and questions of ethics are made complex by their contexts, both local and global.

In particular the poems have explored the ways in which individuals respond to their environment, whether social or topographical, but above all in terms of the tremendous psychological pressures that their ordeals have submitted them to. Accordingly the poems have probed mental issues involving hostility, desolation and alienation, and we can begin to recognise the extent to which Browning's poetry is concerned primarily with inner states.

Across the three poems there has been the common thread of the journey or mission in which mankind steps out of the bounds of convention, or orthodoxy. The central poems of our discussion have revealed Browning's fascination in the challenges and anxieties inherent in human heroic experiments, adventure or voyages of inner discovery.

At the heart of the poems has been the question, expressed explicitly or figuratively, of the relationship of the poet or artist to his or her society (and this area is developed further in the next chapter). In this respect we have tried to show the importance of the nineteenth century's view of the poet as a special individual, a bard or seer.

Methods of analysis

We have made use of the same techniques as Chapter 1 and begun to look in detail at how Browning's specifically literary devices work towards influencing readers' responses.

1. *Poetry*. We have explored the way that Browning employs different metrical forms (including dactyl and anapaest) to create detailed effects and considered how different stanza forms can affect interpretation. We have noted how sound, for example through alliteration, assonance and rhythm, can produce interesting nuances of meaning and mood. Another key feature of our discussion has been to analyse Browning's use of symbol and metaphor and the dynamics working in different narrative forms.

2. *Dramatic monologue.* We have advanced our understanding of the complexities of this special device, recording how this is affected by features of character and point of view, and also how language elements like verb tense, diction, choice of nouns (concrete versus abstract) and sentence types can all operate together towards an overall effect.
3. *Setting.* Each of the poems has a different setting and our discussion has set out to demonstrate the way that setting can work in both literal and symbolic dimensions.
4. *Tone of voice.* A crucial aspect of each of the poems in this chapter is Browning's deployment of irony for both satiric and moral effects. We have also taken note of how the poet employs these elements to elicit interpretations and the extent to which these are affected by the limitations of the dramatic monologue.

Suggested work

To consolidate and further develop the work of this chapter, consider and try to answer the two following questions.

(a) Read or reread Browning's 'The Pied Piper of Hamelin' and describe the Piper's 'mission' in all its aspects. How does the theme of 'betrayal' there resemble that in 'The Patriot' and 'The Lost Leader'? Work out how the rhyme scheme and rhythm differ from those of the other poems in this chapter and describe how these contribute to that poem's satirical effect.
(b) To what extent would you say that Browning's figures are heroic only in so far as they are victims of extreme changes in fortune?

3

Reach and Grasp: Two Artists

'Andrea del Sarto (Called "The Faultless Painter")'
'Fra Lippo Lippi'

> Your business is to paint the souls of men ...
> Give us no more of body than shows soul ...
> Paint the soul, never mind the legs and arms ...
> ('Fra Lippo Lippi', lines 183, 188 and 193)

For practically the whole of his life Browning was very much immersed in the realm of visual arts. He lived in close to proximity to major galleries, most notably the Dulwich, the Uffizi, the Louvre, and the Accademia in Venice. More than any other of Browning's publications, the collection *Men and Women* of 1855 testifies to his fascination with visual art and to the questions concerning how an artist relates to his or her audience. Browning was also intrigued by points of contact between literary and visual arts. Poems such as 'Popularity', 'Transcendentalism', 'Old Pictures in Florence' and 'My Last Duchess', all variously have these issues at their cores. In the dedicatory poem of the collection 'One Word More', addressed to Elizabeth Barrett, Browning draws out the interrelationship of the arts:

> Ay, of all the artists living, loving,
> None but would forego his proper dowry, -
> Does he paint? He fain would write a poem, -
> Does he write? He fain would paint a picture ...
> (lines 65–68)

But of all the poems in the *Men and Women* collection, 'Andrea del Sarto' and 'Fra Lippo Lippi' impart the most richly exciting performances, and humane treatments of art and artist themes as well as themes of the Italian Renaissance.

We have already discussed some of the broad themes relating to art and the artist in 'My Last Duchess' and 'The Lost Leader', topics such as originality in art, responsibilities of the artist-poet, and his or her relationship with the audience. The two poems that form the backbone of this chapter explore more deeply esoteric elements in art such as creativity, production, theory, purpose, and how these impinge upon or derive from the day-to-day business of life.

'Andrea del Sarto (Called "The Faultless Painter")'

The opening poem in the second volume of *Men and Women*, 'Andrea del Sarto' was composed in Florence and was more than likely prompted by a request in March 1853 from the Brownings' mutual friend John Kenyon to obtain or commission a copy of one of del Sarto's paintings.

For his brilliantly luminous portrayal of the painter Andrea del Sarto (as well as of his wife, Lucrezia), Browning's chief debt is to Giorgio Vasari's eyewitness account in his *Lives of the Painters* (first published 1550), a collection of brief sketches of his contemporaries in the Italian renaissance. However, Vasari, a former pupil in del Sarto's studio, is less than glowing in the account of his more talented mentor,

> ... the most excellent Andrea del Sarto, in whose single person nature and art demonstrated all that painting can achieve by means of draughtsmanship, colouring, and invention ... yet had Andrea possessed more boldness of mind doubtless he would have been without equal. But there was a certain timidity of spirit, a diffidence and softness in his nature ...
> (*Lives of the Artists*, Part III, chapter 24)

Del Sarto (1486–1531) lived almost the whole of his working life in Tuscany, apart from his lucrative 'long festal year' at the court of the French king (remembered poignantly in lines 145–218 of the poem), where he produced some of his finest work for the appreciative patron Francis I. Until, that is, 'my Lucrezia' beckoned him back home to Italy.

I would like to explore Browning's dazzling poem by focusing on two important extracts and to use them in order to look closely, first at the theme of art, and then at the character of Lucrezia, and her relationship with del Sarto. In the first passage, lines 68–103, the artist reflects on, among other things, his painterly skills, and then in lines 219–250, del Sarto addresses his beloved Lucrezia, and responds to the arrival of her 'Cousin'.

On a still evening in autumn, del Sarto watches the day fade, from an open window of his house in Florence, and looking across to the small Tuscan town of Fiesole. He and his wife, Lucrezia, have been quarrelling, over some paintings promised for her friend. As a church bell rings, he reflects sadly that she takes no interest in his profession but, worse, his life and work have failed to live up to his early potential. Yet he discovers some consolation in the fact of his renown for meticulous realistic depiction of his subjects.

Passage (i) lines 68–103

> No sketches first, no studies, that's long past:
> I do what many dream of, all their lives,
> —Dream? strive to do, and agonize to do,   70
> And fail in doing. I could count twenty such
> On twice your fingers, and not leave this town,
> Who strive—you don't know how the others strive
> To paint a little thing like that you smeared
> Carelessly passing with your robes afloat,—   75
> Yet do much less, so much less, someone says,
> (I know his name, no matter)—so much less!
> Well, less is more, Lucrezia: I am judged.
> There burns a truer light of God in them,
> In their vexed beating stuffed and stopped-up brain,   80
> Heart, or whate'er else, than goes on to prompt
> This low-pulsed forthright craftsman's hand of mine.
> Their works drop groundward, but themselves, I know,
> Reach many a time a heaven that's shut to me,
> Enter and take their place there sure enough,   85
> Though they come back and cannot tell the world.
> My works are nearer heaven, but I sit here.
> The sudden blood of these men! at a word—
> Praise them, it boils, or blame them, it boils too.

> I, painting from myself and to myself,   90
> Know what I do, am unmoved by men's blame
> Or their praise either. Somebody remarks
> Morello's outline there is wrongly traced,
> His hue mistaken; what of that? or else,
> Rightly traced and well ordered; what of that?   95
> Speak as they please, what does the mountain care?
> Ah, but a man's reach should exceed his grasp,
> Or what's a heaven for? All is silver-grey,
> Placid and perfect with my art: the worse!
> I know both what I want and what might gain,   100
> And yet how profitless to know, to sigh
> 'Had I been two, another and myself,
> Our head would have o'erlooked the world!' No doubt.

Although, like so many of Browning's works, this opens *in medias res*, the situation is quickly and brilliantly elaborated and the reader soon discovers this to be a psychological study in which time and cause are key themes in del Sarto's consciousness. Browning's poem presents a sympathetic picture of an individualist struggling in the midst of everyday distractions, cares and aspirations and at the heart of this is a highly refined dramatic monologue. The intimacy of this form – as we have already seen – can imply candour and spontaneity about the speaker, his relationships and his views. But, this being Browning, we are on the alert for subtle ironic touches.

The chief formal interest of this passage arises from its lively intimacy and also from its modulations, the subtle variations in del Sarto's moods and views and in the vivid tension generated in his relationship with Lucrezia. This centralising consciousness is a stream of ideas locating him within his world of 'four walls'. His mind is constantly probing, assimilating fears of rivalry and anxiety about his place in the world, his marketability, his status in the elite of renaissance masters. His consciousness continually weighs the personal price he pays for all this in terms of his sexual relationship, the fear of a potential loss of Lucrezia, the conflict of desire and constraint. Yet, above all, Browning is anxious to portray the normal man.

This passage is rich in all its implications, so it will help if we can take an analysis in three stages.

(a) lines 68–77

The extract starts with del Sarto boasting of his ability to paint faultless canvasses, that is, without preliminary sketches or studies. 'That's long past', he brags, implying that such groundwork is the stuff of novices, those who still dream of scratching a living ('strive' and 'agonize') and – ideally – achieving fame by their skill. Countless others dream of what he does daily. He is, on his own terms anyway, a success. Unfortunately he is constantly dogged by the nagging thought that by others' standards he is not. Yet, like these dreamers, he too strives, unfailingly – and this reflex of unceasing endeavour anticipates the statement of his philosophy in line 97.

He has no time for these preliminary preparations in another sense too. As lines 189–191 denote, del Sarto is worked off his feet struggling to meet clients' commissions; he is the 'sorry little scrub' that works himself into a sweat. However, as he repeatedly does in this poem, he tries to console himself with the thought that he is the equal of geniuses like Raffael, men who, so he guesses, do not have to make initial sketches or studies.

Typical too is the way Browning reveals del Sarto's character by setting up the double point of view we discussed in Chapter 1. Here the artist boasts that he could count twenty such inferior painters in Florence alone. He achieves a momentary sense of superiority in the reflection that there are many hopeful painters who cannot afford to work in Florence, the hub of contemporary art. The phrase 'and not leave this town' is thus an unwitting admission that he is trapped – the poem has many examples of the constraints on del Sarto. In this way, Browning silently translates his boast into an innocent admission of impotence.

Although in 'Fra Lippo Lippi' the artist is nominally confined, being a monk, his monologue comes across as conspicuously free, as well as being dynamic, tricksy, warmly lascivious and passionate about life. By contrast, del Sarto while physically unfettered, feels bound to Lucrezia, and is manifestly passive, timid, and dreamy:

> So free we seem, so fettered fast we are!
> ('Andrea del Sarto', line 51)

It is no coincidence that while Lippo Lippi emerges in early dawn, we see del Sarto at twilight. The crepuscular del Sarto, 'weak-eyed bat' whose 'four walls make his world' (169–170), also feels constrained by timidity in his art, knocking out impeccable images for a nameless market, so his self-portrait is markedly devoid of free will. For we 'half-men'

>   All is as God over-rules. (133)

For the whole period of the time of the poem, he is also trying to convince his wife of his professional prowess, his potency that not even he is fully convinced of. In addition to an awareness of his shortcomings in art, his consciousness is dominated by acute and constant knowledge that she repeatedly cuckolds him with the anonymous Cousin (line 220 – though there may be others too). At the same time, these are the two main parameters haunting his mind, restless disappointment mixed with earnest desire.

Although Lucrezia will figure more fully in the discussion of our second passage below, we can see here much of her character and her attitude towards his art:

>   ... a little thing like that you smeared
>   Carelessly passing with your robes afloat,— (74–75)

While the phrase 'little thing' is intended by del Sarto here as an understatement, Lucrezia is conversely likely to hear it as an overstatement, since she is insouciant, indifferent to his preoccupations with perfection. With flowing robes she herself seems aloof, gliding in and out of his frame and of his mind: his wife, his muse, his anguish. Not daring to reproach her, he simply remarks on the smudge (she has smudged his marriage too but he merely dotes and defers to her).

In his judgement the 'little thing' is nevertheless a detail of some large importance. The 'little thing' is still less than others can achieve, can 'do'. Del Sarto actually does work, he makes and sells paintings, rather than idly dream about a life in art or deprecating others like a critic, like this 'someone'. At times del Sarto surprises even himself – in this moment of self-appraisal, he is quite relaxed about his perfect little things, his small victories, his 'grasp'.

The extract then focuses most closely on the psyche of Andrea del Sarto, on his drive to paint, and to paint better than others. He is painfully conscious of rivals both in art and in sex – and later in the poem the two will converge.

His wistfulness makes him appear strangely detached and yet he yearns for more. In spite of his tirade against the dreamers, there is a strong streak of the dreamer in del Sarto himself, wishful rather than assertive (his monologue is replete with modal forms: for instance, if only, were I, may, and might).

He has a deep-seated inclination for avoiding painful decisions and confrontation, opting instead to procrastinate (see line 10). He is staunchly passive too, settling for this cosy life of accommodating other people's demands. The quiet end of evening air symbolises this condition of phlegmatic passiveness, the twilight signifying the general sense of cadence that permeates del Sarto's life. In spite of this, the jobbing painter remains resolutely optimistic about his life and future:

> I might get up tomorrow to my work
> Cheerful and fresh as ever. Let us try. (19–20)

He might, but that's for tomorrow anyhow.

But for now, in the tranquil air of autumn he would rather not face his triple demons of doubt, ineffectuality and incontinence. Del Sarto himself is keenly aware of these, of course, together with the other realities of his life but he has a suave capacity for self-deception, and his monologue is vibrantly alive with the tensions between the two worlds. What is more, this capacity should warn the reader of the possibility of unreliable points in his account, and consequently of the scope that this literary double perspective affords for Browning's characteristic ironies.

(b) lines 78–89

> Well, less is more, Lucrezia ... (78)

With this paradox del Sarto tries to convince Lucrezia that the 'less' of their life together is actually 'more' than the lives that most people enjoy (but he also tries to convince himself too – as much of what he ostensibly intimates to her is actually aimed at himself).

For Browning too these details are crucial. The less is more, and details signify. As we have noted, del Sarto incessantly seeks to redeem himself in his own and other's eyes but chiefly those of his intractable wife. He has painted a 'little thing' that others admire (74) but he believes its quality and its significance are greater than its apparent size: quality outweighing quantity, and his special gift is perfect draughtsmanship.

He is judged by 'them' always; he is jealously conscious of shadowy others, whispering, threatening, and disparaging, or so he suspects. He has completed 200 pictures (line 256), which is not many for an artist of his age, and this testifies to the slow, painstakingly meticulous details of graphic truth he strives for (the 'faultless painter'). However, in the words of his supposed critics his paintings fail to capture the soul, even if

> There burns a truer light of God in them ... (79)

In other words while he scrupulously ('low-pulsed') depicts perfect 'arms and legs' on his canvasses, other contemporaries feverishly labour to capture the real soul (the 'truer light') of their subjects and so aspire divinely to heaven. Their studies generate a flame of essential existence by refining their work, transcending the 'now', connecting with the realm of the sublime.

By reaching beyond the body's local detail, the celebrated 'masters' tap into this beauty by way of impressions rather than by relying on the kind of photorealism sought by del Sarto. His own approach is unable to transcend the world of such correspondent realism – because it is rooted in mundane reality.

The work of artists like Rafael, Leonardo and Michelangelo (see line 263) have so many flaws in their natural realism, but their work can subtly conjure a tremendously spirituality. They achieve this not with the detail (the 'less') but with the whole rhythmic form of their works (the 'more'). It is a remarkable, if unintended, admission by del Sarto and a further example of Browning's double perspective, in which a speaker unwittingly exposes his own deficiency by mistakenly assuming we share their view.

And yet, del Sarto does confess that his rivals, with their

> ... vexed beating stuffed and stopped-up brain, (80)

do manage to attain to heaven even though their work remains mundane, 'groundward'. They are in mystical contact with heaven through their 'reach', their artistic aspiration (line 84 – and he has more to say on this further on; see also lines 104–110). Moreover, del Sarto seems to be saying that his contemporaries have Church approval for their work whereas he himself lives outside official sanction, dwelling inside Florence too, either because he lives with a prostitute or because (like Fra Lippo Lippi) he uses recognisable local people in his religious studies. The realm of official religious endorsement is 'shut to me' (84) – as indeed may heaven itself.

Although he reassures himself that he does 'what many dream of' (69), del Sarto appears to be in a constant state of anxiety regarding his artistic niche. He rates himself higher than the jealous dreamers yet enviously inferior to the 'masters'. Despite this, he remains stubbornly convinced of how his realist works are 'nearer heaven'. In contrast to his easy-going, low-pulsed temperament, these other artists are highly volatile, their 'sudden blood' (88) provoked by comments – praise or censure – about their work.

In his work as a whole, Browning is fascinated by the ways in which an artist relates to an audience, especially in terms of the theme of popularity, and this interest is evident here. Lines 88–89 create an impression of other Florentine artists as mainstream and dynamic, constantly in the public eye, their works inciting strong feelings in their audience as in themselves. This fixation with his public reception and the fickleness of popularity is one shared in part with the narrator of 'Old Pictures in Florence', and compare similar themes in 'The Patriot', 'The Pied Piper', 'The Lost Leader', and 'Popularity' itself.

(c) lines 90–103

In tune with this theme of fame is the fact that almost the whole of del Sarto's discourse is based on attempts at rationality. As the middle lines of the passage shows, the painter strives to account for differences between his own self-estimate and that of others. He sets out to vindicate his shortcomings in art and life, though ultimately these self-rationalisations fail. Thoughts of self-defence are usually attended by grinding accusations, which gradually subside into self-consolation (a prominent feature of his discourse is the way it subtly advances through a dialectic series of opposites: dream/strive, brain/heart, groundward/heaven, hope/failure, and so on). These features are even more evident in the third part of our passage.

His thoughts are in fact anything but 'low-pulsed', 'unmoved' or 'placid' but rather, agitated, intense, constantly spiralling in on the same prickly topics. Having opened this passage with a fairly complacent assessment of his career and status, he then discloses his profound disappointment about being debarred from aesthetic heaven (84).

This section begins typically with first-person, 'I'. Whatever del Sarto utters, it is always through the filter of himself.

> I, painting from myself and to myself,
> Know what I do, am unmoved by men's blame,
> Or their praise either. (90–91)

This represents yet another of his grand assertions revealing how deluded he actually is, especially about himself. Not surprisingly, del Sarto takes refuge in these spirit boosting assertions. What he does know is that he paints, not for himself (far from it), not even for Lucrezia his wife, but for her lover politely coded as her 'Cousin'. And the monologue as a whole verifies that he is far from 'unmoved' by critics. Moreover, as we have seen, he paints for money and he is acutely sensitive to what others thinks of him. When critics carp that he has badly depicted Morello – a mountain north of Florence – he claims to be indifferent. Yet he is indifferent to their praise so long as his paintings are,

> Rightly traced and well ordered ... (95)

Revealingly, he is most touchy about any criticism that disparages his graphic realism. After all he is the 'faultless painter'. It is not difficult to see that del Sarto often misses the point that the three great masters have become masters on account of, let us say, the inspiring humanity in their works rather than simply for their pictorial realism. The mountain does not care (96) but del Sarto certainly cares. His assertions repeatedly forget and so undermine themselves.

In a moment of typical incongruity, del Sarto famously asserts:

> Ah, but a man's reach should exceed his grasp,
> Or what's a heaven for? (97–98)

It is a sentiment heavy with meaning and distils in short the process referred to in lines 70–71, of dreaming and doing and failing. The vigour of this aphoristic utterance is in marked contrast to what has gone before, even within this short passage, and it seems to run counter to evidence in the rest of the poem. In sum, a man should always be striving for more than he has achieved or than he believes he is capable of. He urges mankind to make the special effort to succeed, never to be content with what you have.

However, in the end, there is not much evidence of the speaker following his own counsel. In fact, in the case of del Sarto himself, this maxim can more aptly be understood as: a man's reality ('his grasp') is itself always the obstacle to achieving his full potential ('his reach'). He repeatedly identifies a problem and articulates its remedy but then, Hamlet-like, fails to act, both in terms of his work and his wife (Lucrezia seems to exist beyond both his 'grasp' *and* his 'reach'). In reality, his grasp actually ends up cramping his reach (contrast the tenacious 'reach' of Childe Roland or 'The Patriot' and the individual hell it drives them through).

Passage (ii) lines 219–250

Following the previous passage, the speaker's thoughts focus now on his wife. Seeking a scapegoat for his frustration, del Sarto becomes increasingly convinced he has been ensnared by Lucrezia. He turns his 'faultless' attention to a copy of a Rafael sketch and presumes to correct an arm 'wrongly put', pondering that while it lacks a draughtsman's precision, the artist has indeed caught the soul. Lucrezia's infidelity has, he believes, undermined his own work, reducing it to perfect mediocrity. He next escapes into reverie about his golden years under the indulgent patronage of Francis I, the period representing his pinnacle of success – until, that is, a restless Lucrezia beckoned him back to Tuscany. And his reward for this uxorious compliance is to be cuckolded by her prostitution. Yet del Sarto's unflagging optimism holds out the possibility that she may yet reform.

The next passage for our consideration occurs at the moment of Lucrezia's imminent departure for a sexual assignation with a client, euphemistically termed her 'Cousin':

Let us but love each other. Must you go?
That Cousin here again? he waits outside?   220
Must see you—you, and not with me? Those loans?
More gaming debts to pay? you smiled for that?
Well, let smiles buy me! have you more to spend?
While hand and eye and something of a heart
Are left me, work's my ware, and what's it worth?   225
I'll pay my fancy. Only let me sit
The grey remainder of the evening out,
Idle, you call it, and muse perfectly
How I could paint, were I but back in France,
One picture, just one more—the Virgin's face,   230
Not yours this time! I want you at my side
To hear them—that is, Michel Agnolo—
Judge all I do and tell you of its worth.
Will you? To-morrow, satisfy your friend.
I take the subjects for his corridor,   235
Finish the portrait out of hand—there, there,
And throw him in another thing or two
If he demurs; the whole should prove enough
To pay for this same Cousin's freak. Beside,
What's better and what's all I care about,   240
Get you the thirteen scudi for the ruff!
Love, does that please you? Ah, but what does he,
The Cousin! what does he to please you more?
I am grown peaceful as old age to-night.
I regret little, I would change still less.   245
Since there my past life lies, why alter it?
The very wrong to Francis!—it is true
I took his coin, was tempted and complied,
And built this house and sinned, and all is said.
My father and my mother died of want.   250

As in the previous discussion, it will help if we can break down this passage into sections complying with its form. There appear to be three logical parts, which function in a dialectic: (a) lines 219–225: the husband desperately hoping Lucrezia will stay; (b) lines 226–243: in which he struggles to assimilate work with the inevitable cuckoldry; and (c) lines 244–250: where he glumly struggles to evade the wretched truths about his present life.

Since Lucrezia is, in spite of everything, so central to del Sarto's mind, art, and love, I have chosen this passage to allow us to examine more closely the woman herself and her relationship with the painter. The form of the passage is shaped by the subtle changes in the speaker's moods and feelings, as well as by variations in focus and time scale, and further, by rhythmic modulation of the emotional distance between himself and Lucrezia.

Here (as in so many of the poems in *Men and Women*) Browning is fascinated, not by the specific aesthetics of the Renaissance period, but by the psychology of the central character. Yes, he endeavours to communicate the mind of the man as artist, but above all the mind of man as a man, flawless as a painter, maybe, but brimming with the moral and psychological flaws of a human being.

(a) lines 219–225

This passage is a highly visual performance and Browning's great feat lies in achieving so much without having to resort to explicit description. Yet again the conversation, thoughts and silence spur the reader to construct the moment of the couple in the golden studio, suffused with bright rays from the setting sun. (The poem is particularly well-nuanced in the theme of time, but also of capturing time past via the experience of the present moment – through flashbacks to del Sarto's past.) So here we may actually see smiles, hands and eyes, a visitor below, a ruff, stolen French gold, interiors with corridors, and an allusion to his father and mother, plus much more. It must be added though that, because of the nature of the dramatic monologue, Lucrezia herself is always turned elusively away from us.

The opening line of this passage strikes an unexpected parallel with 'Porphyria's Lover', drawing her lover and del Sarto together in watchful sadness at the departures of two women. Here Lucrezia's lover is just as desperately distressed, as his feverish unanswered questioning implies, though with no hint that he will do anything than remain in faithful wedlock. The fact that so many of these questions rely on tone of voice deepens the sense of del Sarto's desolate emptiness.

The poignancy in del Sarto's voice is increased by his rather pathetic 'Let us but love each other' (219), knowing she has betrayed him with her body countless times before ('That Cousin here again?'). He knows this but his utterances become more frantically impotent, peaking miserably in line 223. In matters of sexual transaction he is utterly artless.

Lucrezia prostitutes herself ostensibly to pay off loans made for 'gambling debts'. The deixis in these opening lines suggest del Sarto's surprise – perhaps he sees through her excuse because in line 239 he appears to offer her paintings to sell instead. And in line 223 he desperately begs her to give *him* her smiles, smiles being another euphemism for sex – if, that is, she has any time for her compliant husband. It is his feeble version of fairness and connubial rights:

> Well, let smiles buy me! have you more to spend? (223)

Since there is no sign from her, del Sarto concludes this short section with the solace that while she sells her body, he also sells his skill in art, 'works my ware', and so discovers a congruity between them if only in their chill commercialism. With a forlorn synecdoche – hand and eye and heart – he counts his pitiable blessings.

Lucrezia is at her most shadowy here. Ironically, where del Sarto goes for graphic realism, Browning's own work prefers impressionism. Because of the deception about sex for gambling debts, an unexpected side of her indistinct nature is suggested. Gambling is a nice symbolic touch too because, unlike her circumspect, quiescent husband, it associates Lucrezia with risky pleasures, fate and chance. Does she reply to her spouse's 'smiley' question? of course not, and what her casual departure does do is strengthen the impression of his utter ineffectuality.

His response to her outrageous infidelity is to immerse himself in art and especially its materialism, its 'ware' and 'worth'. Materialism here draws a brief parallel with the Duke of Ferrara and the Bishop of Praxed (see Chapter 4). Del Sarto's eagerness to exchange art for cash contrasts himself with the spiritual artist of Browning's Pictor Ignotus and with his coevals Michelangelo and Rafael. This, his own private world helps to palliate feelings of desire and conflict, burying his self-revulsion in work.

On a symbolic level Lucrezia represents natural physical beauty and the free, unconstrained will (in lines 27–28 del Sarto is troubled that she disfigures this 'perfection' with pearl earrings). As she is his perennial model for the Virgin or Madonna, it is no small irony that his equanimity should be ravished by the physical magnetism of this *puttana*. As such her sexual physicality is a counterpoint to del Sarto's incessant cerebral stirring – as her silence is to his volubility. In conventional terms Browning formulates her as the embodiment of sin while del Sarto images her as Eve-like in her 'serpentining beauty' (line 26).

For a character that does not speak directly, Lucrezia exerts a strong physical presence in the poem, ever present in the consciousness. She is pricked out in fine impressionistic strokes – the turn of her head, a careless swish of her skirt against a wet canvas, her insouciance and indifference to his art and its aspirations. Her husband repeatedly addresses her by name, as if hoping to possess her through its charm, 'my Lucrezia', a name that is indicative itself in containing the word 'lucre' (as his name embraces the word 'art'). And it is difficult not to be reminded of the name of her notorious contemporary, Lucrezia Borgia.

Although he is continually negotiating with her, it is she who dictates the rate of exchange. Nonetheless, one of the poem's core mysteries is why she remains with him. The answer must be that in an age when women were commonly barred from owning property he offers safety, or security, and she has full licence of action. For him, she is his muse (see lines 118 and 132) and additionally brings in cash via her body and her face. In line 241 he shouts across for her to sell a ruff for 'thirteen scudi' and it is highly likely that it is she who is supporting *him*, the perfect painter.

(b) lines 226–243

This section of the passage sees more of de Sarto's response to Lucrezia's impending exit. His first rejoinder here, 'I'll pay my fancy' (226), is a kind of indignation, but the keyword 'fancy' offers a number of possibilities, all based on a notion of 'desire'. On a simple level he means, 'I'll suit myself'. Alternatively, and like Porphyria's lover, he (improbably) relishes his own company, and we get the impression he is accustomed to this forsaken solitude.

As the root of del Sarto's artistic work, 'fancy' is likely to denote 'imagination' and clearly this figures highly not only in his creativity as artist but also in his dreamy perception of Lucrezia. Importantly, it confers solace for him through artistic fantasy to escape the sorrowful reality of cuckoldry (Porphyria's partner finds a more desperate remedy to the unbearable truth).

Moreover, fancy connotes 'skill', so could imply that he will try ardently to supplant her 'Cousin' by knocking out populist, commercial art, and the previous line (225) makes this sense clearer; in del Sarto's imagination the Cousin represents the shadowy, unfocused 'other' that haunts his consciousness (a frequent phenomenon in Browning).

In this section the verb forms change slightly, but sufficiently to reveal a sudden change of tone. So, where, in the first section of this extract, the short questions equated with shock, panic and confrontation, in the second where the tone has slumped into resignation we hear a mild supplication in 'Only let me', followed by submissive appeals. After the 'gold' of earlier sections, now there is only the 'grey remainder of the day'. He has been left with the 'idle' fag-end of the day while Lucrezia's amusement is only just beginning.

In the game of sexual politics del Sarto has lost – long lost – and his next recourse is to 'muse' fancifully on the rosy past:

> How I could paint, were I but back in France ... (229)

His fugitive sorrow swings to the future, desperately striving to evade the awful pain of his cuckolded present. To parallel this feeling, his spoken clauses change to predominantly conditional forms denoting hope and dream in place of resoluteness: 'Were I', 'could', 'would' and 'should'.

If only he could paint the one masterpiece, 'just one more' (230), only this time he would use a new female model for the Virgin. He tries to imply, of course, that Lucrezia is not actually indispensable, but perhaps also that she is the actual root of his inefficacy. Like Lucrezia, we can readily see through his wistful reverie, but we still desire to know how he will deal with an intolerable situation.

He proceeds with an ambiguous assertion:

> I want you at my side
> To hear them ... (231–232)

As we read the first line of this it may seem as if at last del Sarto has discovered a refreshing new tenaciousness. But then Browning's enjambement carries the line over to the predicate that, typically, softens and undermines his apparent hardness, until, in line 234 it dribbles away to a lame supplication, 'Will you?'

We have been here before; we have become attuned to del Sarto's dreamy prevarication. In another desperate manoeuvre to deflect her from her assignation, he even asks his wife to procrastinate too – 'Tomorrow, satisfy your friend'. If he could only get her to hear masters such as Michel Agnolo Buanarotti to endorse his work ('its worth') perhaps she would surely acquiesce: so much has his integrity been sapped away he must reluctantly turn to others. However, this too proving futile, he meekly attempts (in line 235) to wheedle himself between Lucrezia and her client by offering to work up paintings for the Cousin's 'corridor'. Eventually, the passage reaches its crisis at the pronouns 'there, there', with del Sarto fumbling for words or substitutes to avert her libido:

> ... throw him in another thing or two ... (237)

By this point in the poem del Sarto has plumbed the very depth of desperate complaisance. He offers almost anything and everything to appease Lucrezia and to thwart the Cousin's 'freak', his craving for sex with his wife. It is this failure of del Sarto to assert the will that precludes any genuine sense of tragedy about him: he knows what he must do yet cannot, or will not carry it through. Further, his pleading sinks to a comic level when begging his wife to sell a ruff for fourteen scudi, a high price.

This section shambles to a humiliating finale in del Sarto's begging some sign from the supremely indifferent Lucrezia: 'Love, does that please you?' (242). Line 243's exclamation draws attention to the euphemism in the label 'Cousin', and closes with a whisper of del Sarto's belated exasperation. But it is only a whisper, and his words ring hollow in the silent air until it becomes apparent she is unwavering, and his hope collapses:

> I know both what I want and what might gain. (100)

Reach and grasp again. But del Sarto is not a man of great ambition in the first place. His ineffectual desire to be other than he is, in art and love, as well as life, has reduced him to a man utterly careworn, driven ragged with apprehension and a dread of losing 'his' Lucrezia that constantly undermines his ease.

He is cornered by the power of his unrequited love, as by his lack of real ability and by his own diffidence. Rather, paralleling her obedience to the Cousin's call, del Sarto's soul is always at the beck of Lucrezia's sorcerous charm – like a bird to

> The fowler's pipe, and follows to the snare ... (125)

Cadence is a familiar reflex in his monologue, his thoughts routinely lapsing into impressions of confinement, within his four walls, trapped (like the 'weak-eyed bat') inside his own infirmity of will and its ever-present consequences.

In line 135 del Sarto asks himself of Lucrezia the very question the reader has pondered, 'Why do I need you?', since, after all, he believes the three great painters are all unmarried. Then he answers his question in his own half-baked fashion:

> Yet the will's somewhat - somewhat, too, the power -
> And thus we half-men struggle. (139–140)

It solaces him to imagine that his life may after all just be typical.

(c) lines 244–250

There are many moments in 'Andrea del Sarto' when the poem seems less a dramatic (i.e. spoken) monologue than interior monologue, that is the tacit thoughts of the main character. And these last few lines of this extract seem just so, spoken after Lucrezia has left the studio to prepare herself.

The simile in line 244 appears to be for himself only, feeling old and forsaken, one more admission of failure. The admission draws his mind to the word 'regret' (245), indicting and confronting. Although avowing that he regrets 'little', most of his wistful monologue is taken up with conditional forms ('if'), as we have already noted (and this is one aspect of Browning's oblique mockery of him). Given the chance, he would change a great deal, and the rhetorical question in line 241 seems to confirm this section as interior monologue since the question is directed at himself, his constantly questioning conscience. The assonantal pun on 'life lies' (246) ironically points up the fact of his life as built on a quicksand of enervation and self-delusion.

Within two lines, he stumbles on one of the big regrets of his life: abandoning his career at the court of Francis I, and in particular his embezzling of the funds granted to him by the king for buying paintings. That period in his life looms large and recurrently in his memory, although his self-recrimination at least raises him morally above the inconstant and amoral Lucrezia, eager to stoop for her adulterous coin.

Characteristic of del Sarto's dialectic thought-process is a tendency to first deny regret, then to confess his regret, and finally to justify it by way of casuistry. The passage closes with an example of how he rationalises away his sin of embezzlement on the grounds that it allowed him to buy his studio; he was 'tempted and complied',

> And built this house and sinned, and all is said.
> My father and my mother died of want. (249–250)

The same rationalising process is at work in the way he blithely restrains his aspiration, content to work within his 'grasp' to the expense of his 'reach'.

Commentary

In the subtitle to the poem Andrea del Sarto is described as 'The Faultless Painter' and this inevitably spurs a consideration of what kind of artist he is and his broader views on art. In a phrase that looks like an oxymoron, the artist himself describes his work in line 99 as 'placid and perfect'. It is a phrase that seems to imply a causal connection, that the pictures are perfect because placid, serene but maybe docile, perhaps timid, unassuming, even lifeless. Like the word 'faultless', 'placid' is not unreservedly flattering.

The word 'perfect' or 'perfection' comes readily to del Sarto's lips. For instance, of Lucrezia:

> Oh, with the same perfect brow,
> And perfect eyes, and more than perfect mouth ... (122–123)

Her ears too are perfect (line 15) and he remains baffled to understand how she can prick them to insert earrings. The idea of pain in the service of art is alien to him, and he dare not ruffle these images of perfection, only strive to emulate them as best he can by a photographic reality.

Perfection is 'what we painters call our harmony' (34). As he gazes on the autumn twilight, he undergoes a mild epiphany on his life and work, astonished how 'the whole seems to fall into shape' (46). Del Sarto has the artist's perception, seeing God's perfection all around him and especially in the details of everyday life. He struggles then to transmute these quotidian details (including Lucrezia, whom he employs as his life-model) via his imagination into the perfect shape of ever-living art.

But he does not succeed – at least not in the way he believes Michelangelo or Rafael do so well, which is a constant irritation to him. In lines 190–192 he envisages the former castigating del Sarto for his failure to 'plan and execute', which is what del Sarto himself admits to in his 'no sketches', 'no studies'. In front of him he has a copy of a Rafael study and finds 'that arm is wrongly put' (111), but when he sets out to correct the anatomical accuracy of it he runs the risk of destroying the very soul of the painting. In 'Fra Lippo Lippi' this actually runs counter to the advice given by a Prior to the painter Lippo Lippi:

> Paint the soul, never mind the legs and arms ... (193)

The paradox for del Sarto is that the closer a work of art approaches physical perfection, the greater the distance grows from spiritual perfection. His work displays adroit technical facility but lacks spiritual excitement, the capacity to pour his soul onto a canvas.

Del Sarto's attitude to art is the antithesis of 'art-for-arts'-sake'. He must paint what will sell in order to live. He paints to please Lucrezia, his wife, inspiration, and constant model (he cannot afford anyone else) with the hope that with promises of eventual fame he may one day replace her 'Cousin', her client-lover. He is aware too that his 'mother and father died of want' (250) and this recognition of his humble origins has seared a painful stricture on his outlook (as his name 'del *Sarto*' indicates, he is the humble son of a humble tailor). Thus, the notion of a vocation in painting has become a source of energy and pride even though the dull reality is that his 'gain' is on the level of subsistence wages. A 'faultless' worker, he is his own severest critic.

Adding to his wretchedness is the knowledge that what he creates has become a commodity. This is in spite of his self-mythologising thought that 'my works are nearer heaven'. However,

> While hand and eye and something of a heart
> Are left me, work's my ware, and what's it worth?   (225)

The truth is that while other painters aim for divinity, his own work is servile, commodified. Exchanging objects for a fee to unseen merchants, it has become a transaction. Heaven is 'shut to me' and he 'sits here', struggling to do nothing more than earn his own keep. He is thus stoically conscious of the gap between his 'grasp' and his 'reach'.

Barbara Melchiori draws attention to the multitude of references to money in the poem as well as its allied elements such as desire, spending and poverty (Melchiori 1968, pp. 69–70). Art is here an exchange commodity – like sex, in the case of Lucrezia, and they both appear to prostitute themselves, pimping and accommodating clients' desires. So the opening lines of the first passage – 'No sketches first ...' – are likely to mean that del Sarto really has no time to indulge in any professional luxury because he is too busy turning out canvasses just to stay alive and to service Lucrezia's gaming debts.

We can now see the world of 'My Last Duchess' and 'The Bishop Orders his Tomb' from the creator's perspective rather than the consumer's. The Duke of Ferrara acquires 'pieces of wonder' to impress his palace guests; the materialistic Bishop of Praxed eagerly commissions opulent fittings to outdo his rival. The artists, Fra Pandolf and del Sarto, are mere servants who, like the alchemist of 'The Laboratory', create and fashion their goods to order and for extrinsic ends.

'Fra Lippo Lippi'

I have chosen to discuss 'Fra Lippo Lippi' (another dramatic monologue and again by an actual renaissance painter) because, although a fascinating poem in its own right, it will serve as an ideal pendant by which to compare our findings on 'Andrea del Sarto'. In turn, I have selected the following passages for discussion in order to draw out the interrelationship between Lippi's artistic and religious (or philosophical) views, as part of a broader discussion of Browning's Renaissance themes.

This brilliant poem is set in Renaissance Florence on a spring night, towards dawn, when its eponymous friar, Fra Lippo Lippi, is apprehended by the city watch. Mostly in blank verse, it was composed in late 1855 and Browning famously recited the poem at his dinner party in September of that year, reciprocating Tennyson's presentation of his *Maud*, recently published.

Florence has numerous canvasses of Lippi, and again Browning was especially familiar with those in the Pitti Palace opposite his apartment (in fact the poem is set in the very vicinity of the Pitti, on the south side of the river Arno). As Browning later acknowledged in a letter to art critic John Ruskin, his principal source for the framework of Lippi's biography is once again Vasari's *The Lives of the Painters*, although most of the speaker's remarkably curious character is the poet's own invention.

Browning draws out more fully the idea that Lippo Lippi (real name Fra Filippo di Tommaso Lippi) was instrumental in a revolution in painting style – rejecting the old religious, conventionally stylised depiction in favour of a more naturalistic representation. My analysis of the poem will explore Lippi's attitude to art and try to relate it to the religious dimension in his thoughts. In addition, as the poem's title suggests, Browning is fascinated by the man himself, his complex psychology and motivation, what Vasari calls his 'dextrous ingenuity'.

I have decided to spotlight the discussion on two passages, one following on the other, dealing, respectively, with the poem's major themes of religion and art, and crucially the connection between them. Passage (i), lines 270–299, gleans some important features of church orthodoxy, while passage (ii), lines 300–335, explains or applies these to Lippo Lippi's theory of art.

As we have by now come to expect from Browning, the monologue is an eyewitness account, beginning *in medias res*. The setting is the fifteenth century (*il quattrocentro*) and we are late night-time in a Florentine street, dawn rising, alongside Fra Lippo Lippi, artist and Carmelite friar, womaniser and buttonholer *par excellence*. Unlike the fearful Andrea del Sarto, the friar here blazons his identity to the watch and to the reader in the poem's opening line:

> I am poor brother Lippo, by your leave!

He has been detained in the red-light area during curfew and before the watch can arrest him, he interjects the fact that he is currently under the patronage of the powerful Cosimo de' Medici, ('a friend') for whose palazzo he is painting saints. Lippi gives the 'cullion' watch some drinking money so he can discourse with the captain and then sets about justifying his importunate sexual appetite on the grounds that he is after all but a frail human animal, 'a beast' as he puts it.

He then catalogues the torments of his early life of poverty (as del Sarto), fending for himself as a feral orphan on the streets, scavenging rubbish and cast-off food. Sensing an indulgent ear for his childhood scrapes, he becomes more expansive. At age eight, he was dumped by his aunt at the local Carmelite 'convent' (the word convent applies to a community of churchmen as well as to female; line 91), and eagerly he adopts the 'rope' and the 'serge' for,

... the good bellyful (104)

plus shelter, regular meals and the security of the order, symbolised in the 'rope that goes all around'.

Unable to conform to monastic discipline, Lippo Lippi is equally incapable of mastering bookish Latin, and just as the friars consider expelling this recalcitrant urchin they discover his graphic talents, ordering him to 'do our church up fine' (140). However, Lippi is irked by the Prior's interference in matters of art, particularly his injunction to ignore the physical reality of mortal bodies, and instead depict only the souls of saints and churchmen.

Extract (i) lines 270–299

> You understand me: I'm a beast, I know.   270
> But see, now - why, I see as certainly
> As that the morning-star's about to shine,
> What will hap some day. We've a youngster here
> Comes to our convent, studies what I do,
> Slouches and stares and lets no atom drop: 275
> His name is Guidi – he'll not mind the monks-
> They call him Hulking Tom, he lets them talk -
> He picks my practice up – he'll paint apace,
> I hope so – though I never live so long,

> I know what's sure to follow. You be judge! 280
> You speak no Latin more than I, belike;
> However, you're my man, you've seen the world
> - The beauty and the wonder and the power,
> The shapes of things, their colours, lights and shades,
> Changes, surprises, - and God made it all! 285
> - For what? Do you feel thankful, ay or no,
> For this fair town's face, yonder river's line,
> The mountain round it and the sky above,
> Much more the figures of man, woman, child,
> These are the frame to? What's it all about? 290
> To be passed over, despised? or dwelt upon,
> Wondered at? oh, this last of course! - you say.
> But why not do as well as say, - paint these
> Just as they are, careless what comes of it?
> God's works - paint anyone, and count it crime 295
> To let a truth slip. Don't object, 'His works
> Are here already; nature is complete:
> Suppose you reproduce her'- (which you can't)
> 'There's no advantage! you must beat her, then.' 299

One of the first things to strike us about Brother Lippi's monologue is its easy-going chattiness – with elisions (I'm, we've, don't), non-fluencies (for example, line 271), deixes ('that morning-star', 'yonder river', and so on), the whole speech scuttling along. More than anything this style paints for us an image of a slick, quick-witted, streetwise rascal boasting a raffish eye for a woman and a chance. Certainly not what we would generally expect of a monk.

His diction is, of course, conversationally simple, and yet the ideas it conveys are sometimes quite complex or symbolic. So, in examining the above passage I would like to focus on three words in particular (there are many deserving others): 'beast' in line 270, 'Latin', line 281, and 'wondered', line 292. In this first discussion of Fra Lippo Lippi I would like also to think about the poem's theme of religion and then later to tie this in with some thoughts on art.

Lippi's vivaciously intense chatter is set against the tranquil mood of a warm Tuscan night on the brink of cockcrow (he has already missed Matins and will miss Terce). This passage begins with Lippi's familiar smooth talk. First he adopts excessive self-disdain, to unsettle the watch-captain, 'I'm a beast, I know' (270, repeating line 80). This is one aspect of Lippi's elaborate mask-making, one that actually denies the possibility of a mask. By claiming to share a mortal weakness he, of course, hopes the captain will accept him openly as one of the boys. 'Beast' acknowledges his highly-charged sexuality, prowling beneath the pious facade of his monk's habit ('you think you see a monk'; 3). His beastliness is additionally the source of his deep humanity, a counterculture to the moral severity of his overseers.

The next line extends the poem's recurrent imagery of seeing – Lippi sees as certainly as any artist might. 'Certainly' is part of the thread of imagery relating to the notion of security, the thing Lippi prizes in terms of the nourishment and protection in the Church.

The 'morning-star' makes a pert hint at Lucifer, a fallen ex-favourite. The security Lippi finds in the Church imbues his narration with assuredness, evident in his description of 'Hulking Tom', who is in real life the renowned painter Tommaso Masaccio, whom Lippi portrays as his pupil (274; in real life Masaccio was actually Lippi's master). His own hazardous urchin life has given him the percipience to measure faces, to see acutely beneath their masks (note line 114).

It is interesting that Lippi's pronouns 'we've' and 'our' betray a loyalty to his convent. The allusion to 'youngster' echoes the speaker's own adoption by the monks, an idea extended by 'He picks my practice up' (277; yet, ask yourself, does 'practice' refer solely to the tutor's artistic techniques, or also to his moral ways?). Curiously, 'slouches', 'stares' and 'Hulking' stand in marked contrast to Lippi's own quicksilver ways.

The next stage of the passage begins with the injunction 'You be judge!' (280), an apt call to the reader too since the authorial silence of the dramatic monologue transfers the task of judging onto the reader. Lippi continues his attempts to bond with the captain by sharing his lack of bookish learning:

> You speak no Latin more than I, belike.   (281)

We will need to return to this line for extended discussion, but for now we can note how the following line takes up the thought of hands-on learning, 'you've seen the world'. He flatters him as a 'man' after Lippi's own heart, one who has enjoyed a rich direct experience of life:

> The beauty and the wonder and the power,
> The shapes of things, their colours, lights and shades ... (283–284)

This is a beautiful homage to the rich glories of the felt world, felt equally through the senses as through the affections. With the 'changes and surprises', Lippi embraces the whole of life, mutable and capricious, which is the manifesto of his sensual life and what he strives to capture in paint ('With wonder at lines, colours, and what not ...'; 192). The phrase 'Beauty, wonder and power' alludes to the tripartite world of Florence, of art, science (or philosophy) and politics (including religious authority).

Lippi refers to each of these points in turn and, in effect, his relationship to all of them is really what the poem is about: 'art' (284), science or philosophy (290) and politics (283). Art subsists for him in shapes, colours, light and shade. It is through this direct, felt experience rather than through ecclesiastical rites that Lippi venerates God and all his creation, consisting of – as the next few lines catalogue – town, river's line, the encircling mountain, man, woman and child.

These are the 'frame' or trig points of certainty in his life and worship, the objects that delimit his consciousness. They are presented to his attention in immediate relation, framing his sense experience, and rather than the abstruse musings of theology these are what he empathises with. Invariably he accepts the fundamentals of faith as opposed to church dogma and morals, rejoicing only in the truth of their surfaces.

'Frame' is an example of the copious imagery of encircling or containment, like the convent walls and those of the Medici household, those encircling mountains, the 'rope that goes all round' (104 and 367), acting as both a form of security but also as moral constraint. Once again, Lippi's mind is in relentless tension with both of these elements but he repeatedly escapes through a full-on physical encounter with humankind and via the imagination, uniting him as a painter with the creator-God ('and God made it all!'; 285).

'What's it all about?' (290) – in demanding this, Lippi rehearses his simple but moving awe at the world, an awe conventionally understood as the province of science. However, the artist's frank riposte to 'wondered at' is to paint God's works 'Just as they are', to paint exactly as they seem and not to 'let a truth slip' (296). The empiricist Lippi thus affirms the reality of sense-perceptions as the truth of the world, without feeling any need to go beyond, behind or within transitory appearances in search of some deeper or more permanent truth. What we discover through the senses is all there is. No more, no less.

Nature, or the world perceived through the senses, is personified conventionally as female, 'her' in line 298, and acts of perception are entailed in the poem's recurrent imagery of seeing (for instance, in line 271). Lippi characterises the Prior as refuting this view – if nature is all there is ('complete'; 297), then what is the point of art if all it does is to copy, to 'reproduce her'. Because of the Prior's particular theology he would say that, of course, and he would also say, 'you must beat her, then', that is, go beyond what you see – the body – and reveal the soul in man. As the next passage will reveal, Lippi is noticeably perplexed at this. However, before examining his bafflement we should pause and look at the broader implications of what he has said thus far.

To some extent Lippi is a stereotypical bohemian artist (maverick, nonconformist, womaniser, radical) but then we remember he is a monk, a churchman, at least outwardly. In order to have been accepted by the convent he claims to have renounced the world (line 98) but patently this is but lip service, exchanging his vow for a secure life of regular meals, a uniform of worsted scapular and 'blessed idleness' (105; an oxymoron, idleness actually being a sin). His turbulent masculine energy hardly betrays a life dedicated to ascetic piety – in essence he satirises the hypocrisy of the Prior who almost certainly indulges his own libido on the quiet.

Without doubt his religious commitment is perfunctory only and he admits to this, unashamedly privileging his sexuality and sexual appetite over intellect (the 'value and significance of flesh', 268). Earlier (lines 213–214), prompted by the captain, Lippi presents his version of the medieval three-part composition of the human entity: namely, body, mind and soul. Here his commitment to 'flesh' indirectly refers to this, and to the medieval orthodoxy of the contest between flesh and mind – a conflict that Brother Lippi happily resolves, to his own satisfaction at least.

The early doctors of the Church promoted the idea that the mind and the soul were what essentially distinguished mankind from the beast, yet humanist Lippi is concerned only with the man. In our earlier discussion of 'The Lost Leader', we considered the idea of the artist being a part-divine, set apart from other men in terms both of his vision and of the ability to articulate it. However, Fra Lippi, in styling himself as a 'beast', brazenly refutes any possibility of himself as a demigod.

For him art is a function of nature (as 'beast'), instinctual in the same way that sex inevitably is (he tries to support this argument with his metaphor of the mill-horse, in line 254). He looks at man as a whole, not subdivided into boxes. In the words of Browning's Rabbi Ben Ezra,

> '[neither] soul helps flesh more, now, than flesh helps soul!'
> ('Rabbi Ben Ezra', line 72)

While drawing attention to the fact that, as regards truth, there is no primacy of the soul over the body, Lippi asserts that we should understand a person to be the whole man or woman (Browning's reference to the 'beast' may also have in mind the classical Roman novel, *The Golden Ass*).

In his excellent study, *Browning's Hatreds*, Daniel Karlin reckons that Lippi's rage (line 242) refers to his bitterness at being cursed with 'physical longing and immersion in the life of the body' (p. 76). Yet the form of the passage superbly demonstrates again the speaker's skill in articulating the life of the mind in rational argument.

Lippi understands mankind to be in a state of fall (note lines 64–65) and understands this state to be inherent in our humanity. In lines 156–157, after observing a murderer at the altar, Lippi surveys the crucifix and reflects how little have things changed since Calvary. In other words, corruptible human nature is a constant – no matter how much the Church believes it to be redeemable by grace or good works.

Lippi insistently challenges the Church view, believing instead that the natural desire of mankind is hedonistic, the stimulation as well as the gratification of pleasurable acts. Hence his affirmation of the 'beast'. As a prudent churchman himself he acknowledges the right of the Church to go about its dutiful routines, even though it is expressed in a futile process of restraint (he is beset by a variety of moral agencies each seeking to restrain him: the Church itself, together with Cosimo de Midici, and now the night watch).

Beneath the surface acquiescence, he is tenaciously unfazed by threats, warnings, prescriptions or proscriptions. He has evolved techniques for dealing with authority in all its guises, preferring to adopt comic impudence to allay his demons and to slide away. An example of this nimbleness comes in lines 238–239 when he croons another fragment of the *Stornello* – a form of traditional Italian folk song whose words are improvised to suit the circumstances. Lippi slyly alters the line but retains its impertinence:

> *Flower o' the pine*
> *You keep your mistr ... manners, and I'll stick to mine!*

Furthermore, nimbly modifying 'mistress' to 'manners' safely reminds listeners of the rumour that the Prior too has a mistress, innocently reciting an old song (as a cheeky satirical chorus, the *stornello* successfully acts as an ironic counterpoint to the poem's lofty ideas).

How much more spirited is Lippi's monologue than that of Andrea del Sarto's. Along with his easy charm, he has the ready word, an answer for every situation ('I had a store of such remarks'; 127). This flair with language comes, we guess, from his time as an urchin on the Florentine streets where survival depends on having the right patter. He appears now to be mesmerising the guard in a manner Lippi has become accustomed to devise, desperately struggling to wheedle his way out of a theological imbroglio. And to enhance the wordplay, he appears to animate them with some judicious play-acting (360–372).

His reach seems constantly to be exceeding his grasp, pushing and probing – in words as well as action. Although of similarly poor circumstances (del Sarto actually hails from slightly higher social stock), Fra Lippo is easier and more confident, self-possessed, partly as a result of the security offered by the Church and the Medici name, but chiefly because of his brash cheek. Lippi has none of the financial worries nor the encumbrance of a wife and is clearly more promiscuous than the timid del Sarto.

I have proposed the word 'Latin' as another of key words in this section – and in the poem as a whole. In symbolic terms it represents the world of writing, orthographic work, in contrast or perhaps a complement to painting. But crucially it also signifies bookish learning:

> Such a to-do! They tried me with their books:
> Lord, they'd have taught me Latin in pure waste!   (108–109)

In a characteristic swipe of protest against this intellectual education, Lippi 'drew men's faces on my copy-books' (129), seditiously doodling between 'verb and noun'. We have seen of course how Lippi acquired his own peculiar learning on the streets and between the sheets. And yet, for one ill-equipped for intellectual book-learning he is remarkably adroit in articulating his philosophies of aesthetics and epistemology.

In 'One Word More', his epilogue to *Men and Women*, Browning nursed the wish of a symbiosis of the written and the visual arts, citing the artists Rafael and Michelangelo as exemplary practitioners of verse. Yet 'Fra Lippo Lippi' seems resigned to their incompatibility.

The label 'Latin' stands for still other things too in the poem, notably the past, the Church itself, and its hegemony over lives and souls, and symbolising order itself. We need now to examine these different themes.

Strictly speaking, Lippo Lippi is a friar (of the first order of Carmelites), mendicant and contemplative. His convent is that of Santa Maria del Carmine (built 1268, almost completely destroyed by fire in 1771, but still standing and still contains works by Brother Lippi). For him the word 'Latin' is synonymous with the Catholic Church itself, which in turn is bipartite: denoting, on the one hand, home and security, while on the other, a repressive organisation that tries to coerce him into conforming to its precepts on art and morals. In spite of his religious indoctrination since age 8, his essential, individualist character is naturally irrepressible.

'Latin' as 'Church' also represents order, a fixed grammar of life and faith, both of which Lippi constantly struggles to undermine ('They with their Latin'; 242). As such, 'Latin' figures as a 'logocentric' attitude to life, a way of thinking that strives to fix meanings and relationships, usually by controlling the written word. It is a domineering, hierarchical attitude often working in clandestine or masked discourses. So, for example, the common folk of Prato have been conditioned by a form of religious art predicated on an approved, intransigent model of aesthetics. It is a conservative aesthetic that parallels a similarly intransigent political outlook (see lines 318–319).

Lippi confronts this view by endorsing not only the visual but also the spoken way of life, the ever-changing flux of speech, its human warmth and plasticity. He instinctively recoils from any attempt to conscript him into the religious hierarchy – in fact he still thinks of the convent as a one-way deal. Worst of all for him would be the prospect of becoming one of its insidious instruments of power, for example in missionary work. So to obviate this possibility, he more readily identifies with the secular Medici and the captain of the Watch, trilling his amorously flirtatious folk song.

One of Browning's great dramatic ironies of the poem is that, while it is set in the Renaissance, one of the great moments of human cultural history, Fra Lippo is utterly blasé about it and his contribution to it. By dwelling on the commonplace, Browning again debunks cultural mythology – in the same way that Lippi debunks it by depicting his saints as unremarkable, everyday people. What the poem does foreground, however, is the period's conflict and tension between humanist thought and a medieval religious orthodoxy.

That Lippi is a believer is apparent from his own explicit statements; for example:

> I always see the garden and God there (266)
> Changes, surprises, - and God made it all! (285)

However, in lines 289–290 of the passage he expresses a crucial renaissance-humanist distinction in talking of the pre-eminence of mankind. Lines 290–292 articulate one other important facet of the Renaissance, a 'wonder' at the world, a practice that became legitimate once the study of mankind itself became the proper focus of learning. Del Sarto's maxim that 'a man's reach must always exceed his grasp' expresses a variant on this: the only limit to man's reach (for example, in the study of science, art, or philosophy) is man himself, providing he accepts the ultimate overarching limit of God's domain.

Ostensibly a man of religion, Fra Lippo Lippi verbalises the artist's task as that of making sense of the world, using himself as its measuring frame, to 'find its meaning' (315). One solution to the paradox of humanist freedom within the confines of God, to conceive of man as stretching his mind to its utmost,

> Art was given for that;
> God uses us to help each other so,
> Lending our minds out. (304–306)

Another solution lies in the notion that as a creator himself he identifies with God the creator, not the old concept of an avenging God. He accepts the fundamental faith of the Church but not its dogma. In this way – and expressing yet one more tenet of Renaissance thought – he allows himself to frame his own morals, and does so by proclaiming his essence as a man, egregiously, a 'beast'.

As a Renaissance man, Lippi emphasises the flesh – the physical – as a source of truth ('with homage to the perishable clay'; 180). He embraces the empirical, positivist world, symbolised in the poem by the acquisitive materialism of the Medici (see line 99) and the libidinous diversions of sex.

The church, to be sure, takes a different view: that true reality lies in the world beyond the earthly realm of transient mortal experience, which is inexorably locked in the senses. Under this philosophy the ephemeral human life of the world is merely a dream, a temporary event contrasting with that everlasting sphere of truth in heaven. This view can be traced ultimately to the works of the ancient Greek philosopher Plato, who claimed that we could not truly know a realm in which things were constantly changing. Earth perceptions are to be regarded as dreams, shadow imitations of ever-living, and so unchanging, spiritual forms (these forms are thus the basis of knowledge).

This view is hinted at in the words of the Bishop of Praxed:

> ... so must we die ourselves
> And thence ye may perceive the world's a dream
> ('The Bishop Orders His Tomb at Saint Praxed's Church', lines 8–9)

In his uniquely naive way Lippi mockingly spurns this 'idealist' attitude:

> The world and life's too big to pass for a dream ...   (251)

Consistent with the life of an empiricist, he (as Andrea del Sarto too) depicts saints in the bodies of the ordinary people of Florence, painting them just as they are, 'fat and lean' and 'folk at church' (146), deconstructing the life of the spirit. He is unable to oblige or even to understand the Prior's mysticism, manifested in his injunction to

> Paint the soul, never mind the legs and arms!   (193)

Instead, for Brother Lippo Lippi wonder resides in the material reality and this exists in nature, in the very earthly 'changes and surprises' that Platonists detest:

> God's works - paint anyone, and count it crime
> To let a truth slip. (295–296)

Passage (ii) lines 300–335

When it was first published 'Fra Lippo Lippi' was, not unexpectedly, very well received by critics and readers alike. Painter-poet Dante Gabriel Rossetti ranked it among his favourites and in the *Westminster Review* George Eliot described it as 'original and perfect', its dramatic psychology brilliantly rendering the 'racy vigour of a brawny genius' (January 1856).

In poems such as 'Fra Lippo Lippi', 'Andrea del Sarto', and 'The Bishop Orders His Tomb in Saint Praxed's Church', Browning delineates a key phase in Italian cultural history. The two passages I have chosen lie at the climax of the poem in which Fra Lippo Lippi postulates a theory of art that marks the critical paradigm shift of that century, when Renaissance art eclipsed the medieval model, and we should examine the poem in this light.

I have selected consecutive passages because of the strongly interlocking thematic strands of the two: it is difficult to appreciate Lippi's ideas on art without some understanding of the degree to which religion permeated the art scene of quattrocento Florence.

> For, don't you mark? we're made so that we love   300
> First when we see them painted, things we have passed
> Perhaps a hundred times nor cared to see;
> And so they are better, painted - better to us,
> Which is the same thing. Art was given for that;
> God uses us to help each other so,   305
> Lending our minds out. Have you noticed, now,
> Your cullion's hanging face? A bit of chalk,
> And trust me but you should, though! How much more,
> If I drew higher things with the same truth!
> That were to take the Prior's pulpit-place,   310
> Interpret God to all of you! Oh, oh,
> It makes me mad to see what men shall do
> And we in our graves! This world's no blot for us,

Nor blank; it means intensely, and means good:	
To find its meaning is my meat and drink.	315
'Ay, but you don't so instigate to prayer!'	
Strikes in the Prior: 'when your meaning's plain	
It does not say to folk - remember matins,	
Or, mind you fast next Friday!' Why, for this	
What need of art at all? A skull and bones,	320
Two bits of stick nailed crosswise, or, what's best,	
A bell to chime the hour with, does as well.	
I painted a Saint Laurence six months since	
At Prato, splashed the fresco in fine style:	
'How looks my painting, now the scaffold's down?'	325
I ask a brother: 'Hugely,' he returns -	
'Already not one phiz of your three slaves	
Who turn the Deacon off his toasted side,	
But's scratched and prodded to our heart's content,	
The pious people have so eased their own	330
With coming to say prayers there in a rage:	
We get on fast to see the bricks beneath.	
Expect another job this time next year,	
For pity and religion grow i' the crowd -	
Your painting serves its purpose!' Hang the fools!	335

This long passage will be easier for us to discuss if we examine it in a series of three short sections, as follows: (a) lines 300–305, (b) lines 306–322 and (c) lines 323–335.

(a) lines 300–305

In the early part of his own dramatic monologue, Andrea del Sarto sighs,

> Love, we are in God's hand.
> How strange now, looks the life he makes us lead
> So free we seem, so fettered fast we are!   (49–51)

His poem teems with exclamation marks but where del Sarto's exclamations are more often sighs of resignation, such marks in 'Fra Lippo Lippi' usually indicate urgency and excitement. Likewise, when Lippi talks of God it is less in negative terms of vengeance or restraint than excitedly concerning the gifts he has bestowed upon humanity. Lippi lives in order to work within these constraints – they are a discipline that gives significance to his life.

So in line 305 the humanist Lippi embraces his faith at the same time as he acclaims art as God's gift to man. Like del Sarto he may feel that 'we are in God's hand', but he regards art and life as part of a collaborative enterprise instead of a dull compromise. An integral element in understanding Lippo Lippi comes in the first line of the above passage, and especially:

> we're made so that we love ... (300)

The whole of his being is divided equally between love and art – they are the twin engines that power him, and of course they are intimately and mutually codependent.

Mankind in general was made to love and he in particular made to paint. In its many guises, love is a key device in the poem as a whole; first, as *caritas*, 'brotherly' love of mankind; or, second, as *'agape'*, the generosity of the convent in taking Lippi in when he was 8; and third, there is erotic love. Additionally, there is the worldly love of creation, that is of nature and the world. The themes of love and art pervade his whole being.

We have recorded how the convent fails to inculcate in Lippi any genuine grasp of Latin, but there is one singularly noteworthy exception:

> All the Latin I construe is, 'amo' I love! (111)

For him what distinguishes mankind from the animal kingdom is love – it is the cement bonding all of mankind (*'Take away love, and our earth is a tomb!'*; line 54).

This engagement with the world through love is another factor that marks out Fra Lippo from the withdrawn and 'faultless' del Sarto. Accordingly, Lippi cannot 'renounce the world' (96) as the Prior urges – except for its materialism and commerce, which seem rooted in negative sensibilities. This is the reason he declares that 'Art was given for that' (304), that is, to make people aware of creation and to rejoice in it, to draw attention to a world become overly familiar as we pass its objects 'a hundred times' (302). Painting the world, that is, its people, improves it by refreshing our love of it.

His purpose in contriving naturalistic art is not simply to reproduce nature ('which you can't') but to 'beat her then' (299).

His engagement with creation or 'love' is expressed even in his chit-chat with the captain, his 'homage to the perishable clay' (180). By the same token, Lippi's lust for life as well as libido are as clearly evident in his artwork as in his unflagging sexual stamina. Thus he adopts a slightly amoral view of sex – as a kind of loving homage to mortality.

In effect, love is Lippi's religion. As a renaissance humanist it is an extension of his philosophy that

> God uses us to help each other so ... (305)

Humanism has often – down to today – been given quite a loose diversity of interpretation. However, Renaissance humanism was an intellectual movement that arose largely due to rediscovered classical ('pagan') works of Rome and Greece, and this allowed mankind to become the centre and yardstick of his own studies. In this particularly humanist form of faith (i.e. deism), God came to be seen as less interventionist, less controlling in the minutiae of daily actions, and more as a distant, supreme power, that granted mankind an enormous scope for exploration of his potential and to reach beyond his grasp ('as far as doth reach the mind of man', in Christopher Marlowe's *Doctor Faustus*, circa 1590).

God had, so to speak, taken a step back and permitted humanity to discover and define itself, to reimagine its own morals, and explore the universe, on condition that it did not contradict scripture.

So it is in this context that we can situate Lippi as a renaissance pioneer, lover and painter of man as man. His religion commences with man and then works upwards, an attitude that reverses the medieval model and that suffuses his concept of art, as we will see below. It follows that he is a disciple of *Christ* incarnate (Christ the man) rather than merely a servant of the *Church* (he is affirming too that through art the Church itself must come to 'better' see its own world anew, reappraise its outdated dogma). Though a failure at Latin learning and at monkish discipline, Lippi's boisterous and unruly charisma doggedly stamps his vision of art.

What the autocratic Church regards as his lapses are in fact the wonderful apotheosis of his humanity. The poem seems to say that by way of

Lippi's art theory, human nature will always win through and, though the medieval-minded Church may try to repress nature, Lippi glorifies and revels in it. In his ebullient loyalty to this ideal, he sketches all who attend the church, fat and thin, saints and murderers, the clear inference being that art is amoral, autonomous, and transcends petty issues of local politics. Rooted in nature, Lippi's art, in this one point at least, resembles Andrea del Sarto's: that is, Lippi's everyday men and women populate his frescoes of religious and divine heroes.

Thus he honours life in its most egalitarian – simple folk are mythologised through art, his 'homage to the perishable clay' (line 180). By the same token, the reverse applies – that saints, like artists and priors, are essentially perishable clay themselves, flesh and blood: 'paint anyone', and paint the truth (line 295). So Fra Lippo assembles a pantheon of great saints and moral imagery infused with earthbound frailty and raucous sexual innuendo. He glorifies God as a shout in the street, a deity itself rooted in the quotidian mundane.

So with the acute eye of a fine artist, Lippi is prewired to recognise the eternal in the everyday; for instance, as the 'cullion' grabs him by the throat he detects in him the face of Judas, while, in his comrade, there is a slave clutching John the Baptist's severed head. Lippi transmutes the ordinariness of everyday life into living art (while settling a few personal scores along the way) by means of penetrating the ordinary in mortal nature, and doing so with a sparkling irreverence:

> He's Judas to a tittle, that man is!
> Just such a face! (25–26)

God too was an artist, a maker of the flesh of the universe (lines 266–267), as Christ the carpenter was a maker (recall too that starvation on the Florentine streets has turned Lippi into a desperately sharp observer of faces, their nuances and intentions, learning the 'look of things'; lines 115 and 125).

(b) lines 306–322

In this next section of the passage, we see Browning extending and deepening the view of Lippo Lippi as a believer. God is *'lending* our minds' – it would be quite inaccurate to conceive of Fra Lippo Lippi as anything but a believer. The notion of 'lending' in line 305 vividly underlines the humanist theme – Lippi is an iconoclast, yes, but, for all that, still a deist, a humanist but never an atheist. Minds are returnable to God at due date.

An aside suddenly punctuates his stream of discourse when Lippi once again draws painterly attention to the cullion's (or scoundrel's) face, convinced of his potential as Judas for some canvas. He is easily distracted by such visual possibilities – and most of all by a woman's shape – though not perhaps with any particular aesthetic or spiritual object in mind.

Thoughts of faces and bodies remind the speaker of the Prior's troubling mandate to 'paint the soul':

> If I drew higher things with the same truth! (309)

It is difficult to imagine how he could do so, paint the soul that is, especially as by definition it would be non-physical. In any case, Fra Lippi makes a distinction between art and religion such that – painting the soul would be to usurp the 'pulpit-place', the divine office of the Prior, for which he has neither qualification nor inclination. On the other hand, the painter does strike an important distinction here, insisting that art is not in the pay of religion or, by extension, of politics or commerce because to do so would be to degrade art. Art would then not have intrinsic value but become secondary, an instrument in advertising these other functions.

By declaring 'interpret God to all of you!' (rather than to 'us'), Lippi is here satirising the Prior's voice. By joking that the Prior is terrified by what sins people will get up to when he is dead, the artist is adamant that people are not by nature evil:

> The world's no blot for us ... (313)

Avowing this, he logically repudiates the Church's dogma of original sin, the stance that human beings are congenitally wicked as a result of the Fall of Adam and Eve (see line 266).

On the contrary, the world is not 'blank' – it is good, the sanguine artist pleads, but it is a mystery, intensely so, and it is the artist's task to interpret for the viewer:

> To find its meaning is my meat and drink. (315)

And if that sounds polemical, there is yet more mileage for the sardonic monk, aping the Prior's voice on the theme of artistic duty. Where the Church understands the duty of art as to make congregations more diligent towards mass and morals, Lippi recoils: why do this through art when you can scare people back to their 'duty' through hair-raising objects, like bells and crucifixes:

> What need of art at all? A skull and bones,
> Two bits of stick nailed crosswise ... (320–321)

Mildly blasphemous, Lippi's charming irreverence keeps the watch at bay for a moment or two.

His scathing point is, of course, that conventional church symbolism has become stale, moribund and impotent. These are among those things 'we have passed/Perhaps a hundred times', and now hardly anyone notices, graphically supporting his point that art has the great power to continually refresh our ways of responding to familiar ideas and objects.

(c) lines 323–335

In the final section of our analysis, the speaker's excitement unexpectedly intensifies. In his spirited, facetious wit, Lippi comes buoyantly alive, joking here about St Laurence being 'toasted' on one side (in the course of his martyrdom on a griddle, Laurence reportedly urged his torturers to turn him over as he was now done on one side). At Prato Cathedral, his newly painted fresco of the saint has been 'scratched and prodded', vandalised, scraped almost down to the bricks of the chapel. The painter reacts quite temperately, in the light of this terrible desecration, but he appeases his resentment with yet another scoff:

> The pious people have so eased their own
> With coming to say prayers there in a rage ... (330–331)

The simple brainwashed worshippers have assiduously carried out the dirty work for the Church, censoring his avant-garde images.

Lippi is likewise cheered by the fact that the mutilation both confirms his view about religious indoctrination and holds out the possibility of extra commissions in renovating it. His painting and the desecration similarly 'serves its purpose' (335), corroborating the validity of his experimental views. The fresco had successfully achieved what all the older daubings had failed to do, that is, to evince a response out of its viewers.

The new style of art that irks the Church and its stooges is, of course, realism or naturalism, confronting and challenging the orthodoxy of stylised figure-painting, a hangover from the medieval period (for example, compare the work of Rafael or Lippi with that of, say, Simone Martini or Duccio in the previous century). As we have already noted, 'Fra Lippo Lippi's' approach is to depict naturalistic, identifiable figures, replete with all their faults and infirmities. Browning's own approach parallels this experimental drive with his own 'grotesque' psychological sketches of historic figures (his poem 'The Patriot' presents a similar example of the individualist persecuted by a timid and reactionary multitude).

What then could the Church's possible exception be to realism? One simple answer is the view that saints and other luminaries derive their mystique and, accordingly, their mythic power through their distinction and remoteness from the ordinary people. To depict saints in everyday faces would be to rob them of their mystifying unattainable stature, and thus diminish their power to subdue. The less simple answer is hinted at in lines 298–299 of the poem:

> 'nature is complete:
> Suppose you reproduce her' - (which you can't)

Lippi's argument is succinct: nature, earthly life, is a mere copy, a dream, of the real, true life existing only in heaven. So, on these terms, art must be at best a copy of a copy, and consequently a distortion of the truth. In other words, 'Since you cannot reproduce the truth of nature, any attempt to do so would simply create a falsehood.' And, he guesses, the Church could never, logically, sanction a falsehood.

Lippi's art theory is thus a direct challenge to the Prior's stipulation that the artist should paint only that mysterious and ultimately elusive soul. Lippi's brash riposte is that this decree is not rationally feasible or even desirable: how could he possibly disentangle body and soul, they being logically the same indivisible entity:

> ...soul and sense grow sharp alike,
> He learns the look of things ...   (124–125)

When this is all added up and rationalised, the only course open to Lippi, one that may not satisfy the Prior, is, with comic impudence, to paint the truth of the body in its full and graphic detail.

Commentary

Quite apart from anything else, the dramatic monologue enables a poet to inject a great naturalistic air to a character's speech and situation; it is first-person, straight from the horse's mouth. Another important advantage is naturalism. Because the poem's structure appears to emanate from within the character him- or herself, the monologue imbues emphasis, priority and sequence to what the character regards as significant. Form and content merge and are one: Far Lippi is his monologue and the monologue is Fra Lippi.

In *Browning's Hatreds,* Daniel Karlin describes this poem as a 'soliloquy' (p. 76). However, we should challenge this view on the grounds of the presence of an audience, albeit a silent one, and soliloquies need not require an audience. In addition to Lippi's voice we hear ventriloquised a host of other voices in their different layers – beside himself, there are the Prior's voice, a fellow brother at Prato (325), folk voices in the *stornello,* an anonymous voice (106), a 'sweet angelic' voice (370), the 'good fat father' (93–96), and even a white mouse has its say, 'weke, weke' (11).

Although the Watch-captain himself does not speak, he is rather more than an interlocutor a kind of interrogator, literally so as a watch-man, and as such he is the validation of the speech. It is an extensive speech, but it does include asides and some of the lines may even be interior monologue (if all of its 392 lines are monologue, then Lippi is a garrulous prattler and the captain would likely be asleep by its close). To the extent that it is a dramatic monologue, the poem puts us in the role of the captain as Lippi's confessor and judge, and, accordingly, we should become wary of the speaker and his self-amplifying words since we have only Lippi's version of Lippi. He is artist of the verbal as well as of the visual deception.

Thus his character is revealed as much by the manner and the form of the speech and what he does not say, as by its formal statements. The naturalism of the poem exists in its slice-of-life content (it is Lippi's habitual life rather than a crucial moment in it) and this extends to the form of the poem. Because it is contoured organically rather than chronologically, his attention flips back and forth, to the past and then forward again to the present, and so on. There being only the one voice means we must try and read between his lines to develop a fuller impression.

Lippi's monologue aptly demonstrates his view of the role of art to disrupt, polemicise and reacquaint with chaos. On account of his disruptive propensity he emerges as a subversive force ('I've broken bounds'; line 223). His chief target, of course, is not the watch nor yet the Medicis but the Church whose desperate clinging to past forms is the butt of his satire, subverting its sclerotic medieval aesthetics. While he is all too aware that the Church is his landlord and paymaster, he recognises that it represents order, tradition and decadence and Lippi seeks to subvert this with all the power of his new order of art.

Browning perfectly harmonises his nature to the dramatic monologue; Lippi's narrative form is his own intimate kind of chaos breaking with existing forms of narrative. Lippi's is a highly energised oration characterised by dazzlingly streetwise virtuosity of patter, deception, and evasion. The voice drives energetically forward, through the speaker's intense passion for aesthetics as well as via the obvious impulses of libido and self-preservation. A man in love with life and art.

Browning imbues the poem with both an authentic sense of the past and a bold relevance to the contemporary: quattrocento Florence and nineteenth-century England, local Italian light rendered in the idioms of art and the diction and mercurial wit of Victorian cockney.

Conclusions

1. In this chapter we have been able to compare two of Browning's mature dramatic monologues, and thus analyse the consciousnesses of two almost coeval artists. We have observed how, although both artists live in similar straitened and stressful circumstances, each has exploited different means of coping with them.
2. Adopting a 'comparison' approach has enabled us to see more clearly how the two main characters – one secular, the other 'religious' – respond to important themes, including authority, religion and relationships.
3. Women figure very highly in the lives of the two and impinge on their careers in different ways, but women are presented as a foil to the men

and their artistic themes rather than as rounded characters with any convincing sense of internal lives.
4. Both painters adopt realistic techniques of portrayal but the two differ in the degree to which they are able to articulate their ideas. Lippo Lippi has a less distracting domestic life and this appears (on the surface at least) to allow him the objectivity needed to formulate a coherent theory of art. Andea del Sarto is preoccupied with the way his private life and his moral infirmity have hampered his career; Fra Lippo Lippi is more concerned about the degree to which authority figures – church, politics and police – curb his private life and his revolutionary theory.
5. Although these poems are set in an historical period, Browning hopes to generalise their situations to his own period to show the perennial difficulties and challenges that confront artists and authors as a whole; these include issues concerning fame, economic privation, the relationship between private and artistic life, pressures against originality, and the role of the imagination.

Methods of analysis

1. *Comparison.* Adopting a 'comparison' approach has helped us in the task of analysis because the poems can act as a mutual source of stimulation and contrast for the reader. In this way it is easier to draw conclusions about different attitudes, approaches and strategies adopted by characters and author in parallel texts.
2. *Dramatic monologue.* Browning's use of the vehicle of the dramatic monologue has encouraged us to focus on the relevant details of each character's consciousness. By obliging us to examine the language of their discourse, we have scrutinised features such as diction, figures of speech, word classes, direct speech, form and point of view. Nuances in lexical choice have been the gateway to understanding character and subtle changes in tone and mood.
3. *Poetic technique.* We have looked closely at Browning's use of sound on its different levels; for example, rhyme, rhythm and metre, caesurae, plus alliteration and assonance (for example, alliteration is at times used for sensuous effect and at other times as a means of drawing the reader's attention to important lines or themes).

Suggested work

In order to get a broader grasp of Browning's views on art, try some of the other poems referred to in this chapter. For example, 'Pictor Ignotus' or 'Old Pictures in Florence' are very useful here and I would recommend reading them to analyse the ways in which these differ from the poems under discussion in this chapter. In particular pay close attention to how individual monologues are adapted to express their different characters and the attitudes to themes of art expressed in them. How far is Andrea del Sarto's maxim 'a man's reach should exceed his grasp' borne out in each of these?

4

Religion – Fears and Scruples

'He said true things but called them by wrong names'
('Bishop Blougram's Apology', line 996)

'The Bishop Orders His Tomb at Saint Praxed's Church'
'Bishop Blougram's Apology'
'Caliban Upon Setebos; or, Natural Theology in the Island'

Introduction

Given the pervasive influence of the Christian religion upon almost all aspects of Victorian life, private and social, it is no surprise that Browning's own childhood was nourished by parents of firm religious commitment. The Brownings themselves were dissenters, Christians who opposed state intervention in religious matters, and who established their own faith doctrines as well as founding their own churches and schools. Church Dissent is a broad label applying to convictions as diffuse as the Quakers, Methodists, Anabaptists and Unitarians.

In particular, Browning's parents subscribed to Congregationalism, a movement distinguished by its strict commitment to the autonomy of the local congregation, and so opposed the Anglican policy of the supremacy of bishops. The family's dissenting principles are sometimes cited as the chief reason why in his early teens Robert could not attend Oxford or Cambridge university, because – until 1855 – places were limited to communicants in the established Church of England (Browning, however, consoled himself with the memory that his hero Shelley had been expelled from Oxford on religious grounds). In 1828 he did briefly attend the new London University.

Robert's early literary compositions were encouraged and published by the family's Unitarian friend William Johnson Fox in his *Monthly Repository*. It was Fox's enlightened radical politics – he was sometime Liberal MP for Oldham – that helped moderate Browning's early religious fervour.

In mature years Browning's beliefs fluctuated between rationalist doubt and an unformulated deism, while he cultivated an enduring fascination with philosophy, especially metaphysics and ethics. While shedding his youthful Shelleyan idealism, he retained a lifelong commitment to broadly Christian values (professing an extensive knowledge of religious texts) – a point that made him both sceptical of his wife Elizabeth's avid spiritualist leanings and highly scornful of what he saw as the pomp of Roman Catholicism. Both of these elements feature strongly in the poems under consideration in this chapter.

During the Victorian period, other, more global currents in the intellectual life began to impact on religious belief in Britain. The nineteenth century witnesses intensifying schisms in Protestantism, most famously in the Tractarian crisis (more on this below). Such rifts often go hand in hand with religious doubt that results from radical scientific advances. For example groundbreaking discoveries in geology and related sciences, together with radical theories in secular philosophy and sociology, increasingly undermined the bases of revealed religion.

Browning's poems do not on the whole evidence any particular religious affiliation, though there are hints of figures, themes or archetypes that ultimately derive from his Christian background. As well as the poems under analysis in this chapter, it is well to keep in mind some of those discussed in previous chapters that have broadly religious elements; for instance Christian analogies in 'Childe Roland to the Dark Tower Came' and 'The Patriot'. Religious controversies are conspicuous in the dramatic monologues of 'Andrea del Sarto' and 'Fra Lippo Lippi', while we have already discussed in Chapter 1 the spiritual implications in the closing lines of 'Porphyria's Lover':

> ... And all night long we have not stirred,
> And yet God has not said a word!   (lines 59–60)

'The Bishop Orders His Tomb at Saint Praxed's Church'
Rome, 15—

Like 'My Last Duchess', this popular poem is now a favourite anthology piece and yet, amazingly, in its day the poem went virtually unnoticed. However, among people whose opinions Browning valued, the poem was very warmly received. For example, art critic John Ruskin commended the poet's love of the Renaissance, adding in reference to this poem:

> I know no other piece of modern English, prose or poetry, in which there is so much told, as in these lines, of the Renaissance spirit, - its worldliness, inconsistency, pride, hypocrisy, ignorance of itself, love of art, of luxury, and of good Latin.
> (*Modern Painters*, Volume IV)

And in her letter to Browning, Elizabeth Barrett (Robert's most forthright critic) praised the poem's metre as a 'new thing', while in another she rhapsodised that

> St. Praxed's is of course the finest and most powerful ... and indeed full of the power of life ... and of death. It has impressed me very much.
> (letter to Robert Browning, 21 July 1845, *Love Letters*, p. 134)

On submitting the poem in 1845 to the editor of *Hood's Magazine*, Browning remarked that it was 'a pet of mine, and just the thing for the time – what with the Oxford business'. The 'Oxford business' referred to the Oxford or Tractarian Movement of the 1830s and 1840s, an attempt by several Anglican theologians to reinstate pre-Reformation doctrine and rituals (the movement derives its name from *Tract XC*, 1841, by John Henry Newman who argued that there was little significant disparity between Anglican and Roman Catholic faiths).

As a protestant Nonconformist by upbringing and disposition, Browning was always nauseated by Catholic pomp and ritual, along with what he regarded as its hypocritical and repressive dogma – exactly what was highlighted in 'Fra Lippo Lippi'. Other poems too denounce Catholicism in its diverse manifestations, for example 'The Confessional' and 'Soliloquy of the Spanish Cloister'.

Like 'Fra Lippo Lippi', 'The Bishop Orders His Tomb' is situated in Renaissance Italy, in Rome though now, and once again Browning debunks conventional Victorian notions of the Renaissance period. Here the narrative focus is on the fading Bishop himself, not in a modest presbytery as we may expect, but in his 'state chamber' (11), a fact that prepares us for his reflections on a bourgeois life of decadent hedonism. The moribund bishop is intended by Browning as an allegory of the Roman Catholic Church itself.

With varying degrees of angst, his thoughts vacillate between the present business and past memories (namely, his mistress and his rival Gandolph, his tomb and his posthumous reputation at the hands of his sons, musings on the Church and art). Once more it is these personal elements that generate the form of the poem. The Bishop's mind is not at all concentrated, as we may have expected, on the future, of the eternal soul after death, but is consumed by a living will, a struggle to dictate to the future his legacy of power and reputation.

Now, after a lifetime of easeful acquisition and pleasure, the Bishop of Saint Praxed, in Rome, lies on his deathbed encircled by his recalcitrant sons. Faust-like, at this eleventh hour he faces the prospect of death – if not damnation. He has long deliberated on his tomb, detailing to his attendant sons some precise points of its style and decoration. The tomb itself is to be of basalt, a very dark mineral, bounded by seven rose-peach-coloured columns, his statue to recline on this slab while on his knees rests a lump of deep blue, semi-precious lapis lazuli.

The poem begins, less *in medias res* than in the time-honoured narrative style of treating readers as one of his listeners, 'Draw round ...' (2). The Bishop recalls fondly his passionate love for the mother of his children and how he outwitted his rival, Gandolf, for her love. Nevertheless, the memory of Gandolf rankles. And thus, while the Bishop desperately strives to console himself that he avenged his rival by ordering for him an inferior tomb of 'onion stone', together with a commonplace inscription (ELUSCEBAT, 'he was illustrious'), he is fearfully conscious that the same thing will almost certainly happen to his own tomb.

To obviate this likelihood, he desperately pledges to his children all his material wealth (which they are due to inherit regardless), including villas, horses and valuable manuscripts. Throughout the poem his mind flits between past and present, and the yearned-for future, concluding on the unresolved rivalry with his predeceased adversary.

For discussion I have chosen the following extract because it embodies so many of the poem's key themes, of time, emotion, materialism and the will, especially as they relate to the topic of religion.

> For Gandolf shall not choose but see and burst! 50
> Swift as a weaver's shuttle fleet our years:
> Man goeth to the grave, and where is he?
> Did I say basalt for my slab, sons? Black -
> 'Twas ever antique-black I meant! How else
> Shall ye contrast my frieze to come beneath? 55
> The bas-relief in bronze ye promised me,
> Those Pans and nymphs ye wot of, and perchance
> Some tripod, thyrsus, with a vase or so,
> The Saviour at his sermon on the mount,
> Saint Praxed in a glory, and one Pan 60
> Ready to twitch the Nymph's last garment off,
> And Moses with the tables ... but I know
> Ye mark me not! What do they whisper thee,
> Child of my bowels, Anselm? Ah, ye hope
> To revel down my villas while I gasp 65
> Bricked o'er with beggar's mouldy travertine
> Which Gandolf from his tomb-top chuckles at!
> Nay, boys, ye love me - all of jasper, then!
> 'Tis jasper ye stand pledged to, lest I grieve
> My bath must needs be left behind, alas! 70
> One block, pure green as a pistachio-nut,
> There's plenty jasper somewhere in the world -
> And have I not Saint Praxed's ear to pray
> Horses for ye, and brown Greek manuscripts,
> And mistresses with great smooth marbly limbs? 75
> - That's if ye carve my epitaph aright,
> Choice Latin, picked phrase, Tully's every word,
> No gaudy ware like Gandolf's second line -
> Tully, my masters? Ulpian serves his need!

> And then how I shall lie through centuries, 80
> And hear the blessed mutter of the mass ...

One thing that the reader is most likely to notice here is the Bishop's use of metaphor, as in line 50, 'see and burst'. This tells us a number of things – he is a very confident orator, one accustomed to addressing groups, and to expressing himself in heightened rhetoric. He is a man habituated also to pleasure and ease, used to giving orders, as he does now. The speech teems with colourful tropes, mostly metaphors and simile, like in the next line:

> Swift as a weaver's shuttle fleet our years ...

What a marvellously evocative simile for mortality, both in enunciating the speed of life passing and in the 'weaving' image, suggesting a brilliantly complex interplay of ideas which could actually refer to his own manipulative manner. With increasing fright he feels the waning of his powers and the imminence of his death (line 80) – though, ironically enough, there is no hint yet of a loss in his power of speech. However, Browning mixes his speech with all sorts of other hues and layers.

The language of his monologue is by turns extremely conversational ('marbly' in line 75, 'mouldy' in 66, 'mutter' in 81), then formal and direct, and amusingly churchy, as in the next line, 'man goeth to the grave'. He also likes to lard his speech with poetic archaisms reminiscent of biblical lexis: 'twas and 'tis, ye, wot; and its syntax (for example see line 63).

At first it appears that the Bishop is using asides, like in line 53 – his sententious spiritual point about the 'grave' suddenly bringing to mind his own physical grave. Then we discover that the whole speech itself is actually constructed of asides, each one triggering off the next, each one tending to undermine the force of the earlier. So line 53 satirises the Bishop's blatant materialism by way of its contrast with a hackneyed piety from some distant tract.

In answer to his question in line 53, yes, the Bishop did order 'basalt', a very expensive mineral, evoking classical, imperial Roman tombs, and quite often he does sound more like a minor Roman emperor than a devout prelate. The word 'meant' in line 54 is an important marker of the theme of 'will' because what we and the sons witness here is an attempt by this reprobate to impose his will on the future after his death. He is trying to shape posterity and its opinion of him. Hence his painstaking designs for the tomb.

It is not difficult to imagine how diffident his sons must feel in the face of this pompous, domineering father – who is nevertheless supine to their mercy. With typical Browning irony he is their father in both senses – Catholic patriarch and also paterfamilias, begetter of this forbidden fruit of lecherous loins. He is a man of the world, of many worlds, but chiefly the sensuous one (it is worth remembering that he has taken vows of chastity, poverty and obedience!).

The analogy with a Roman emperor gathers more credence in the subsequent lines and asides. Exacting materialist, he insists on the fine details of a sumptuous mausoleum:

> The bas-relief in bronze ye promised me,
> Those Pans and Nymphs ye wot of, and perchance
> Some tripod, thyrsus, with a vase or so ...   (56–58)

The imagery refers to the trappings of paganism, Pan and Nymph being classical spirits, while, in line 60, 'tripod' is associated with a heathen altar of the oracle and 'thyrsus' is the wand of Bacchus, god of orgiastic inebriation. As if this were not sufficiently grotesque, his next line juxtaposes paganism with the image of Christ, the 'Saviour', on the Mount.

The ironies deepen in both complexity and comic effect. The 'saviour' is doubtlessly one on whom, after a life of illicit fornication and hedonistic materialism, the Bishop pins his forlorn hopes for redemption. The 'Sermon on the Mount' was where Christ set out the beatitudes that would guarantee salvation, and Browning mischievously slips this in here for satirical contrast (the opening line of the poem works in the same way with its reference to 'Vanity'). Since, by definition, the poet cannot intrude comment directly into a dramatic monologue, he drops in hints of the moral standards by which the bishop may be judged, controlling from outside how the poem reads.

Accordingly the beatitudes stand in stark contradiction to the Bishop's dissolute life style. These were enumerated by Christ in his Sermon on the Mount, and Browning intends them as tacit allusions by which to beat the Bishop: poverty, meekness, righteousness, mercy, pacifism, and love or charity (see *Matthew* v. 3-10).

Browning employs the same juxtaposing irony in the following lines. First, Saint Praxed – or Prassede in Italian – was actually a female saint, though at line 95 the Bishop mistakenly believes she was a man. She was beatified on account of her selfless sacrifice – along with her sister – in helping Christians who were being persecuted by the Romans in the second century (the bishop fondly believes she was present at Christ's Sermon on the Mount). Clearly Browning wants to draw the contrast between the self-centred bishop with the altruistic saint who risked her own life in the service of others.

Imagining her with a 'glory' or halo, the minister regards her as merely another hollow detail in the adornment of his own tomb. The ironies gather: Saint Praxed is to share this spot with Moses bearing the 'tables' of the law, the Ten Commandments, many of which the Bishop has joyfully violated. Eccentrically sandwiched between these two upright figures is to be an erotic scene in which Pan is caught in the act of twitching off a Nymph's underwear!

His sons should by now be sniggering at this but their father suddenly breaks from his honeyed reverie to notice that they are in fact stupefied. In a paranoid aside he turns to Anselm, his trusted favourite:

What do they whisper thee ... (63)

His current life is now one of unrelenting anxiety, of how other people regard him but, more urgently, whether the fruit of his loins will honour his intentions after his death. His natural suspicion is that they are grasping materialists, intent only on his wealth, 'To revel down my villas', that is, pawning the buildings to fund a good time (65; note the plural here too). Like father like sons.

Their dreaded revenge would be to party away the father's money and then bury him in a miserable beggar's tomb, ignominiously 'bricked over' with 'gritstone' or some cheap, ugly limestone ('travertine') from the hills north-east of Rome (66). At this point we may recall the opening line's reference to 'Vanity' as a denunciation of the churchman's arrogance. Even more ignominious to him is the thought of himself as the butt of Gandolf's chuckling derision (contrast line 50).

One of the many fascinating features of this protean monologue is the way the Bishop's anxiety repeatedly draws him into reverie, especially of the horrors of what may come. After the climax of terror in line 67, his ire subsides and instead he tries a softly-softly approach with his boys, 'ye love me', while all along suspecting they probably do not.

He settles for jasper as the stone for his tomb, though this is still a very expensive material. He has changed his mind from the basalt of line 53, and he will change it again in 101, to lapis lazuli, a semi-precious stone, a great lump of which he has stolen and buried in his vineyard (see lines 36–42). Lapis is not the piece to adorn the tomb since he has already earmarked the lump to sit somewhat farcically on his effigy's knees.

'Tis jasper ye stand pledged to ... (69)

This word 'pledged' is interesting because a major percentage of the poem's anxiety relates to the idea of the sons making binding promises (for instance, see line 56) and the Bishop's evident uncertainty about his will. The word 'orders' in the poem's title points to the old man's domineering, authoritarian attitude, controlling as much as he is able.

More than anything, for the Bishop the pre-eminence of his will is an important theme here. For him, hell represents the demise of his will, the fact dawning abruptly on him that death will render him absolutely impotent. A man accustomed to getting his own way, having things just how he likes them, he now recognises that the old easy ways are nearing the end, 'fleet' as the weaver's shuttle.

And yet the prospect of meeting his maker appears to leave him far from fazed. Only the prospect of leaving behind his precious bath and all the rest of his possessions causes him any trouble. His sons will have to seek out the jasper 'somewhere', and there seems a fat chance of that. In his advanced dotage now, he appears to be increasingly confused and disillusioned: 'Do I live, am I dead?' (13). Thus he dizzily believes he has 'Saint Praxed's ear'.

More promises follow: horses, valuable ancient Greek manuscripts and beautiful women with sensual legs. Blatantly acquisitive of bloodstock, he collects manuscripts, but not for their intellectual content, only their value as powerful investment collateral, as well as for the power inherent in exclusive ownership. As for women, he is able to offer his boys a choice of mistresses. His has been a life epitomised by power, lust and materialism, in fact the diametric opposite of what Saint Praxed and her 'ear' might stand for.

Additionally, his grand plan relies on his sons adhering to his deathbed instructions about his epitaph. Even today Latin carries some peculiar gravitas, and it comes as no surprise that, as with the horses, manuscripts and women, he insists on the finest quotation. Marble has its own language of power (98) yet only something from the great 'Tully' will adequately enrich it.

Marble's own language derives from its quality, rarity and association with the classical period. Marble and Latin even today exert a powerful fascination, while Marcus Tullius Cicero (106–43 BC) is still highly rated as among the most eloquent of Latin orators. Typically, the man whom the Bishop rejects, Ulpian, was renowned as an upright lawyer – while Tully, the man he embraces, had a reputation for wily disreputable skulduggery.

The Bishop's thoughts inevitably return (in line 80) to an earlier anxiety – prestige in death. All this hoped-for grandeur is for one thing only: to impress spectators of his tomb. A man who appears to have achieved nothing lasting in life (he is anonymous within the poem), seeks the assurance of eminence in death. His mind is constantly preoccupied with thoughts of his nemesis, Gandolf, an anxiety only partly palliated by recalling how he once bested Gandolf out of the fairest mistress, and topped his rival's tomb with a cheap citation from Ulpius.

Facing recumbence 'through centuries' (80), he clings onto these minor exultations in the hope that they may bring relief from his relentless mental turmoil, lulled by the blessed 'mutter' of the mass. Even religion, supposedly his vocation, is reduced in Browning's satire, to the irreverent euphemism of a 'blessed mutter'.

Commentary

To compare churchmen in at least one circumstance, the Bishop of Praxed is the antithesis of Fra Lippo Lippi's Prior. Where brother Lippi's Prior is the essence of Platonism, Praxed is a disciple of empiricism. Platonism is the philosophy of the unseen, unsensed; Praxed follows a philosophy of tangible materialism. So if we see the Prior's thesis as representing Renaissance Catholicism, then the Bishop's cupidity is both its obverse and its everyday actual reality – at least according to Browning.

Having said that, the poem deals less directly with Catholic doctrine than with what Browning regards as the materialism and hypocrisy of its proponents and with the morality of one of its churchmen. All of these elements seem here and elsewhere to be rooted in power and its abuse. It is the loss of this power, both ecumenical and secular that deeply worries the Bishop here; the image is of a man who has enjoyed a long lease of power and luxury, only now to be faced with the fast-approaching prospect of an eternity deprived of them. Yet he appears to us oblivious of the doctrinal implications of death and any transcendent afterlife.

In reality the Bishop fears posterity – namely people – more than he fears God. For him the afterlife is pretty much like his earth life – an eternity of gazing

> ... up into the airy dome where live
> The angels, and a sunbeam's sure to lurk ...   (23–24)

It is unlikely that Jesus wants him for a sunbeam and doubtful anyway that he actually conceives of himself in these terms.

Again, Browning teases out a perceived distinction between faith and church, between spirituality and institution. He does so because he considers that established religion quietly makes them separate, yet intentionally confusing the two in popular imagery. And in fact the title of the poem makes an ironic extension to this idea: the bishop is not 'ordering' his soul, his moral account, but ordering a material afterlife – the tomb – as an extension of the bodily life. This marks a kind of psychological immaturity in him as well as moral blindness – and both elements contribute impudently to Browning's satire.

While our bishop gives little evidence of any zeal of faith, he pins his future hopes on Saint Praxed to pray for his soul (since no one else is likely to, not even himself):

> And have I not Saint Praxed's ear to pray ...   (73)

Yet, given her celebrated piety she may not relish association with this hedonistic materialist and there must be a strong chance that he is already damned.

Saint Praxed is to be yet another servant to minster to his bidding, a bidding that he insists should continue beyond his death. In this respect the word 'orders' in the title is intended to show us a man accustomed to marshalling his subordinates. In fact there is not a great deal of ordering of anything final (and there are frequent changes of mind) and Browning uses this again as symbolic of a vainglorious materialistic man, much exercised by the prospect of a loss of power, the looming failure to impose his will beyond the grave. For him religion has become a means to wealth, sensual luxury and power – that he must abandon or divert into an imposing tomb.

This theme of the will occurs frequently in the poems under our consideration. For example Andrea del Sarto's feeble resolve is blunted by matrimonial issues while Lippo Lippi's will had to be judiciously masked in the face of the Church's absolute will. In 'Childe Roland' it appears to be stuttering willpower alone that gets the hero through, and in 'The Laboratory' the assassin's will must be exercised through the medium of an alchemist. The men of 'My Last Duchess' and 'Porphyria's Lover' become energised by the physical power of imposing their will on abject women.

As in previous poems, Browning effortlessly matches the verse to the subject. Once more delivered in blank verse, the poem's metre is low key, its regularity offset by enjambement and caesurae. The central character of the Bishop is the (almost) exclusive source of the poem's form and meaning – though some of this meaning is not as the speaker intended. Again the first-person dramatic monologue is relaxed, and conversational, a tone accentuated by means of its discourse markers (see lines 2, 3 and 34, but there are many examples) and the usual markers of conversation (colloquialism, repetition, flashback of memories, asides, non-fluency and ellipsis).

It is no surprise that the poem's form is loosely that of a Catholic Mass, his sons as acolytes. The stages of the service are: induction (line 2), commemoration of the dead (8), confession, of sorts (37), consecration (82) and *Nunc Dimittis* (119). Thus in its function as ironic framework it works as a black mass. The inherent looseness of the poem's linear organic form and its unities of time and place are offset by its singleness of voice and the diverse range of its allusions (as well as by a feeling of the church's enclosure).

The narrative voice is also, of course, the main driving-wheel of the poem, coalescing desire and anxiety (so that they are seen as one quality). The poem also draws a great deal of its interest from the character's sensuality, especially in the visual sphere (where he has a weakness for subtle colours and shapes), often producing amazingly beautiful touches:

> Peach-blossom marble all, the rare, the ripe
> As fresh-poured red wine of a mighty pulse.... (29–30)

and

> Blue as a vein o'er the Madonna's breast ... (44)

Many commentators go so far as to describe Browning's monologue style here as 'stream of consciousness', a narrative device famously associated with the novelists James Joyce and Virginia Woolf. Browning's 'stream' is an attempt to capture the apparently haphazard semi-conscious workings of the mind, proceeding by association and immediate stimulus, and drawing together items from seemingly disparate spheres. In this poem and 'My Last Duchess' he skilfully brings the techniques of the dramatic monologue to a new pinnacle of distinction, integrating into his verse qualities that had previously been the reserve of the novel.

'Bishop Blougram's Apology'

> My first thought was, he lied in every word ...
> ('Childe Roland to the Dark Tower Came', line 1)

Writing to his friend Edward Chapman in January 1856, Browning was anxious to get hold of a copy of that month's number of the Catholic Journal, *The Rambler*, and in particular an unsigned review of his extended monologue 'Bishop Blougram's Apology', which he had published the previous year in the *Men and Women* collection.

Contemporary readers of the poem quickly came to identify Cardinal Nicholas Wiseman as the model for Bishop Sylvester Blougram. Wiseman had been consecrated bishop in 1840 and then, in 1850, was raised to the newly created position of Archbishop of Westminster, and thus controversially head of the Catholic Church in England, controversial because many

Protestants feared this as an expression of Catholic political ambition in the country (the opening to the poem appears deliberately phrased to irritate religious sensitivity – see line 3 for instance).

Curiously, the basis of Browning's eagerness to read *The Rambler* was his belief that the unnamed reviewer was none other than Cardinal Wiseman himself. The reviewer was not in fact Wiseman but Richard Simpson, who nevertheless regarded the poem's theology as 'scandalous' and 'abominably untrue', the poem overall being a rare if sceptical delight (Litzinger 1970, pp. 185–186; Houghton 1968).

In addition to being modelled on identifiable individuals, the poem is unusual in being set in to Browning's own contemporary period. As well as its glance at Wiseman and the expanding profile of Roman Catholicism, there are references to, for example, A. W. N. Pugin (line 6), leading architect in the Victorian Gothic revival and to Count D'Orsay (1801–1852), artist, wit and socialite, acquaintance of Napoleon III, in addition to the German theologian David Strauss (lines 577–599). There is a reference too in line 938 to the Crimean War which blundered on between 1853 and 1856.

The point of these and other close references to Browning's own period is that they bring the details of the poem's theological concepts into sharper relevance. The poem emerged at a time when the fierce polemics that followed on the Oxford (or Tractarian) Movement (see Chapter 3) later became intensified by the savage controversy around Wiseman's appointment as Cardinal, and potential Papal intervention in British religious and political affairs. Contemporary readers would have little difficulty in immediately recognising the currency of the furore dramatised in this poem.

A Synopsis of the Poem

The poem is one of Browning's most heavily nuanced, a point that has led many critics to accuse its main character and even Browning himself of casuistry. But it is also one of the poet's most cryptic monologues, sounding unexpected depths of religious ideology and evasion.

In the main body of the poem, the eponymous Bishop is the sole speaker, lecturing, browbeating and patronising his relatively inert auditor, Gigadibs. The poem has a coda spoken by another, presented by an unidentified speaker, possibly (but not certainly) Browning himself. The opening lines give some idea of the setting of the poem, evening in the Bishop's residence following a service in a church designed by Pugin, possibly St George's, Southwark. Gigadibs has set the Bishop on his course by criticising those who profess faith and enjoy its privileges, while harbouring profound doubts.

The first 100 lines or so of this prolix address set out the ostensible motives behind it. In the wider perspective there have been charges in the press, both anti-Catholic and hostile to Blougram, in the context of Cardinal Wiseman's appointment in 1850 and its perceived threat to the established Anglican Church. On more personal terms Blougram prepares to shield himself against the view that he nursed ambitions to become Pope, refuting this on the grounds that as a non-Italian he had no chance. And the third string is the widely held view that Blougram is a sceptic and a sensualist, not fully committed to Catholic doctrine. It is to these that the stolid Bishop responds with his 971 lines of versified refutation.

Blougram's answer aligns himself at times with his fellow bishop, that of Praxed: he vigorously rebuffs the old journalistic cliché that all churchmen should be ascetic, eschewing worldly diversions of politics, comfort and even pleasure. This rejoinder opens up the two principal avenues of the monologue: the relationship between faith and scepticism, and the ethics of a churchman in the world.

A conspicuous feature of the Bishop's strategy is his use of figures of speech, an early example of this being his figure of the mortal life as a voyage. There is nothing especially novel about this analogy, each individual having his or her own cabin for the voyage (100–101), its furnished accommodation reflecting the social class, wealth and aspirations of the traveller. We are a continent away from the journeyings of Childe Roland. The cabin is, however, the preserve of the believer, and contrasts with the atheistic 'landsman'.

Blougram next skilfully acknowledges that he does not possess all the answers to questions of faith, thereby shrewdly blocking off Gigadibs's possible lines of attack (161–167). To further wrong-foot his listener, the churchman himself disarmingly adopts the position of a sceptic, professing that faith in God is uncertain and may be relative:

> And now what are we? unbelievers both …   (173)

It is a masterly stroke since it allows him to build up the possibility of faith ('The Grand Perhaps!'; 190) from below rather than struggle to defend it from the received position.

To try to show the symbiotic intricacy between faith and doubt, Blougram next introduces the allegory of the chessboard (212). Unbelief and faith are actually defined by one another but from a personal point of view he chooses faith since a life in the Church has exalted and enriched his existence, curbing the unacceptable excesses in his nature, the 'cabin' in which he voyages. He thus presents himself as a realist, claiming to recognise the practical limitations of himself and of theology (though some would argue that this is unacceptably complacent, or even backsliding on his part).

At each point in his thesis, the Bishop anticipates Gigadibs's reaction – making it a one-sided, pompous-sounding homily. He contemptuously posits the different reasons people may have for professing faith, such as to emulate the nobility (424). Would Gigadibs's model be Napoleon Bonaparte or Shakespeare, or possibly Martin Luther? none of these was, Blougram claims, anywhere near perfect, and in any case we have only the popular, outward and heroic image to judge them by: 'hearsay'. Faith, argues the Bishop, is not a matter of exemplars, science or history – our faculties are too limited – faith refers to the metaphysical and so transcends worldly issues of evidence and proof. However, he does add that faith may be something instinctive, that Gigadibs was born with faith, but has since tried his best to suppress it:

> Trust you an instinct silenced long ago ... (630)

The passage I have chosen for analysis (lines 647–675) occurs at this point in the monologue, when Bishop Blougram realises that Gigadibs's next line of attack may be to denounce head on all possibility of faith, and so completely undermine his Christianity, a vulnerable target in this gritty game of chess. The Bishop makes another of his consummate feints.

> Pure faith indeed - you know not what you ask!
> Naked belief in God the Omnipotent,
> Omniscient, Omnipresent, sears too much
> The sense of conscious creatures to be borne.   650
> It were the seeing him, no flesh shall dare.
> Some think, Creation's meant to show him forth:
> I say, it's meant to hide him all it can,

> And that's what all the blessed evil's for.
> Its use in Time is to environ us,
> Our breath, our drop of dew, with shield enough
> Against that sight till we can bear its stress.
> Under a vertical sun, the exposed brain
> And lidless eye and disemprisoned heart
> Less certainly would wither up at once   660
> Than mind, confronted with the truth of Him.
> But time and earth case-harden us to live;
> The feeblest sense is trusted most; the child
> Feels God a moment, ichors o'er the place,
> Plays on and grows to be a man like us.
> With me, faith means perpetual unbelief
> Kept quiet like the snake 'neath Michael's foot
> Who stands calm just because he feels it writhe.
> Or, if that's too ambitious – here's my box -
> I need the excitation of a pinch   670
> Threatening the torpor of the inside-nose
> Nigh on the imminent sneeze that never comes.
> 'Leave it in peace' advise the simple folk -
> Make it aware of peace by itching-fits,
> Say I - let doubt occasion still more faith!

In terms of its discussion of religion, the passage can be navigated by using three interesting points of diction: 'sears' (649), 'ichors' (664) and 'faith' (675 – as well as at 647 and 666). Using these words as cornerstones of our discussion enables us to consider the passage in the three parts controlled by them: (a) lines 647–654, (b) lines 655–665 and (c) lines 666–675.

(a) lines 647–654: 'sears'

Bishop Blougram has been prompted to focus on faith through the question raised by Gigadibs at line 598. However, to introduce his defence the prelate suddenly makes a surprising (and quite choleric) declaration of strategy, implying that he discards the dogmatic concept of faith:

> I show you doubt, to prove that faith exists.   (602)

Up to this point Blougram has been content to dwell on religious scepticism or doubt. His retort now stresses the enormity of the question:

> Pure faith indeed - you know not what you ask!

By 'pure' here the Bishop means unqualified by circumstantial elements, like references to biography or the mediations of individual religious groups and cults. The next couple of lines help make this point a little clearer:

> Naked belief in God the Omnipotent,
> Omniscient, Omnipresent ...

Gigadibs wishes to focus the exchange on the divinity of God, goading the speaker into a definition of the Godhead itself. But, as we will discuss in more detail below, this is an area that Blougram wishes to avoid in order to secure more wiggle-room to impose his own definitions.

The reason he does propose is that for 'conscious creatures', or humans, to attempt to penetrate the essential nature of God it would be impossibly blinding – we just do not have the mental capacity to comprehend entities such as omnipresence or omniscience. Like staring at the sun, such probing or 'seeing him' cannot be 'borne', as likely to 'sear' too much the rational consciousness. Mankind cannot easily bear such reality and thus 'no flesh shall dare'. For this reason, he argues, we have been encouraged to look more safely at his Creation, the material handiwork – of nature, life on earth, the cosmos. Moreover, he claims that Creation thus hides the essential truth (and some would say Blougram's monologue itself does this better).

There is reverence too in Blougram's baulking at divinity, as there is in his fallback position, Creation being at least a sign or expression of God's existence, his DNA being firmly imprinted on it. The same reasoning extends through the oxymoron in line 653:

> And that's what all the blessed evil's for.

If God has created all the universe, then the property of evil too, as part of that nature, must be his work, and so is 'blessed'.

(b) lines 655–665: 'ichors'

Mankind is a creature of 'Time' – we are mortal – so the Creation myth helps to cocoon ('environ') us with a useful narrative, a 'shield enough' to safeguard 'our breath, our drop of dew' (these are conventional images of the human body or life – but also 'breath' hints at the soul, as in 'Fra Lippo Lippi', lines 184–186). Eventually then we become able to bear the 'stress' of the 'truth of Him', God (line 661). Referring back to line 649, Blougram introduces yet another metaphor – just in case Gigadibs does not quite catch on: the searing truth of God is like the burning tropical sun and we with exposed brain, or 'lidless eyes', would wither up immediately were it not for the deceiving myth.

'Disemprisoned' (659) is a curious word here – or anywhere come to that. Blougram/Browning clearly chooses it to imply 'liberated' but he wants to retain the concept of the original prison in 'environ' (and the passage has other hints of the theme of containment). In this way the word retains both the idea of freedom and its obverse, constraint. This foible is consistent with the passage's many other ironies and paradoxes.

Unlike the imagination ('eye') and the feelings ('heart') the mind is vulnerable to the enormity of ideas such as the concept of ' God'. But time and earthly life gradually 'case-harden' the intellect in order to survive, in the way that an insect's carapace is a resilient, protective shield. In the word 'harden' Blougram is further hinting that as we grow older we grow duller, our receptivity and inventiveness ossifying – unlike the mind of a child, that 'feels God for a moment' (663–664).

This view owes something to the philosophy of Blake and of Wordsworth, the latter expressing it succinctly in his *Ode: Intimations of Immortality* (1807): infancy is the unique period of that innocence in our lives that enables us to joyously envision the complex moral truths of Nature:

> Heaven lies about us in our infancy!
> Shades of the prison-house begin to close
> Upon the growing Boy ...   (lines 66–68)

Significantly, both poets employ the metaphor of 'light' for 'truth' and each regards the process of maturing as one of incarceration.

Unlike Wordsworth, Blougram's verse is duller, more prosaic, its verbs more indicative. He is eager to impose his vision on what he regards as a dull-witted Gigadibs (see line 669 too). But it is a poem as much about language as religion. So he attempts to rouse poor Gigadibs with an array of ingenious tropes. The child comprehends God, bareheaded and fleetingly, until time moves on, 'ichors o'er the place' (664), and as it grows to become an adult, the vision fades.

'Ichors' shouts at us off the page as a term reassigned from a pagan to a Christian context (Blougram, a man of much paradox and irony). Originally signifying the blood of the ancient gods, it has come to mean a balm, a positive, promoting health – yet Blougram employs it in a more negative sense, suggesting again a protection, a crust or scab forming over a wound or, metaphorically, implying a process of forgetting (where normally a wholesome process, the speaker now equates experience of God as akin to a lesion).

(c) lines 666–675: 'faith'

The word 'faith' in line 666 takes up again the theme introduced in the start of this passage. After his general dismissal of Gigadibs's impossible questions about the nature of God, the speaker turns to his own particular view of a different question, that of faith. Blougram slips from objective issues about the nature of the deity, into a more subjective view: his own response to God, through faith.

As we have come to expect, Blougram responds with shock tactics, and with yet another paradox:

> With me, faith means perpetual unbelief
> Kept quiet like the snake 'neath Michael's foot ...   (666–667)

This oxymoron is not quite what we expect of a bishop and we generally consider religious faith to be strong belief backed by a sense of firm conviction. Yet with a paradox, Blougram gives himself room for a resolution, entering via the smart conceit in the following line. As usual, Browning highlights his key points through alliteration, here in line 667 using the repeated /k/ sound to emphasise the illustration (note too the alliterative /s/ in line 650).

This conceit in line 666 forms one of the cruxes to Blougram's overall thesis. Having at the outset declared that 'nature of faith' was to be his treatise, his Apology, he warns that in contrast to Gigadibs's demand, there was to be no absolute or dogmatic answer to the question of faith (lines 161–172).

In simple terms there is no such thing as constant faith, in that sense of an unchanging steadfast conviction, issued from God. Instead, faith must be earned. If this has a Catholic chime about it then the good Bishop does not mean, by this, to earn grace through kind works, only that faith must be constantly tested and hardened by enduring the torment of doubt. Which draws his mind to yet another allegory, that of Saint Michael, who is conventionally represented as crushing the serpent or dragon Satan as it coils beneath his feet (see *Revelation* xii. 7–9).

Line 668's brilliant oxymoron – setting 'calm' against 'writhe' – vividly condenses this idea. The adverb 'calm' glances back to similar imagery in the passage, 'borne', 'bear' and 'ichors', while 'writhe' draws together a multitude of references to turmoil: sears, stress, wither up and so on. The experience of unremitting stress implicit in 'perpetual unbelief' may also make us aware of how so many of Browning's characters find themselves in this state of permanent tension or trauma (think of Childe Roland, Lippo Lippi, the Patriot or the narrator of 'The Laboratory'). Line 657 here contemplates a time when 'we can bear its stress' but Browning's poetry is more realistic in rarely holding out any promise of relief.

Doubt defines and affirms faith. This strikes a quite visual allegory but Blougram doubts if his listener's intellect is up to it ('if that's too ambitious'; 669 – and he intends this for us too!). Which prompts him to yet one more smart allegory for Gigadibs, and extra alliteration to spell it out. Taking his snuff-box from a pocket, the Bishop draws the analogy of doubt acting like a pinch of snuff to constantly rouse the feeling of awareness.

'Inside-nose' (671) is clumsy, but we get the general idea. It is not exactly 'string theory' and yet it does not quite work through the 'doubt/faith' correspondence as convincingly as does, say, Saint Michael's figure. Snuff or indeed other irritable compounds can be used to make us aware of just how calm things are up our nasal cavities. And yet other counsels oppose:

> 'Leave it in peace' advise the simple folk … (673)

And I, for one, am inclined to agree with them.

The final word of the passage draws us back to its first line, reminding of the key point:

> … let doubt occasion still more faith! (675)

In the context of the whole discourse this 'pure' or 'naked' line puts the point most succinctly. In turn this succinctness may also afford fuel to those who believe that Blougram indulges his prolix sermonising, loading every point with trope and parable, chiefly for his own delectation (and the thought of that sweet pain rumbling in his nostrils may imply a certain perverseness of character).

Commentary

The Bishop's monologue is described in the title as an 'Apology'. In literary terms an 'apology' (or '*apologia*') is not strictly speaking a statement of regret or a plea for forgiveness but an outline of the writer's opinions or stance on a particular issue. Browning, however, is happy that the idea of contrition should hover about Blougram's monologue and this works to satirise the Bishop in the poem: it is anything but an apology.

This monologue is a complex but impromptu response to Gigadibs's inquisition. The genial setting of this conversation piece ('a final glass for me') should not blind us to the fact that Bishop Sylvester Blougram has a steadfast agenda and that he is as uncompromising as the Duke of Ferrara. While he is not contemplating murder, he is not to be diverted from the serious theological and ecclesiastical points at issue. This should be seen within the context of contemporary anti-Catholic hostility following Pope Pius IX's moves to re-establish Catholic bishops in England. At the same time, a mid-century suspicion emerged that Catholic doctrine was beginning to infiltrate Protestant ideology (in fact in 1851 Parliament passed the 'Ecclesiastical Titles Act' forbidding Catholics to use the title 'Bishop').

As an apology, the Bishop's discourse can be described as teleological, that is, his discourse has a specific purpose and its arguments tend toward a preset conclusion, though here conclusions are more implicit than overt. The form of the above extract reflects this sense of purpose: (a) the Bishop questions human capacities to grasp the essence of God, especially if this equated with faith, then (b) he sketches the ways people adjust to this limitation, concluding (c) with a new definition of faith in the light of (a) and (b).

For this reason his dialectic argument often comes across less as a relaxed chat than as a lecture, with the intention of undermining preconceptions about faith. By the same token, the conversational setting does have thematic function. Bishop Praxed presides in conditions of very comfortable living, immured from the ghastly socio-economic issues of the day. The setting also lends the impression that Blougram regards the quest for truth as a type of after-dinner game, and whatever we think about the speaker's character we sense that he is an expert in the fine nuances of language, a brilliant driven strategist in the machinations of power play.

To understand the thrust of the passage we should first put it in the perspective of the poem as a whole, beginning with the theological context.

In the opening section to the poem, Bishop Blougram arrogantly sympathises with Gigadibs's position as auditor and assures him that he himself finds theology a difficult subject: 'every whit as hard' (line 158). This has the advantage of blunting his listener's objections even before they surface. Also early on, the Bishop sets out his aim of discovering truth:

> I promised, if you'd watch a dinner out,
> We'd see truth dawn together ...   (16–17)

and truth or reason is to be the basis of his treatise.

In another tactic designed to outsmart young Gigadibs (half the age of the speaker) Blougram confesses that his faith is not a fixed entity, being neither absolute nor unchanging (162), adding for good measure that he does not know all the answers to theological questions (165). Having cleared the field of potential explosives, he proposes that they start from first principles (rather than fiddle around trying to tweak the niceties of an established creed) and like many philosophical theories he begins with a (kind of) definition of man:

> Grant I'm a beast, why, beasts must lead beasts' lives!
> Suppose I own at once to tail and claws ...   (349–350)

(This is consistent, of course, with contemporary evolutionary theories and with his explanation in the passage that mankind is not equipped to bear the stress of actually facing God.) He admits that like all human beings, deep down he is animal in origin, and that his theology must accommodate this limitation.

Blougram repeatedly claims to be a realist ('we speak of what is; not of what might be'; 346) and this imparts a patina of truth to what he does say. For example, not all men are of equal ability and there be some who are intellectuals and so marked out in their field. He uses this distinction to justify the different levels of comfort that prevail in society. The Bishop presents some examples of these exceptional men: he admires Shakespeare, of course, also Napoleon and Luther as outstanding achievers, if controversial for their aims. And yet, when everything is totted up, they are still only men, mortal, still rooted in the beast:

> That even your prime men who appraise their kind
> Are men still ... (388–389)

Blougram really aims to distil religion into its purest form, its most absolute precept, which is faith, and the clever touch is to use doubt to enable this. Even if we are repulsed by the man himself his ideas have a whiff of reason.

Blougram sees the chief threats to religious faith in the mid-Victorian period as twofold: on the one hand, a growth in materialism promulgated by advanced industrial processes, with a general increase in profits and wealth among the elite classes (line 550); and on the other the burgeoning effect of rationalism, science and secular philosophy (line 632).

Matthew Arnold's poem 'Stanzas from the Grande Chartreuse', published in the same year as 'Bishop Blougram's Apology', expresses more lyrically the widespread awareness of threats to traditional patterns of faith. Arnold's poem, however, represents a more personal response to the mid-century crisis in established religion, the growing sense of scepticism in the wake of tumultuous changes in science, industry and society.

> Wandering between two worlds, one dead,
> The other powerless to be born,
> With nowhere yet to rest my head,
> Like these, on earth I wait forlorn.
> Their faith, my tears, the world deride -
> I come to shed them at their side.
>
> (lines 85–90)

A similar strong feeling permeates both poems, of a long era coming to a close, a reshaping or redefinition of faith in the face of the new realities. Arnold's feeling of uncertainty and of impotence very much animates the passage under analysis and its yearning to hold onto the essence of the past belief but in a new idiom. Blougram yokes the vocabulary of contemporary scepticism to elaborately reassert its relevance to faith (other poems from Browning's *Men and Women* 1855 that address this spiritual unease include *Saul, Cleon* and *Karshish*.)

Barabara Melchiori writes that Browning 'does not wholly satisfy us that "faith means perpetual unbelief"' (Melchiori 1968, p. 16). This is of course correct, or partly so. The poem gropes towards a possibility of faith by examining the diverse ways of dealing with unbelief

> ... how can we guard our unbelief,
> Make it bear fruit to us? (180–181)

A main part of Blougram's mission is, while fumbling on from a position of scepticism, to investigate the different meanings of the word 'fruit'. Through the process of the chessboard analogy, and by repeatedly acknowledging the ever-presence of doubt, he hints at the delimitation of faith. So, in lines 648–649 of the passage he does not deny a definition of God as 'Omnipotent, / Omniscient, Omnipresent', only that these concepts are too difficult for mankind to embrace. So even if we believe, it is not easy to say what actually is the object of our belief.

A turning point for Blougram himself, a chink in the door, is that unbelief itself is every bit as vulnerable ('how can we guard our unbelief'). Because of our nature as humans there will always be

> The grand Perhaps! (190)

Doubt is innate. Humans can never be absolutely or finally convinced of anything, and the niggling possibility of, say, transcendence, even of a deity, keeps open the door for faith (this skirts close to St Anselm's Ontological Argument for God, but Blougram has eyes on two other routes instead).

Doubt is legitimate, he argues, for a number of reasons (603). As in the case of Saint Michael's writhing serpent it acts as a challenge that – if overcome – will reinforce faith. Further, doubt is a realistic position based on human nature and on free will, and thus underpins his definition of humanity.

He steps beyond this, however, adding that free will is God's way of saying that a man's reach should exceed his grasp (622–625). However, returning to the passage again, he arrives at a preliminary conclusion, that because of a lack of certainty, faith and scepticism will never be finally resolved:

> ... faith means perpetual unbelief ... (666)

At the same time, even if we were able to follow reason or rational philosophy we do not always desire to do so. And in any case there are plenty of distractions and irregularities in life and society that prevent or displace the will into a compromise (886–887). Furthermore, Blougram doubts that reason in itself can be pursued to any final point of an objective solution and that ultimately men often prefer instinct as a guide to principles or action (line 825 on).

When this is all totted up, do we think he has clinched it? has the Bishop established a convincing grounding for the existence of God? Logic can be a capricious force in the philosophy of religion, since it is ultimately a human construct. Blougram's scepticism could just as easily lead to atheism, or indeed Satan worship, or even the veneration of Father Christmas. Natural Theology also renders *The Bible* and other scripture in an ambiguous area of status (while many believers do insist on their viability). His stress is for the most part negative, cutting away what is not valid or sound, and his argument, for faith of some kind, is often eloquent (and Natural Theology is heavily satirised in 'Caliban Upon Setebos').

The narrator of the poem's coda, a sceptic himself, is irascible in condemnation of the Bishop, which is of course one important function of the coda:

> For Blougram, he believed, say, half he spoke.
> The other portion, as he shaped it thus
> For argumentary purposes ... (980–982)

Blougram draws us along the tortuous paths of his labyrinthine and prolix 'Apology' and at heart it may all be an April Fool's trick, an elaborate exercise in rhetoric and a means of bullying the long-suffering Gigadibs.

In the coda, the strange appendix to the poem (lines 971–1014), the focus suddenly pulls away in a very filmic manner, its voice commenting in part on Blougram's hypocrisy (believing only 'half he spoke' and calling true things by 'wrong names'; 980 and 996). The speaker reveals that in the monologue the Bishop was trying only to defend himself against 'cavillers', petty objections.

The poem closes with the revelation that Gigadibs has emigrated to Australia to take up farming, closing ambiguously with a prayer that he has 'studied the last chapter of St. John', St John's being the last of the gospels. The narrator could mean by this that he hopes Gigadibs has abandoned established religion, to pioneer farming in the new land. On the other hand, the final chapter of St John's gospel refers to Christ's disciples sharing a meal and then eschewing material comforts, to spread the word of God abroad. This would seem unlikely to refer literally to Gigadibs himself, but this interpretation would be a brazenly ironic swipe at Blougram's life of hedonism.

Clearly, the voice in the coda is neither that of the Bishop nor of Gigadibs himself; so who *is* the unattributed 'speaker' here? Many critics agree with Woolford and Karlin (1996) that the speaker is in fact Browning himself, *in propria persona*, presenting in the coda his own views on the two characters and to warn the reader not to take too seriously the churchman's words. In reality it is impossible to say conclusively who the speaker of the coda is and it is not particularly relevant whether we think Browning agreed or not with the speaker.

More fruitful is it to discuss what the coda contributes or detracts from the whole piece. In simple terms, the coda suddenly gives perspective and vividness to the whole conversational setting. The new perspective gives the cue to challenging and even undermining Blougram's heavily one-sided utterances, casting his convictions into a new light of potential speciousness and perdition. At the very least, the coda renders a sense of conclusion to the poem, through its detachedness and apparent objectivity.

Another important function of the coda is that its revisionary viewpoints actually inject some distance between the Bishop and Browning the poet. The narrator takes unexpected control of the poem and the reason for this may be that, unlike most of the poems we have discussed so far, there is no obvious integral irony or satire controlling interpretation. Which may be why Browning thought it necessary to add this in the more explicit format of a coda. Perhaps the ultimate ironic coup is Gigadibs himself, the ex-literary man driven to a bucolic life in the barren antipodes, abandoning civilisation – if so then this swipe at all that the Bishop stands for would have been less easy to achieve through the rambling mouthpiece of Blougram.

'Caliban Upon Setebos; or, Natural Theology in the Island'

In the poems we have considered so far in this chapter, Browning can be seen to be exploring inauthentic or 'bad faith' religion. In other words, he is anxious to expose bogus belief whether in the form of hypocritical churchmen, counterfeit doctrine or, in other poems, authoritarian religiosity ('Holy-Cross Day') or plain exploitation of eager and vulnerable minds ('Mr Sludge, "The Medium"', and 'Mesmerism'). It is easier to see what he disapproves of, of what for Browning does *not* constitute faith. Religion per se is not to be understood as the equivalent of faith.

In 'Caliban Upon Setebos' Browning analyses a form of faith that enjoyed a brief but popular vogue in the mid-1800s, the Natural Theology referred to in the poem's subtitle. It is a form of faith loosely based on scientific methods, a form that is challenged by Bishop Blougram (see 'Bishop Blougram's Apology', line 819).

Caliban, Setebos and the island of the poem all have their immediate origins and springing point in Shakespeare's *The Tempest*, the playwright's final and certainly most fantastical drama. While it is not necessary to know the play intimately before tackling Browning's great poem, a reading of it will certainly enrich the experience as well as convey the kinds of themes that Browning is concerned with. In any case, this moving and powerful play is well worth reading or hearing in its own right.

'Caliban Upon Setebos' was original published in the 1864 collection *Dramatis Personae*, a book more commercially and critically successful than any previous Browning publication. Following the death of his wife three years earlier, Browning had settled once again in London where the hot talk of the day was the continuing crisis in religious faith, a theme that had long held Browning's fascination, and in particular the phenomenon of Natural Theology.

In Britain the mid-century storm concerning religion had arisen in large part as a response to fast-changing horizons in science. Darwin's publication of *Origin of Species* in 1859 had been the detonator to critical debates about religious truths as well as raising a storm regarding the essential definition of mankind itself. The implications of the evolutionary hypothesis threatened fundamental scriptural wisdom with regard to creation and the history of man (a controversy that can still polarise dispute today, more than a century and a half later).

Religious scripture – the accumulation of received 'knowledge' on miracles, prophecies and the divine nature of Christ – had been vigorously challenged in, for example, David Strauss's *Life of Jesus* (1835) and by Ernest Renan whose own *Life of Jesus* appeared in 1863. Together, these books interrogated the historical accuracy of the gospels, positing that they actually represented at best allegorical truths or even wishful thinking in terms of their messianic perspectives. Thus, as a response to this kind of scepticism, Natural Theology arose as a faith system that did not rest on the scriptures but employed reasoned observation of the natural world to draw conclusions about transcendental causality.

In lighting on Shakespeare's figure of Caliban, Browning discovered a superb platform for discussing Natural Theology, a phenomenon that is absent from the play itself. In Shakespeare's *The Tempest*, Prospero recounts in Act One, scene two, how twelve years earlier he, as Duke of Milan, had been ousted by his brother Antonio and cast adrift at sea with his 3-year-old daughter, Miranda. Washing up on a luxuriant island, Prospero employs magic to bring it under his total hegemony, partially liberating an airy spirit, Ariel, and enslaving the only other resident, Caliban. A primitive and the aboriginal owner of the island, Caliban is son of a witch Sycorax, who long before the arrival of Prospero had informed him of a god, Setebos. Prospero has been teaching him language – until, that is, Caliban allegedly attempts to rape Miranda.

Nevertheless, Browning's poem is in fact set in a period just prior to the start of the play's action, some time after Prospero's colonisation of it. All the same, Browning happily usurps some of Shakespeare's themes of nature versus nurture (including language), the ethics of colonisation, virtue versus vengeance, and the concept of forgiveness.

A Synopsis of the Poem

Before getting to grips with an extract, it will be useful to get a reasonable grasp of the poem's narrative as a whole. At the start, Caliban has withdrawn into the comparative safety of his cave-den. Away from earshot of Prospero – so he believes – he lies flat, cooling his belly in the slushy mire of a pit. There Caliban responds in a highly sensual manner to his natural environment, at one with bees, spiders, flowers and the tickling water newts.

At the thought of Prospero's tyranny the tone suddenly turns grimly cool. For respite he desperately conjures the memory of Setebos:

> ... that other, whom his dam called God. (16)

It was his mother, Sycorax, who had linked this deity Setebos with the moon, and the son now idly speculates on the nature and power of this god.

There next follows a series of speculations by Caliban, each beginning: 'Thinketh,' (by which he actually intends '*I* think'). Caliban has observed very closely the behaviour and nature of the animals around the island and bases his conclusions about the god on these, in turn using Setebos's supposed power to fill in gaps in his explanations about the island's phenomena. There is none of Blougram's theological doubt here; Caliban is fully convinced about the nature of his tutelary deity:

> ... He made all these and more,
> Made all we see and us, in spite: how else? (55–56)

The monologue here sounds as if the speaker is echoing the distant words of his mother. Yet it is a divinity with limitations: he could not make a copy of himself to be a mate, as was the case in that other garden, Eden.

Caliban speculates on his own potential creativity, making a clay birdman and pinching it into life. He hopes that, like Prospero's Ariel, it will carry out his vengeful will on vexatious creatures. The theme of vengeance, so implicit in *The Tempest*, is never far from Caliban's thoughts and, after pondering the flight of his clay 'mankin', he speculates on the consequences of mutilating it, plucking off limbs until it resembles an egg.

Further cruelty is contemplated, in gratuitously ripping off a crab's pincer (105) and in torturing a blue jay (118). For Caliban these are a re-enactment of what he understands is the wantonness of the deity, since he instinctively attributes his own adversity and misfortune to the immanent will of capricious divinity. Pain and misery represent the revenge of Setebos on earth, on the natural world, 'out of spite' at his inability to reach heaven:

> ... he cannot soar
> To what is quiet and hath happy life ...   (144–145)

If Setebos is thus limited in power, then by Caliban's reasoning there must be some superior entity. And Sycorax had asserted that 'the Quiet made all things' (170). Sycorax begat Setebos and Setebos begat the Quiet. Setebos existed only to 'vex' or disrupt all of creation, 'vex' being one of Caliban's shibboleths since it has become one of the key principles of his own life and that of nature – his mind in a state of constant vexation, paralleling the chaos of the world,

Caliban has built a mysterious construction resembling a shrine to the Quiet, of spikes of trees and turf, bearing a moon motif, topped out with the skull of a sloth. However, he fully expects the 'terrible' Setebos any moment to spoil it with a hurricane, just for spite (199).

The passage I have chosen for analysis and discussion appears at this point in the monologue, beginning with an account of yet another of Caliban's constructions, this time redolent of Elizabethan construction methods:

> So it is, all the same, as well I find.
> 'Wove wattles half the winter, fenced them firm   205
> With stone and stake to stop she-tortoises
> Crawling to lay their eggs here: well, one wave,
> Feeling the foot of Him upon its neck,
> Gaped as a snake does, lolled out its large tongue,
> And licked the whole labour flat: so much for spite.   210
> 'Saw a ball flame down late (yonder it lies)
> Where, half an hour before, I slept i' the shade:
> Often they scatter sparkles: there is force!
> 'Dug up a newt He may have envied once
> And turned to stone, shut up inside a stone.   215
> Please Him and hinder this?—What Prosper does?
> Aha, if He would tell me how! Not He!
> There is the sport: discover how or die!
> All need not die, for of the things o' the isle
> Some flee afar, some dive, some run up trees;   220

> Those at His mercy,—why, they please Him most
> When ... when ... well, never try the same way twice!
> Repeat what act has pleased, He may grow wroth.
> You must not know His ways, and play Him off,
> Sure of the issue. 'Doth the like himself: 225
> 'Spareth a squirrel that it nothing fears
> But steals the nut from underneath my thumb,
> And when I threat, bites stoutly in defence:
> 'Spareth an urchin that contrariwise,
> Curls up into a ball, pretending death   230
> For fright at my approach: the two ways please.
> But what would move my choler more than this,
> That either creature counted on its life
> To-morrow and next day and all days to come,
> Saying, forsooth, in the inmost of its heart,   235
> 'Because he did so yesterday with me,
> And otherwise with such another brute,
> So must he do henceforth and always.'—Ay?
> Would teach the reasoning couple what 'must' means!
> 'Doth as he likes, or wherefore Lord? So He.   240

One of the pervasive problems for readers encountering this brilliant poem is the very language in which it is articulated. Caliban's discourse marks another major stride forward in Browning's art, this time by completely matching the form of the poem to its subject. The novelist James Joyce once jokingly asked for a painting of the city of Cork set in a frame of corkwood. And Browning does something of the same thing here: the poem is less *about* Caliban than actually *being* Caliban.

The passage demonstrates that apparent 'problems' are in fact the matter of the poem. Typically, Caliban does not often use personal subject pronouns – so we read here 'Wove' (205), 'Saw' (211) and 'Spareth' (226 and 229). But he is inconsistent, because in lines 212 and 223, for instance, he does include the pronouns 'I' and 'he'. In *The Tempest* we learn that although Prospero has been teaching him language, Caliban appears to be unable (or reluctant) to use standard English, giving rise to ambiguities in the text. But this language is in fact the essence of Caliban.

The word 'so' is another of Caliban's keywords for two reasons. On the one hand, it signifies resignation in the face of his impotence against gods and master: things are thus and always so. On the other hand, the word signifies a causal relationship, the result of Caliban's febrile attempts to explain and connect occurrences and phenomena.

His construction projects are likewise defective and collapse less from poor assembly, weather or circumstances than by wilfulness on the part of some power figure. In the passage, he uses anthropomorphism to account for why his painstaking wattle fence was 'licked flat' by a wave acting like a lolling tongue. In a marvellously imaginative rationalization of disaster, the sea had felt Setebos's oppressive 'foot upon its neck' and was forced to vex his wattle fence. Conversely, the 'foot upon the neck' serves to remind the reader of the fact that the speaker is an indignant slave to the white settler on *his* isle.

Caliban's wattle fence is an example of the monologue's imagery of constriction and control, which are integral to the theme of power. Similarly, the animals here – tortoises, snake, a squirrel and hedgehog – are members of the island's teeming wildlife which have become subject to Caliban's own attempts at power and regulation. The whole of this erstwhile paradise is in a constant turmoil of struggle within a hierarchy of forces (which forces include the divine as well as the human inhabitants).

The speaker is at the playful mercy of divine powers from all quarters, including the heavens, as he recounts the day he was almost struck by a meteorite, horrified by the 'force' that could hurl this:

> 'Saw a ball flame down late (yonder it lies)
> Where, half an hour before, I slept i' the shade ...   (211–212)

Caliban is both awestruck and alarmed by the baffling secrets of the world about him.

(Is it an anachronism that this primitive should be aware of 'half an hour' – as he is of the 'month' in line 294? Or are these simply droppings from Prospero's casual idiom?)

The reference to a meteorite situates Caliban in the context of space. But then the next few lines locate him immediately in the world of the Victorian theological controversy with the revelation that he has unearthed a fossil lizard:

> 'Dug up a newt He may have envied once
> And turned to stone, shut up inside a stone.   (214–215)

This stone connects to the earlier reference to an egg, and is one more instance of 'imprisonment' imagery: the 'newt' is 'shut up', and for spite (notice how Caliban animates everything with a motive force). 'Turned to stone' has terror-striking Old Testament resonances, but for now Caliban shrugs it off with typical fatalistic stoicism.

We must return later to discuss the Darwinian implications of this fossil and its important implications for theology but it is interesting to note here that Browning himself had an unusual fascination for live newts. He seems to have spent much time in observing them and in a letter of 1846 to Elizabeth he describes his delight in their movements (in terms not unlike Caliban's), concluding 'What a fine fellow our English water-eft is' (*The Love Letters*; Volume I, pp. 370–371).

Caliban next attempts to conjure his familiar genius to hinder Prosper, the use of his shortened name emphasing how the colonial interloper flourishes at the expense of the aboriginal (216). He feels himself even more the victim when he muses on how both Prospero and Setebos persecute him for their 'sport' (the word 'sport' here may recall another very apt Shakespeare comparison, from *King Lear* where Gloucester, like Caliban, abused and tormented by enemies, famously complains:

> As flies to wanton boys, are we to th' Gods;
> They kill us for their sport.   (4.1.36–37)

Caliban figures himself as such a victim of unseen gods.

Yet, Caliban notes that some of the creatures do manage to escape death at the hands of malicious intentions, by diving or running up trees. He may be thinking back here to lines 100–108 when he considered the crabs at his mercy and how he could on a whim simply select one for torture and let others go by (compare too lines 97, 203 and 210). In employing this image Browning is probably vilifying the Calvinist doctrine of 'election and reprobation' – that some are held by destiny to be favoured for heaven while others are preordained to damnation.

The ellipses in line 222 indicate Caliban's frustration at his inability to discern any consistency in the behaviour of either Prospero or Setebos that could lead him to understand their retribution. He can discover no moral grounds ('discover how or die!') and he resorts either to keeping clear of their wrath or adopting trusted methods of appeasement, 'Repeat what act has pleased' (223).

This failure of his 'science' to predict a pattern in the ways of God or Prospero leaves him bewildered and yet his inquisitive alertness is persistently driven to know and then formulate precepts. However, because his life depends upon it, he resorts to a familiar religious formula:

> You must not know His ways ...   (224)

Not understanding God is also part of the game. Ineffability must be the cause. This inability to divine an outward explanation drives him to a subjective moral injunction, along the lines of 'Thou shalt not ...'. And Caliban's thoughts abound in self-imposed moral sanctions (the word 'must' appears three times in the above passage alone) and this is part of his formula for Natural Theology: observe natural behaviour, extract patterns and conclusions, formulate beliefs and ethics. This inconsistency ought to be enough on its own to destroy any credibility in Natural Theology – until, that is, Caliban invokes the well-known get-out clause, that we must not nor cannot know the ways of God (compare *Isaiah* 55: 8–9).

Which is why he repeatedly focuses on the victimised animals around him, often identifying himself with them. He cannot be sure of the ways of Setebos and he has even tried to emulate his vagaries. The allusions to the harmless squirrel and hedgehog (or 'urchin') in lines 226 and 229 are a case in point. Caliban spares these creatures both of whom gratify him in their different ways: the squirrel that is unfazed by his power and the hedgehog that is so fazed. With typical anthropomorphism he attributes human feeling and motive to each. Caliban probes his way in the power hierarchy and like Prospero he likes to play at god (see line 168).

Accordingly, what irritates his magisterial dominion is that these meagre beasts will assume that he is consistent in his mercy or spite. For him it is the very unpredictability that is the mark of a true divinity.

> Doth as he likes, or wherefore Lord?   (240)

Once again he projects human thought and reason onto the animals, implicit in his words, 'counted', 'saying', 'because'. Ironically, while believing himself to hold dominion over these animals he identifies with them, assuming that they share his conscious rationality.

Curiously, Caliban finalises at least twenty of these intense speculations by intoning the phrase 'So He'. In thematic terms this reinforces Caliban's reasoning faculty, since the word 'so' first observes and then posits a cause. At the same time, on an ecclesiastical level, this phrase has a reverential, antiphonal effect as in a religious liturgy, revealing a love of the poise and rhythm of the language.

In *The Tempest* Caliban reviles Prospero with:

> You taught me language; and my profit on't
> Is I know how to curse.   (1.2. 365–366)

Language is one characteristic element in the paraphernalia of colonialism. Yet Caliban has probably the most beautiful poetry in the whole of the play, partly because he is so sensitive to all of nature in the island. Browning continues that idea in his own verse where Caliban's phrasing is richly Keatsian in its abundance of sensual music. In the above passage every line has a voluptuous, almost palpable, texture of alliteration and assonance. Note for example, the /s/ susurrating through lines 206 and 215, and the /m/ humming away in line 220. Each line has a luxuriant fluidity of vowel sounds – and at least eight of them (including 210, 220, 229) have the full gamut of basic vowels: a-e-i-o-u. The whole poem yearns to be voiced aloud and, to appreciate Caliban's special music, you should try reciting his lines. The effect is to reinforce an impression of how the speaker responds ecstatically to his sense environment, resonating this back in his intricate verse-speech.

This music is deceptively complex yet perfectly natural sounding: once again Browning breaks up the blank verse with caesurae and unexpected ellipses, with non-fluency elements, to give the whole a fresh spontaneous surface.

Caliban's mind moves on, believing there will be 'no change', that Setebos will remain the same dread force and he will have to 'live in fear of Him' (242). Once again speculating on the metaphysics of godhead, he becomes sanguine and wonders if Setebos could actually 'vex' the ultimate divinity, the Quiet, or even metamorphose *into* the Quiet 'as bugs grow butterflies'.

He repeatedly stresses the cruelty of Setebos and confides that he avoids the sunlight and the open landscape in case he is caught dancing. Isolated and bereft in his own silence, Caliban's life force triumphs all the same, despite all the intimidation, in the hope that he too can one day dominate the power structure. He does, however, remain terrified just on the possibility that Setebos is eavesdropping, and accordingly sets up an insurance policy, sacrificing a kid goat to the god, just in case.

For the time being, Caliban consoles himself with a song of hatred and the prospect that the remote, aloof Quiet will one day 'catch and conquer Setebos'. But then, the tone suddenly plunges. A monologue that begins in a great feeling of happy abandon to miry nature ends in desperate panic. All at once, with hope melting swiftly away, the sky falls silent when a raven 'scuds' off, and Caliban fears that it will inform on him to Setebos about his mutinous 'prattlings'. Apocalyptic omens start to clash about his head, a portent of death (the 'pillared dust') looms before him, until Caliban in desperation prostrates himself before the gathering catastrophe.

Commentary

First things being first, we should not overlook he poem's epigram as a pointer to available interpretations:

> *Thou thoughtest that I was altogether such a one as thyself.*

Taken from the Old Testament, *Psalms* 50:21, this quotation features God warning to mankind of its place and its duties in venerating God. Clearly it speaks of differences, and in particular Caliban's struggle to establish his niche regarding what he understands as the lords over him: Prospero, Setebos and the Quiet. He also spends much of his time identifying those creatures below him over which *he* has power, meditating, 'Are these such a one as myself?'

Crucially, in *The Tempest,* referring to Caliban as a 'slave', 'not honour'd with/A human shape', Prospero imperiously defines him as a sub-human form, bereft of normal rights. This has contemporary Victorian reverberations because the grounds on which nineteenth-century plantation owners would often validate the violent abuse of their slaves was to presume them non-human, quasi-animal life forms. Caliban is the apotheosis of the slave, devoid of human rights, in a constant condition of fear.

Power and fear form the chief criteria of differentiation within Caliban's sphere and they are, in his mind, the joint bases of the island's fluctuating hierarchy. His fitful mind is constantly aware of an 'other' that shadows him in different forms, vexing his quiet. The title's epigram also raises the question of the nature of God, that God may be merely a total fabrication, made in the image of man (a question triggered by Darwinism too). However, the gods that Caliban dreads are inscrutable Old Testament figures of tempest and vengeance, and in this Psalm the tenor is very much one of bullying and coercion.

'Caliban Upon Setebos' takes up questions of Natural Theology, and examines its tenets in the light of evolutionary knowledge. It examines it in a form of language which itself is part of both of these disciplines and is a directly communicated expression of Caliban's nature. This is achieved partly through Browning's familiar grotesque style, a style that takes the reader aback by heightening non-natural perceptions, expression or occurrence (for example see 'Porphyria's Lover', 'The Laboratory' or 'Childe Roland').

Browning's contemporary Walter Bagehot described him as the master of the art of the grotesque, a style that works by incongruity for satiric effect or macabre comedy. Whether the poem is a satire or not is a question we must return to later, but for now we can note here that the poet cultivates this style in order to create a distancing effect from the subject of its perceptions. Caliban himself delights in this form with its luxuriant tropes, ellipses and inconsistent grammar, so much so that it often appears to be an assertion of his refusal to become westernised, making the reader too a victim of his control.

Part of the difficulty of the language for the reader springs from Browning's attempt at something akin to Early Modern English form. But he brilliantly compromises this colonial English to produce something that is actually subversive of it. Because of the non-standard elements in his language some of his words convey extra force by their instability, for instance 'vex' and 'envy' carry complex suggestions, of power, conflict, hatred and desire. This suggests a form of internal language that is in a state of rapid flux, becoming a private idiolect as a baulk against the politics of Prospero and the gods.

At the start of the monologue, Caliban revels in the joy of his private space, reposing secure from the sleeping Prospero and Miranda. Language too functions as an aspect of his private space. The issues in Caliban's speech here often reveal that he is trying to give expression to ineffable, transcendent realities, to say true things and call them by the right names. The passages in the poem that begin 'Thinketh' are a fumbling towards a designation of the power of gods, their omnipotence and arbitrariness in a language limited by what Prospero has imposed on him (it is worth remembering too that the spelling and punctuation are all Browning's – Caliban makes no distinction between 'he' and 'He' or 'god' and 'God').

(a) Caliban

In choosing the name 'Caliban', clearly Shakespeare wished to include the notion of 'cannibal' and he may have been influenced by Montaigne's 1603 essay 'Of the Caniballes' (the play is usually dated to around 1611). For Elizabethan audiences the 'salvage' or savage figure was a curiosity, part man, part barbarous beast (in fact two of *The Tempest*'s characters consider shipping Caliban to England to exhibit him in freak shows). For Victorian readers, the figure of this 'slave', half-man, half-beast, also held out the prospect of the evolutionary 'missing link', evinced in the wake of Darwin's theories.

Unlike Shakespeare, Montaigne accepts the 'savage' man on his own terms, recognising that newly discovered tribes had their own religious faiths and a regularising society. However, in contrast to these American tribes, Caliban lives in almost complete solitude, in the poem dwelling mostly within his own thoughts. What Browning is fundamentally interested in is Caliban's mental processes within the colonial paradigm.

Prospero (and to some extent Setebos) represents a classic colonising presence on the island, backed by force and with intent to impose its alien culture on the aboriginal vassal, by way of 'nurture'. The Victorian settlers and missionaries themselves liked to adopt this simple formula, evangelising western and Christian values, typically in the process of enslaving the indigenous races, backed by superior military forces.

Caliban is, of course, vividly conscious of these tyrannising forces, in the shape of Setebos and Prospero, and a large measure of his angst is due not simply to the fact of violence and intimidation but really its unpredictability and its inconsistent exaction (for instance note lines 236–240). He repeatedly revisits the power/terror situation and frequently articulates ways of evading vexation and wrath. This secures for him a form of internal autonomy, a sovereign inner space or refuge like his miry cave. However, the fact that he necessarily expresses this in English language reveals the extent of his indoctrination. He ironically expresses his resentment in the colonist's own medium.

(b) Setebos

At the beginning of the poem, Caliban takes refuge from the attentions of Prospero and at the end he cowers 'flat' from the supposed thunderbolts of the vexatious Setebos. And between these terminal points he portrays the brutal world that confines him.

Shakespeare probably adopted the name 'Setebos' for his play from the 1577 travel account by Robert Eden, *History of Travaile*, in which he records Magellan's observation of the Patagonians who,

> 'roared lyke bulls and cryed upon theyr great devill Setebos, to helpe them'.

Browning invents all the rest of the detail. In the poem itself Caliban believes Setebos has made and now lives in the moon (he made the sun to keep him warm but did not create the stars). It was Setebos who made the world as a bauble to spite and sport with, a retaliation for not being allowed to reach heaven (146–147 and 149).

Our image of Setebos is of course defined within the boundaries of Caliban's anthropomorphic powers of intellect and observation, as well as language. After observing the animals on the island, Caliban stresses the limitations on the powers of Setebos. Between lines 11 and 124 he makes the surprising revelation of Setebos's weaknesses which thus seems to necessitate concocting another divinity that overarches this local god, namely the Quiet, which oddly is also derived from weakness. This 'ultra' divinity is colder, more petulant and enigmatic, resting more distantly off than the more intimate Setebos, which fact according to Caliban accounts for why that god permits suffering in the world.

Physical description of Setebos is spare though Caliban is impressed by his being 'many-handed', like a 'cuttle-fish', or octopus. This is most probably a metaphorical description, of the god's quasi-omnipotence, its ability to range anywhere, widely across the island. More apparent is the god's character, which is invariably irascible, dedicated to misrule – Caliban employs the keystone word 'vex' some five times of Setebos, a relentlessly tormenting force, constantly troubling the mental life (Caliban has learned his words largely from Prospero and 'vex' looks much like a word used by that sorcerer of him – 'craft' in line 186 could be another such).

At first, however, Setebos appeared as Caliban's hoped-for messiah and even as a confederate avenger, especially as a curb to Prospero's autocracy. Yet now there are occasional hints that he is losing hope in this deity, his faith transferring to the Quiet (especially given the suspicion in line 203 that Setebos is in league with Prospero). The point is, of course, that Caliban is utterly inconsistent in his understanding and estimate of this god, a god he himself has invented to account for his misfortunes and the inscrutable goings-on in nature, based partly on projections of himself.

(c) Religion

Critic Stefan Hawlin, in speaking of the 'savage' Caliban's language, notes that he 'speaks his own semi-animal version of English' (Hawlin 2002, p.169). Compared with that of, say, Andrea del Sarto or the Duke of Ferrara, Caliban's English-as-a-Foreign-Language *is* extremely halting at times, ungrammatical (for example lines 75 and 244), and his odd omission of personal pronouns is frequently bewildering. He is often guilty of Blougram's (996) 'saying true things but giving them wrong names'. His use of those '-eth' suffixes is at first perplexing and often inconsistent (see line 240 – though sometimes Browning leans upon him for metrical reasons). Caliban may struggle with his year 6 SATS test but his frequently complex syntax is more often right than wrong and he is able (just about) to draft complex religious thoughts – and, we might add, in a remarkable vocabulary: solace, vexed, overscale, prodigious, choler, consecrate, exercise.

'Caliban Upon Setebos' has two principal gods: Setebos, deriving from Sycorax, and his own creation, the Quiet (Caliban describes Prospero as 'lord of the isle' but his magical dominion over nature qualifies him as, if not quite a god, then at least a demigod). His confusing omission of the pronoun 'He' produces for the reader too an effect of conflating Setebos, the Quiet and Prospero, all of which relate to power, creation and control over him, coalescing as the vague, domineering 'Other'.

As an exponent of Natural Theology, Caliban's religious ideas in the poem begin and end in observing natural objects and events. Unsurprisingly, he is a superstitious observer of nature; he repeats actions which appear to bring good, or at least reduce ill to himself, attributing the result (including inconsistencies) to the mood of a deity (see lines 223–234 and 240). Setebos, which Caliban fashions in his own image, has become a source of genuine terror and a focus of superstitious propitiation (for example in the idea of sacrificing a goat; lines 271–272).

But what is the character of this god? omnipotent? omniscient? omnipresent? Caliban seems to believe he is all three. His idea of Setebos is as an active god permeating all of nature (unlike the Quiet which is a more contemplative member) and as such shares elements of Wordsworth's pantheistic nature, a 'spirit that rolls through all things' (though lacking an implicit moral dimension). However, these impressions of a divinity do not betray any specific traces of Prospero's Christianity. Perhaps deriving in part from his mother, Sycorax, they now appear to spring from his own intimate relationship with nature, in particular the simple human urge to account for mysterious phenomena.

(d) Natural Theology

Why does Caliban believe in anything, anything at all? Well, of course his mother introduced the name and the idea of Setebos, and much of Caliban's spiritual consciousness is bound up in concepts about power and fear derived via Prosper. Without Sycorax's idea of a 'god' would Caliban have dreamt up his own? Choosing *The Tempest*'s almost pristine island allows Browning to evince this type of fundamental question in an Edenic setting, ideally receptive to concepts of Natural Theology.

We have noted in the 'wave' example how Caliban likes to see a divinity at work in purely natural episodes (lines 209–210), which is in essence the operation of Natural Theology.

Early in the poem Caliban outlines some of the key facets of his god, and crucially its creative aspect:

> 'Thinketh, He made thereat the sun, this isle,
> Trees and the fowls here, beast and creeping thing.   (44–45)

and

> He made all these and more,
> Made all we see, and us, in spite: how else?   (55–56)

He cannot give external reasons for this other than by analogy 'I do: so He' (108); the starting point is often by correlation with himself. A crucial element in this starting point is the observer's own intense inquisitiveness, possibly tweaked by fear. Caliban's internal conversation frequently resembles a catechism of relentless speculation and answer, which gradually resolves itself into a dialectic of explication; for example in line 110 he poses a question about God's handiwork being rough, which is then questioned at lines 127–129, and then he decides it by proposing a 'something' higher than Setebos, viz. the Quiet (129–133).

To many contemporaries of Browning, Darwin's discoveries and the theories based upon them appeared to strike at the very core of accepted religious beliefs. Yet through Caliban's reactions, Browning investigates not the issue of whether Darwin's theory refutes the existence of God, but rather, by what processes did the concept of God first emerge and grow. And he answers the question by presenting the thought processes through which a god would come into being and develop.

The contemporary debate about Natural Theology can be traced to two books in particular: William Paley's seminal *Natural Theology* of 1803, and Bishop Butler's *The Analogy of Religion* (1736), plus the philosophies of David Hume and J. J. Rousseau. Paley considered that the earth, indeed the universe, is too complex in its diversity, efficient symbiotics and self-regulating processes for there not to be a sentient power behind its origins and dynamics. Natural Theology does not necessarily describe God (for example whether or not it is providential), whereas Caliban does discuss Setebos in detail, musing on his power over crabs and birds and so on. Caliban believes Setebos to be more often neutral:

> 'Thinketh, such shows nor right nor wrong in Him,
> Nor kind, nor cruel ... (98–99)

Is Caliban's simplistic anthropomorphism, based as it is on fear of the unknown, then, Browning's satirical comment on Natural Theology? Is Caliban in his frightened, victimised solitude creating a fetish, merely fulfilling a human psychological need (as Setebos allegedly made the sun just to keep himself warm)? Is it that the primitive man's reasoning is too crude and unsophisticated to be understood as nothing more than a spoof of natural fundamentalism? Some critics, such as Robert Bristow and Iain Finlayson, believe so, while others, including Philip Drew and Isobel Armstrong, see the poem as less a critique of theology per se than a confrontation with Victoria Darwinism. To modern eyes and mind the poem's emphasis on anthropomorphism renders it more a satire on religion per se, and the poem's epigram can be seen to support this interpretation:

> *Thou thoughtest that I was altogether such a one as thyself.*

Caliban's botched reasoning and contradictions mean that the viewpoint of the reader becomes superior to that of the character, allowing Browning's irony and, ultimately, powering his satire on the subject of Natural Theology. However, what lingers as most striking about 'Caliban Upon Setebos' is less the facts of a primitive man's thinking processes than the modernity of Browning's approach. It is a masterpiece of expressive style and ranks alongside 'Childe Roland' in terms of its radical approach to psychological expressiveness. However, any feeling of progression which that poem's linear form presumes is ultimately precluded here, eliciting a great sense of paralysis. Caliban's gods offer no escape or redemption, and consequently his intellectual ache seems unremitting.

Conclusions

The three poems under review in this chapter all discuss – among many other things – various themes connected to religion. However, as we have come to expect of Browning, they do so in oblique, off-centre or grotesque formats. The obliqueness of his approach takes many expressions, and strongly impinges on the way he presents elements such as character, language and narrative chronology. The Bishop of Praxed, Bishop Blougram and Caliban represent an eccentric group of people yet they all discuss topics of faith in terms of how it affects them uniquely rather than as notes towards a philosophical treatise per se. These topics have included moral problems, the afterlife, the relationship of faith and scepticism, grounds for belief, and the relation of mankind to its cosmos.

We have noted that because of Browning's remarkable mastery of the dramatic monologue form, it has not been possible to readily detect the poet's own views on these topics, but in any case this may not be as valuable as the individual reader's own interpretation and enjoyment of a text. The deployment of the dramatic monologue is distinctly effective in constructing a sense of intimacy and of spontaneity to the poems, placing their experience in close proximity to the reader.

It is important to remember that while I selected these poems in order to discuss themes related to religion, they are not concerned exclusively with religious topics and can equally be approached in regard to, say, art, ethics, determinism, colonialism, psychology, historicism and so on.

Methods of analysis

In this chapter we have approached these poems employing the same broad range of techniques as in previous chapters. Although focusing on basic elements such as character, narrative and themes, these are best regarded as starting points only, as ways into Browning's dramatic monologue. As such we have attempted to show how other discourse features such as point of view, tone of voice and chronology can affect the reader's interpretation.

We have also tried to stress how sensitivity to Browning's important methods of irony and satire can radically affect our shifting relationships with a text. Above all it is crucial to see a text as a whole, in all its multiplicity of techniques, devices and voices, tones and so forth. The reader's relationship with a work is itself dynamic and organic, never definitive or absolute, and so it is important to reread a work several times after an initial analysis in order to becomes aware of the range of possibilities it offers.

Suggested work

Using the techniques applied in this and previous chapters, read Browning's 'Holy-Cross Day'. After describing the character of the speaker, examine the methods of his interior monologue (particularly the conversational features) and discuss the attitudes to religion that it reveals. How does Browning bring irony and satire to bear on the poem and what conclusions would you draw about his use of them there?

PART 2
THE CONTEXT AND THE CRITICS

5
Browning's Life and Work

No writer writes in a vacuum, and quite often an understanding of the wider context in which he or she writes will help with an understanding and interpretation of their work. To get a fuller purchase on the social, private and artistic contexts of Browning it will be useful to get some idea of the social, political and philosophical currents and forces that made his period and work so distinctive.

With this in mind the three chapters of this part of the study will discuss these contextual elements, beginning with a brief biography of Robert Browning. Chapter 6 goes deeper into the Victorian literary scene, including a look at some of Browning's explicit views on poetry, and the final chapter takes a look at a sample of interesting critical works.

1812–1832 Browning's early life

In the year that Robert Browning was born, 1812, Britain was still at war with Bonaparte's France. The early (and late) Romantic poets were still alive – Wordsworth and Coleridge, Keats, Byron and Shelley – and Browning grew up under the inspiring influence of their artistic lights. In that same year Charles Dickens was born. Jane Austen had recently published *Sense and Sensibility* (and was busy at work on *Pride and Prejudice*). Beethoven was aged 41, Schubert 5 and Mendelssohn 3. Slavery had been abolished in Britain, though the Americans continued to purchase slaves for their plantations from British ships. Steam engines were in a state of relative infancy, the industrial revolution was about to erupt prodigiously on the sleeping cities, and since Britain was essentially an agricultural nation, its men and women lived largely by the seasons and the transit of the sun. Houses continued to rely on candles for light. Italy, where the Brownings were to spend their married life, was still a collection of city states carved up between Austria, France and Spain.

William IV, last of the Hanoverian kings, reigned over the 'United Kingdom', and his successor, Victoria, would not be born for another eight years. The Victorian period, in which Browning would become one of its bright literary stars, was some twenty-five years off.

Browning was born on 7 May into a comfortably well-off, middle-class family, his father, Robert, earning about £200 to £300 a year as a clerk at the Bank of England (an omnivorous book collector, who also indulged a great passion for drawing). His mother, Sarah Wiedemann, ten years older than her husband, was a dedicated nonconformist Christian, and aged 40 when Robert was born and then baptised at the local Congregational chapel where his parents regularly attended worship. His only sister, Sarianna, was born two years later, in 1814.

Solid details about Browning's boyhood are quite scanty, largely due to the fact that he himself did much to obliterate the record, and for information we rely heavily on the memoirs of his sister. However, at the age of 7 or 8, Robert Browning registered as a weekly boarder in the Reverend Thomas Ready's school nearby in Peckham where he appears to have been by turns both disruptive and the victim of bullying. The school conferred a customary grounding in Greek and Latin classics as well as a training in the gentlemanly sports of boxing, riding and dancing. Yet, at this time (and more significantly), he had unrestricted access to his father's extensive and eclectic library, estimated at about 6000 volumes. Under the influence of his mother, he was inculcated with a strong interest in religion but also developed a keen interest in biology (there was an extensive menagerie of animals at home and in mature years Robert maintained a small flock of geese and a pet owl).

Aged 12, Browning compiled his first collection of lyric poetry, 'Incondita', most likely prompted by his growing friendship with Eliza and Sarah Flowers – both of whom in their youth composed music and poetry

(Sarah wrote hymns and is now best known for her lyric *Nearer My God to Thee*). Eliza – nine years his senior – was probably an early crush for Browning and he gave her privileged sight of the manuscript of 'Incondita'. Hugely impressed, she secretly forwarded them on to William Johnson Fox, politician and editor of the *Monthly Repository*, though he remained unconvinced of their value for publication. Nevertheless, Browning continued to be fond of Eliza for the rest of her life and she was the inspiration for his first major poem, *Pauline*.

'Incondita' was eventually destroyed by Browning in 1884, along with much of his other early work and letters. However, two of its verses were copied out and thus preserved by Eliza: 'The First-Born of Egypt' and 'The Dance of Death'. Curiously, each of these reveal a marked youthful debt to Coleridge and Byron rather than to Shelley, later a more important influence, and they clearly attest to the liberal culture of Browning's home at a time when Byron especially was regarded as a notorious deviant.

With his departure from Ready's school at the age of 14, tuition for the adolescent Browning over the next two years was chiefly conducted at home, in Italian, French and music. He was in effect self-taught, with his reading regularly supplemented by enthusiastic visits to London galleries, notably the celebrated Dulwich Picture Gallery 'about a green half hour's walk away over the fields' from their home in Camberwell. For about eight months in 1828 he attended the newly established London University, and his departure from the university marked the end of his formal schooling.

More significant for his poetic development was Browning's introduction at about the age of 15 to the poetry of Percy Bysshe Shelley. Born in 1792, Shelley had attracted attention as much for his radical socialism, his debts and his (failed) attempts at founding a commune as for his experimental poetry (his wife Mary was already more renowned, as the author of *Frankenstein*). Regarded by the establishment as a dangerous fanatic and fantasist, Shelley was nevertheless passionately committed to the cause of social justice, and his verse intensely reflects both this and his immersion in spiritual idealism.

Browning was a mere ten years old when his hero drowned in a mysterious accident near Lerici off the north-west coast of Italy. It was five years later, in a profoundly significant moment, that his cousin presented him with a copy of Shelley's *Miscellaneous Poems*. He quickly thrilled to the music of its deliciously seductive worlds:

> Thy dewy looks sink in my breast;
> Thy gentle words stir poison there;
> Thou hast disturbed the only rest
> That was the portion of despair!
>
> ('Stanza: Written at Bracknell')

Acutely overwhelmed by the life as much as by the verse of this idol, the teenage Browning adopted the full Shelleyan package, embracing political idealism, vegetarianism, atheism as well as striking the 'poetic' posture. He later confided to Elizabeth Barrett how he had barely survived for 'a couple of years & more on bread and potatoes' in zealous emulation of Shelley's vegetarianism.

Throughout Browning's life Shelley's verse remained central among his favourite reading (proudly introducing the poetry to Elizabeth Barrett during their courtship) and his first major poems, *Pauline: A Fragment of a Confession* (published anonymously in 1833) and *Paracelsus* (1835), clearly owe much to the sway of Shelley. The most explicit acknowledgment of his love of this luminary occurred in 1852 when Browning penned the so-called 'Essay on Shelley' (see Chapter 6 for more on this).

In early nineteenth-century England, a middle-class man on reaching the age of 21 might have been expected to fix on a career in one of the secular professions – the law, the military or medicine (in 1829 Browning had briefly attended medical lectures at Guy's Hospital in London), or perhaps banking (as his father and grandfather had). But even at this age, Browning had determined on a life as a poet, though with little outward evidence of talent (his *Pauline* had sold no copies) other than the sympathetic backing of his loyal parents. Browning later spoke, with some irony, of this time in his youth and the 'audacious obstinacy which had made him, when a youth, determine to be a writer and nothing but a writer'. Among his close-knit society he had developed a robust reputation as a confident educated raconteur, a cosmopolitan with a strong taste for satire.

In politics he had come to share his father's progressive liberalism and, not unnaturally, this, along with his mother's evangelical nonconformism, was to colour his adult life and its poetry. But it was to be an arduous struggle for anything like critical recognition.

1833–1844 Browning's early career

At this period of his life, Browning's literary ambitions were increasingly expressed in a passion for theatre, a passion transformed into full commitment after witnessing, in October 1830, a performance of *Hamlet* at the Haymarket Theatre. In the title role was the foremost character actor of the day, (William) Charles Macready, a charismatic performer who was beginning to eclipse even the celebrated Edmund Kean.

All the same, Browning continued to nurture his poetic talent. He was later to claim that it was watching the great Kean that had inspired him to write *Pauline*, published anonymously in 1833 with financial assistance from one of his aunts. This long sentimental poem, heavily influenced by Shelley, was favourably reviewed by editor William Fox. Nevertheless, sales flopped and the philosopher J. S. Mill found it 'bewildering'.

Unabashed by this juvenescent disappointment, Browning pressed on with other literary projects in both poetry and drama. It seems to have been during an extended visit to St Petersburg in 1834 that Browning prepared his biographical drama, *Paracelsus,* based on the life of a sixteenth-century alchemist and visionary. It was with this work that his literary circle began to expand. A confident, vivacious socialiser, he became increasingly acquainted with W. J. Fox, through whom he came in contact with other major contemporaries like Charles Dickens and the satirist Thomas Carlyle who was to become an important friend for the rest of Browning's life. While his circle comprised diverse literary figures whose lights today glow less bright, perhaps the most significant influence in this early phase was the formidable Macready of whom Browning was to become a close ally and protégé.

Over the next twelve years, the fruit of this timely alliance included five plays, two volumes of lyric verse and Browning's notoriously obscure poem *Sordello* (1840). This long work traces, in part, the relationship between a writer and his readership, particularly, and the failure of the latter to grasp the subjective poet's intentions. Ironically this 'failure' is one that later dogged Browning's own ambitious efforts to break into the commercial theatre, with a series of disastrous setbacks.

Throughout these early troubled years, Browning persevered with his verse writing, searching for an authentic voice as well as the wider readership that would vindicate his choice of career. Like his heroes Keats and

Shelley, Browning had to suffer a long apprenticeship of embittered frustration during which he laboured to articulate his ambitions in more accessible forms.

Eventually taking Browning under his artistic wing, Macready – now increasingly a fixture on the London stage – encouraged the young writer to realise his ambitions as a dramatist. Over the next few years there appeared a series of plays, written with Macready himself in mind as their leads, beginning with *Strafford* in 1837 and ending with *Colombe's Birthday* in 1844. None of these received more than a handful of performances and they were invariably staged as a personal favour from the long-suffering actor-manager (although success in the theatre never came Browning's way, an important by-product of his efforts was the dramatic monologue, which Browning would bring to its highest level of development).

1845–1846 Elizabeth Barrett

During the tumultuous period with the London theatre, Browning continued to publish verse, the costs of printing being borne by his father, beginning in 1841 with the series *Bells and Pomegranates* and then in 1842, *Dramatic Lyrics*. The latter, which includes 'My Last Duchess' and 'Porphyria's Lover', attracted negligible sales, yet this volume does establish the poet's mastery of the dramatic form and in a voice distinctly his own.

At this time of his maturing artistry, across town a female poet had attracted considerable celebrity among her circle of London literati. In 1844 she published her two-volume *Poems* to much acclaim, and she was well known for her bravura poetic output and spirited translations. Elizabeth Barrett had by this time a significant body of verse to her name, and her status as a rather successful writer was in marked contrast to Browning's, whose poems were hardly known at all. Her disability and virtual imprisonment in Wimpole Street by her father made Elizabeth all the more intriguing as a result of her physical inconspicuousness.

Browning came to meet Elizabeth Barrett via the intervention of John Kenyon, Robert's wealthy second cousin, and a regular visitor to 50 Wimpole Street. Browning was already familiar with her striking poems, one of which in the 1844 collection had made a complimentary allusion to himself, and he was moved on 10 January to write directly to her, famously opening perhaps the most celebrated exchange of love letters between two poets:

> I love your verses with all my heart, dear Miss Barrett ...

Kenyon had previously attempted an introduction but been thwarted by her chronic illness. The narrative of their quickly intensifying relationship is by now a familiar one, the basis of their friendship being a mutual admiration for the art and intellect of the other. She became effectively Browning's first dedicated critic – though neither poet appears to have composed specifically for or about the other.

Equally familiar to readers is Elizabeth's enforced internment at number 50, but what is not so clear are the definitive reasons for this. There is, of course, her overprotective, tyrannical father who, after the death of Elizabeth's mother, had himself become inordinately insular and fanatically religious. Elizabeth herself had become immured in Wimpole Street through long-term infirmity, having contracted tuberculosis in her teenage years and subsequently developed a dependency on opium. Current medical theory attributes her complex illness to a form of multiple sclerosis.

The couple's first, clandestine, meeting was 20 May 1845 and over the next few weeks and months their love developed rapidly, strengthening their common ground in terms of teaching, literary criticism and, of course, personal affection. Although her father's plans for Elizabeth centred on her continued celibacy and devoting herself to God, she secretly came to think of Robert as wholly replacing her father in her affections. The courtship has been variously characterised, and mythologised, in numerous romantic and fanciful versions (even her beloved spaniel, Flush (1840–1854), has come in for energetic treatment, notably in Virginia Woolf's eponymous novella).

The famous letters are, perhaps surprisingly, not the effusive slush of popular legend. Without doubt the correspondence traces the growing feelings of intimacy between the two but they also contain discussions of their literary art, feedback on each other's verse, and are frequently densely argued, often with a certain obtuseness (usually arising from the protocols of courtesy). Gradually, too, Robert convinced Elizabeth that he was intensely in love with the real woman, and his occasional and furtive visits to number 50

Wimpole Street culminated, after fifteen months, in their secret marriage on 12 September 1846, followed by elopement, in flagrant and rapturous contradiction of all her father's intentions for his daughter.

1846–1855 Italy

At first the newly-weds took refuge in the London hotel of a friend, Mrs Alna Jameson, who then accompanied them on the escape to Italy, settling first in Pisa. And then, in the following April, after some wanderings around Tuscany, the Brownings determined on Florence to become their long-term Italian home, with occasional interludes in Rome and winters in nearby Bagni di Lucca. They settled in Italy at a moment of great political turmoil as Italian republicanism began to gather momentum, Elizabeth being especially sympathetic to the Italians' struggle to overthrow Austrian oppression.

In March 1849, Elizabeth gave birth, to a boy (Pen) – in the same month that Robert received news of his mother's death. In the same year, the Tuscan populace rose up against the Austrian power, forcing Grand Duke Leopold, governor of Tuscany, to flee to Naples. The Brownings' apartment – Casa Guidi – was situated opposite the Austrian's headquarters in the Pitti Palace and they enjoyed a grandstand view of ecstatic crowds celebrating emancipation. Alas this was to be short-lived, as the Austrians soon drafted in massive troop reinforcements to install a more despotic administration, restoring Leopold to the Pitti.

In spite of all the public and domestic upheaval, the Brownings continued with literary composition. Elizabeth's affirmations of her deep love for Robert are expressed in her *Sonnets from the Portuguese*, published to great success in 1850, probably the most memorable of which is the penultimate, number 43:

> How do I love thee? Let me count the ways.
> I love thee to the depth and breadth and height
> My soul can reach ...

In this period Robert composed the pieces destined to appear in his first major literary success, the much-admired collection *Men and Women* (which includes 'Childe Roland', 'Bishop Blougram's Apology', 'Andrea del Sarto' and 'The Patriot').

Early in the following year Robert was delighted to accept a commission from a former editor, Edward Moxon, to compose a Preface to a new edition of *Letters of Percy Bysshe Shelley*. This was completed during the December in Paris and the new volume appeared early in 1852, though without any great commercial or critical notice. To make matters even worse, the collection was hastily withdrawn after it emerged that all but one of the 'newly discovered' letters were forgeries.

Although the *Letters* was utterly discredited, Browning's Preface has prospered as one of the few formal delineations of his literary ideas. Though entitled 'Essay on Shelley', the article has little to say about Shelley as such, being instead very much about Browning himself, poets and poetry in general (for more on this essay, see Chapter 6).

1856–1889 The death of Elizabeth, and Browning's later career

Over the next few years, Browning's social life gradually took up more and more of his time and attention. As the public profiles of the Brownings flourished among the British literati, they increasingly attracted the acquaintance of established writers and artists, including the poets Walter Savage Landor and William Allingham, the novelist Charles Kingsley and the Pre-Raphaelite poets, as well as John Ruskin. Frederick Tennyson – brother of Alfred, the recently elevated Poet Laureate – was a frequent visitor to their apartment and his presence coincided with Elizabeth's deepening fascination with spiritualism. The mid-Victorian vogue for spiritualism, antithesis of the century's growing materialism, expressed itself as an interest in a variety of channels: notably parapsychology, mystical eastern religions, telaesthesia and clairvoyance. Elizabeth's intense fascination was fostered by Frederick and others, much to the derision of Browning (who in his poems 'Mesmerism' and 'Mr Sludge the Medium' satirised the practice as bogus exploitation).

It was in the 1850s and 1860s that Robert's standing as a poet reached its highest critical and commercial altitude. Yet Elizabeth's work was still the more widely saleable, and this point was magnified even more by the appearance in 1856 of her 'novel-poem' *Aurora Leigh*, to massive sales, repeat editions and widespread commendation. *Men and Women*'s publication in 1855 was also greeted by immediate high sales, but Browning became dispirited when these failed to sustain. He was not to enjoy a financial success anywhere near that of Elizabeth's – at least not until the appearance in the winter of 1868/9 of his novel-poem, *The Ring and the Book*.

During the 1850s Elizabeth Barrett Browning's health, never particularly robust even in temperate Italy, increasingly deteriorated and she eventually died in Florence in June 1861, from an incurable bronchial illness. Her funeral and its processional route was attended by scores of Florentines. Now alone, Robert became progressively determined to quit Casa Guidi and in August 1861 he and 12-year-old Pen departed for England, ostensibly to arrange for his education.

From the 1860s on there was a striking rise in the popularity of Robert's poetry. In 1863 a three-volume edition *Poetical Works* was published and was very favourably saluted by the literary press. The following year his very popular volume, *Dramatis Personae*, appeared, containing some new work as well as reprints of earlier verse ('Caliban Upon Setebos' is a notable newcomer). This was the most successful, financially and critically, of all his publications to date. In a letter of 1865 to Isa Blagden, Browning modestly attributed his new-found popularity to his being now more visible to the London critics, the key architects of taste ('gossiping and going out') – he also believed that at last the earlier poems had 'found their time'.

In the long period of his preparation of *The Ring and the Book*, Browning received further recognition when he was made Honorary Fellow of Balliol college, the honour coinciding with the appearance of his new *Poetical Works* which appeared in six volumes. Eventually, in the winter of 1868/9, *The Ring and the Book* saw the light of day, serialised in four volumes. This ambitious verse-narrative – an experimental murder mystery, set in Rome, and reported from diverse points of view – was inspired by an old book that Browning turned up on a Florence market probably in 1860. A great success on all counts, it represented the crowning point of the poet's stock.

Attracting widespread popularity, together with some material wealth, and even offers of marriage, this period in Browning's life was in immense contrast to the 1840s with their stamp of rejection and near-despair. He felt more relaxed too about expressing political views in public – he described himself as a liberal, though he did not agree with Irish home rule and so refused to support Gladstone's bill of 1886. In all likelihood he might have described himself in general terms as open-minded and reformist, but he did not share Elizabeth's progressive position particularly, on the question of female emancipation.

Nevertheless, Browning's company and opinions were sought out and he increasingly mingled amongst the political elite and aristocratic circles. He received honorary degrees from Edinburgh and Oxford, and then in 1881 (and to Robert's mortification) The Browning Society was founded. At the same time, new literary success was tempered by problems in connection with his son Pen, whose private life had become dissipated and who had struggled in his studies at Oxford. Moreover, Robert's later poetry did not attract the same glowing critical reception as the volumes of his middle period. Yet, by this point his reputation was at last secure.

In later years Browning loved to visit Venice out of the season and in due course he purchased Palazzo Rezzonico. It was there that he died on 12 December 1889; he is buried in Poets' Corner, Westminster Abbey.

6

The Context of Browning's Poetry

Romanticism
The Victorian literary scene
Three Victorian poets
Browning's Views on Poetry

Romanticism

The origins of Romanticism lie in the closing decades of the eighteenth century and in the decline of classicism (or more strictly neoclassicism, since this was essentially a revival of the thought and aesthetics of ancient Athens and Rome). Where classical perspectives of the Enlightenment epoch emphasised objectivity and universal truths of permanent authority, Romanticism puts the stress on individuality, subjective ways of seeing, with personal or local truths, in which imagination plays a new and crucial role. Such truths are no less valid but derive from different sources or attitudes to reality. Not for the first time, these radical ways of seeing and writing originate on the continent, British Romanticism deriving substantially from German philosophy. It is an exciting and revolutionary vision, predicated on groundbreaking theories of perception and imagination, which not unsurprisingly were derided and belittled by classicist viewpoints.

The principles of the new Romantic vision were disseminated through the writings of, among others, Samuel Taylor Coleridge whose *Lyrical Ballads* collection of 1798, co-written with Wordsworth, is a clarion call for the new individualistic way of thinking and writing (see Chapter 2 for more on the background of *Lyrical Ballads*). Other important early Romantic poets include William Blake, Christopher Smart and James Thomson, but their radical new work was marginalised by old-school critics as sentimental, 'mad' or 'dangerously subversive'.

Romanticism – like all historic concepts – does not suddenly emerge fully formed in any one particular year (and there is far from consensus about the meaning of the term, even among the original Romantics), nor is classicism swept away completely. Rather, Romanticism evolved from a series of interconnected currents and trends, part philosophical, part political, all revolutionary ways of looking at the nature and status of man. These ways are literally revolutionary in the impetus that the new republican vision invests in the revolutions of France and America, a momentum that resonates throughout the Victorian era, in Italy and Germany, and on through to the present day.

The times were a-changing, and on a massive scale. Romantic thinking became translated into new concepts of human rights, in justice and democracy, permeating the ideologies of J. S. Mill, Thomas Carlyle and Karl Marx. There are repercussions in all areas, even for instance in the world of the traditionally immutable religious establishment, evidenced in the splintering of dogmatic Church authority into numerous dissenting chapels. The new humanist-romanticist paradigm readily permeates the world of Victorian art (principally via the highly seminal writings of John Ruskin), noticeably in the work of J. M. W. Turner, Samuel Palmer and eventually the artists of the Pre-Raphaelite Brotherhood (such as Hunt, Rossetti and Millais). The accent throughout is now on the individual imagination as the source of reality and validity, individual ways of seeing and understanding.

Nevertheless, and at the same time, the Victorian period witnessed far-reaching progress ('progress' is one of the catchwords of the Victorians) in science, engineering, global exploration and industry. Subjectivism and relativism cannot claim a monopoly on all of nineteenth-century thought and, as we have suggested, classicism does not disappear completely. Victorian Romanticism becomes wedded to a rising materialism (or 'positivism') and the two rub shoulders in the new sciences, the new economics and radical politics. Nor is the burgeoning wave of optimism and prosperity necessarily portioned uniformly throughout the whole of society – as the overcrowding and disease in the large industrial cities attests.

In terms of science, a new generation of researcher is fascinated by knowing the physical world in original ways, focusing on the behaviour and structure of observable, quantifiable phenomena, in all its scales from the microscopic of the lab to the imperial mapping of the world and beyond. An enormous expansion in the realm of science stimulates new schools of knowledge, including chemistry, palaeontology, cartography, metallurgy, ethnology and anthropology. Technology and the new industries based on it are rooted no longer in the speculative and abstract, but firmly in the physical sciences. Art and literature too are linked to the new materialism, as is political science (Marx and Engels describe their philosophy as 'social realism' in response to the material deprivation of capitalism's new victims).

The Victorian literary scene

Crucially, the new technology of the Victorian epoch is responsible too for triggering a boom in reading materials in a profusion of diverse forms. The last great leap forward in printing processes had occurred some four centuries earlier with Gutenberg's movable-type presses. Now, a state-of-the-art leap in Victorian printing technologies plus new access to cheap paper-making techniques open the way to large-scale print runs, with attendant cost reductions and improvements in copy and illustrations. It is no simple coincidence that there is an expanded mass readership, ready and eager to devour the increased output. Early religious 'schools' followed by the 1870 Elementary Education Act hold out the promise of free universal literacy to working class children (up to age 13), all of which becomes expressed ultimately in the great surge in demand for printed matter, particularly in newspapers, journal-magazines and literature in its all broadest possible senses (in the nineteenth century more volumes of poetry were published than in the whole of the two previous centuries combined).

Victorians in all age groups and classes, from the nobility to the nouveau riche, to the squalor of the mighty cities, men and women read profusely.

To meet the demand there emerges a new class of professional author, male and female, in all ranks of the burgeoning range of formats: penny-dreadfuls and bodice-rippers through serial stories promising love, adventure, mystery and crime, to the three-volume novel in the growing circulating libraries. Hand in hand with this upsurge in prose forms, the new generation of Romantic poets begins to make its fresh voice heard aloud.

In the realm of prose, the market fosters a new form of secular humanism and social conscience, building on the work of Jane Austen and Walter Scott. The subject matter of commercial literature broadens in its scope and begins to embrace social issues of poverty and injustice (though not the radical solutions required to solve them). The increased demand for fiction helps develop the careers of a new generation of female novelists (though women are not yet encouraged to use their own names) that included George Eliot, Elizabeth Gaskell and the Bronte sisters.

Although the poets of the later Romantic generation – Keats, Shelley and Byron – had carried the torch forward to the second decade of the century, any further evolution is disrupted by the premature deaths of all three of them, Byron surviving until 1824, and dying in the Greek war of independence. Although Wordsworth and Coleridge live on, their verse has lost its early rebellious vigour and they endure in the public notice by and large on their early reputations (Wordsworth becoming an establishment figure as Poet Laureate from 1843 to his death in 1850, when the laureateship was handed on to Tennyson).

After a lengthy hiatus, the old Romantic order is gradually supplemented by new figures, the mantle of public voice and conscience passing to the notable figures of the period: Matthew Arnold (1822–1882), Elizabeth Barrett and Robert Browning, Christina Rossetti (1830–1894) and Alfred Lord Tennyson (1809–1892) (other poets of this period to consider include Thomas Beddoes, Emily Bronte, Ebenezer Elliott, James Mangan and Alice Meynell). Among the finest of Victorian poets, Gerard Manly Hopkins, while composing his verse in the nineteenth century, withheld publication of it work until the early 1900s.

Indicative of the melding of Victorian Romanticism and materialism is the extent to which both Browning and Tennyson differ so much from the early Romantics: on the one hand, there is a readiness to ground poetry in contemporary realism employing corporeal settings, tangible contexts with which characters interact naturalistically, and on the other a strong tendency to respond via sensation and symbolism. In poems such as 'Childe Roland', 'Caliban Upon Setebos' and 'The Laboratory' the realist landscape or scenario plays a decisively active role in reflecting back the psychology and emotions of their speakers, becoming quasi-characters in themselves.

Inevitably, the Victorian poets wrote under the bright afterglow of the Romantics's powerful dynamism yet they share their progressive aesthetics as well a general overarching theme of the 'growth of mind'. The poets listed above tend to stand out from the greater throng of poets because they retain a sense of their own personal focus or commitment. For many other Victorians there is often a blurring of the focus, a feeling of indebtedness and dullness of language. The early Romantics were able (in Coleridge's words) 'to bring the whole soul of man into activity' in a way that the Victorians never quite realised.

As a result of the general constraining effect of moral propriety typical of this age, the Victorians are less inclined to be forthright on key social, political or religious matters that dominate the latter half of the nineteenth century. Mainstream, popular Victorian poets took from the Romantics what was immediately obvious and socially acceptable, converting themes of nature and commitment into pastoral and sentiment. Tennyson's early verse stands conspicuously out from this trend by exploring psychological themes and strong emotion in an early, and accessible, symbolist technique. By the same token, he laboured hard to satisfy ordinary public taste, seeking overall a tone of harmony or unity with a formidable attention both to the supple nuances of language and to the versatility of poetic techniques. Because of his regard to taste, Tennyson is often acclaimed as being more in tune with his society and closer to its popular literary audience than ever the Romantics were.

Let us now turn to discuss in more detail the life and work of three of Browning's contemporaries, beginning with Tennyson himself.

Three Victorian poets

(i) *Alfred Tennyson*

Born in 1809 in Somersby, Lincolnshire, Tennyson was the fourth of twelve children of the village rector. Like Browning, he had access to his father's grand and eclectic library, such that his early education was largely conducted at home. The year 1827 marked both the publication of his first collection of poetry, which also included work from two other brothers, and his first term at Cambridge University (though in a fine tradition of great poets he did not complete his degree). His time as a student is chiefly remembered for his making the acquaintance of Arthur Hallam, later to become his closest friend and literary champion.

It was Hallam who urged Tennyson to publish his first important and solo collection, *Poems, Chiefly Lyrical*, in 1830. This was (unsurprisingly) reviewed most favourably by Hallam in the *Englishman's Magazine*, chiefly in terms of its original use of symbolism. A more demoralizing reception was afforded by *Blackwoods Magazine* (that had also panned and demoralised John Keats for *his* first collection, some twelve years earlier). Tennyson's talent did not attract general recognition until 1832 with a volume simply entitled *Poems*, which applied symbolist technique to his characters' psychological states (it contains the popular poems 'The Lady of Shalott' and 'The Lotos-Eaters').

Among the poems for which Tennyson is remembered today, *In Memoriam* stands out most distinctly; it is still a moving experience to read even a selection from its one hundred and thirty beautifully elegiac stanzas, composed in memory of Hallam who had died in 1833 while on holiday in Vienna.

> I shall not see thee. Dare I say
> No spirit ever brake the band
> That stays him from the native land
> Where first he walked when clapst in clay?
> No visual shade of some one lost,
> But he, the Spirit himself, may come
> Where all the nerve of sense is numb;
> Sprit to Spirit, Ghost to Ghost.
> (XCIII, 1–8)

In Memoriam is by no means a difficult or metaphysical composition and there is no especial impression of transcendence, yet, rather, it beautifully represents a sustained and sincere meditation on the theme of human mortality. An unmistakeable tone of nobility, together with a stoic optimism typical of the age, lifts the poem away from any suggestion of melancholic excess. Above all, this was the volume that established Tennyson as the voice of the age.

In Memoriam was not published until 1850, and the absence of Hallam's advice and support markedly reduced Tennyson's poetic activity. Then, in 1842 he published a new *Poems*, which revises and reissues some early verse but also includes his still-popular 'Ulysses'. The great success of *In Memoriam* attracted royal endorsement in the form of his Laureateship and (in 1883) a baronetcy. His later collections are certainly worthy of attention: for example, *Maud and Other Poems* (1855; including the music hall favourite 'The Charge of the Light Brigade') and his enormously popular Arthurian epic, *Idylls of the King* (begun in 1832 and not published until 1859), based on Malory's medieval cycle, *Le Morte d'Arthur*.

Tennyson's verse achieved greater sales than any other poet of the period, and the admiration of his followers respected him both as teacher and as bard. He was – like Browning – heavily influenced and inspired by Keats, especially for his use of rich imagery and sensuous cadences – the latter evidenced in Tennyson's sonorous musicality and his strong commitment to poetic metre. His voice and subjects are also, and characteristically, concerned with a moralistic stance. Like Matthew Arnold later, Tennyson was increasingly conscious of the gathering crisis in religious faith in the face of scientific discovery and social upheaval.

He continued to compose into his 80s, and died in 1892. He is buried alongside Browning in Westminster Abbey.

(ii) *Christina Rossetti* (1830–1894)

Rossetti was the youngest child of a family of prolific artists and poets, (including Pre-Raphaelite painter and poet Dante Gabriel Rossetti). Her father was an Italian political exile who in 1831 became professor of Italian at King's College, London, Christina being fluent in both English and Italian. A devout member of an evangelical strain of the Church of England, she rejected several offers of marriage on the grounds that the religious credentials of her suitors were either too Catholic or too lax. She is remembered for a very pious, retiring life, for example refusing to watch Wagner's *Parsifal* on account of what she deemed its pagan mythology. Unfortunately, her nascent career was repeatedly punctuated by bouts of recurring illness diagnosed variously as tuberculosis and congestive heart failure. However, in spite of this impediment she socialised avidly in her brother's circle of friends, which numbered James McNeill Whistler, Algernon Swinburne and Lewis Carroll.

Rossetti's publication of *Goblin Market and Other Poems* in 1862 was (and remains) immensely popular. Though worldly popularity clashed with her commitment to religious piety, much of her poetic output can be seen in allegorical terms, as moral parables derived from religious stories. For instance, one of her earliest poems, 'Up-Hill', is a fable about the struggle for salvation:

> Does the road wind up-hill all the way?
> Yes, to the very end.
> Will the day's journey take the whole day long?
> From morn to night, my friend.

In her own day, Rossetti was especially acclaimed for her daring experiments in image and form, for instance in 'The Iniquity of the Fathers Upon the Children', which employs dramatic monologue to explore the subject of illegitimate children (she campaigned zealously for the rehabilitation of prostitutes and unmarried mothers). One of her brothers argued that her work was motivated by 'two great powers – religion and affection' and it is true that much of her writing crusades against social injustice. For example, her intensely dramatic lyric 'A Royal Princess', whose royalties were used to relieve deprivation among starving Lancashire mill workers, is a satire on inequality and poverty.

She is admired today, however, for two works above all: her lyrics for the Christmas carol, 'In the Bleak Mid-Winter' and, of course, the highly sensuous *Goblin Market*. The latter vividly demonstrates two other key strands in her work: the Gothic grotesque (eccentric twists of fate involving goblins, ratels, lizards and serpents) along with a ludic mockery, both quirky and trenchant:

> Laura bow'd her head to hear,
> Lizzie veil'd her blushes:
> Crouching close together
> In the cooling weather,

> With clasping arms and cautioning lips,
> With tingling cheeks and finger tips.
> 'Lie close,' Laura said,
> Pricking up her golden head:
> 'We must not look at goblin men,
> We must not buy their fruits:
> Who knows upon what soil they fed
> Their hungry thirsty roots?'

(iii) *Matthew Arnold (1822–1888)*

Poet and critic, Arnold was educated at Winchester, Rugby School (at which his father Thomas was the illustrious reforming headmaster), and Oxford where he enjoyed a distinguished career as university teacher. High-spirited, with a remarkably versatile intellect, Arnold was a fashionably dressed social lion, who in 1851 was appointed inspector of schools. This eminent post was one he was to retain almost to the end of his life and was indicative of the two celebrated themes of his life, culture and education.

Arnold's first published poetry collections were almost entirely ignored at the time – *The Strayed Reveller and Other Poems* in 1849 and *Empedocles on Etna and Other Poems* which was issued in 1852. Although primarily a poet at this time, his *Poems, a New Edition*, printed when he was 31, is noteworthy for its preface in which he set out some of the terms on which he was later to become widely acclaimed as a critic, rejecting allegory as a device and favouring clarity and simplicity of style. As a counter to prevailing attitudes, Arnold was a firm advocate of an impartial and rational basis to literary criticism, his work demonstrating the strong influence of the writings of Wordsworth and Goethe.

His presence as a formidable critical voice emerged strongly following his appointment in 1857 as professor of poetry at Oxford. Over the next four years Arnold published a series of highly influential essays that fixed his reputation as the spokesman of the new liberal humanism – though in truth he seemed less *of* the Victorian world, than hovering above it. The most polemical of these – especially in terms of its lasting impact – was 'The Function of Criticism at the Present Time' published in *Essays in Criticism* (1865).

This essay has carried a most far-reaching sway on twentieth-century literary thought because, for almost the first time, Arnold tackles the issue of the formal role of the critic and the basis of his or her response to literature in a complex *modern* world. The critic is delineated as a member of the elite whose moral duty it is in a time of flux and turmoil to rigorously uphold the ideals of liberal culture (Arnold shared the Victorians' view of 'modern' as a period of crisis arising from the accretion of various inimical historic forces, chiefly scientific and sociological).

Arnold argues that criticism must maintain a position of disinterestedness, remaining aloof from the 'practical view of things'. Nevertheless, he felt passionately that while the creativity of a writer or artist was much more vital than the critical faculty, criticism should be construed as the 'endeavour in all branches of knowledge, theology, philosophy, history, art, science, to see the object as in itself it really is'.

In lots of ways *Essays in Criticism* was profoundly seminal, not least for Arnold himself who further developed its central moral idea, while his focus gradually turned almost entirely from literature to social and theological interests. Inspired by a fervent zeal for bringing culture and criticism to the British middle class, his crusade got under way with the challenging *Culture and Anarchy* in which Arnold launched his central tenet about the role of culture.

He had turned away from conventional religion and, styling himself a Christian humanist (playing down religion's supernatural dimension), he sought to discover – or justify – a new authority to meet and deal with the growing problems of social unrest in western society. He believed that the traditional authority – the Church – was increasingly impotent and its role should be replaced by culture, an authority founded on the belief that mankind is instinctively motivated to do good.

It is clearly a bold enterprise, rooted in a particular definition both of humanity and of culture. His radicalism takes up the influence of the philosopher Thomas Carlyle in terms of his essential trust in the positive nature of man – though he is miles apart from the latter's far-reaching doctrine of the pre-eminence of the supernatural.

Throughout his life, Arnold continued to compose profound and tenaciously original poetry and in particular he is remembered for 'The Scholar-Gipsy',

'Thyrsis' and 'Dover Beach', the latter of which brilliantly evokes, in free form, an ominous foreboding of schism and impending crisis:

> The sea of Faith
> Was once, too, at the full, and round earth's shore
> Lay like the folds of a bright girdle furl'd.
> But now I only hear
> Its melancholy, long, withdrawing roar,
> Retreating to the breath
> Of the night-wind, down the vast edges drear
> And naked shingles of the world.

Browning's Views on poetry

We have noted already the extent to which Browning's essentially unstructured education contributed to his liberal development as a poet. Essentially an autodidact, he was given licence by his father to encounter and cultivate avant-garde ideas. So, for instance, at a time when Shelley's ideas and verse were regarded as at best disreputable, at worst toxic, Browning was left to immerse himself in the idealist poet's neoplatonism and leftist politics.

From an early age he expressed a commitment to writing, first of all for the theatre and then poetry. Yet, even as an established writer he was generally casual in the routines of work, not one (as Tennyson for example) to regulate himself in fixed, timetabled hours of composition. As Elizabeth described it, he waited for the 'inclination'. He was also self-effacing about the worth of his output. To an acquaintance who elevated his work above Elizabeth's he responded, 'You are quite wrong – she has the genius, I am only a painstaking fellow; The true creative process is hers, not mine.'

In addition to the express influence of the Romantic poets, Keats and Shelley especially, plus Shakespeare, literary figures admired by Browning include John Donne, Walter Savage Landor and from the eighteenth century Thomas Chatterton and Christopher Smart. In art and social philosophy, he fell under the sway at different times of the ideas of Ruskin, Carlyle, William Fox and J.S. Mill. Elizabeth herself was of course a primary influence, often providing direct feedback, even to the extent of

Browning needing to redraft his work (as in the case of 'The Laboratory'), and although Browning derided Tennyson's later style it is difficult not to see a poetic interplay of ideas and forms between these two giant figures of the century.

All the same, Browning could never be described as 'mimetic' and he consciously strove after a unique voice. As one aspect of his commitment to objectivity, Browning held that although all writers begin by emulating their trusted favourites, an original voice emerges only when they have discovered a 'moral end and aim ... it creates, and imitates no longer' ('Essay on Chatterton', 1842). While this of course represents a formidable challenge, Browning sought to attain success by recognising that while, on the one hand, his art aspires to the objectivity of science (objective of reception or result), on the other, it is embedded in the everyday reality of men and women ('Andrea del Sarto' and 'Fra Lippo Lippi' are in essence indistinguishable from the people of Victorian London).

The notion of the 'objective poet' is echoed in Browning's celebrated 'Essay on Shelley' of 1852, where he distinguishes this position from the 'subjective poet'. In the latter case, the approach to poetry is inextricably bound up with the reader's apprehension of the biography and feelings for the poet himself or herself. Browning is not speaking here of the poetry itself, but of the poet. The 'subjective poet' is more private in his or her tropes and allusions, mystical, introvert, aspiring to God.

The subjective poet is one who is

> ... impelled to embody the thing he perceives, not so much with reference to the many below as to the one above him, the supreme Intelligence which apprehends all things in their absolute truth, - an ultimate view ever aspired to, if but partially attained, by the poet's own soul.

The objective poet – like the Browning of the dramatic monologues – passes outside of his or her poetry and the work subsists as autonomous, without reference to any causes behind it. By contrast, the work of the subjective poet is intrinsically bound up in the life of the poet himself or herself – so in order to appreciate the writing we must also understand the biography. The 'objective poet' begins and ends in the everyday, making his or her tropes a matter of open public communication. Except in formal contexts, Browning the man of the world always dissociated himself from Browning the poet.

This critical distinction of objective and subjective taps into a pervasive aesthetical attitude which prevailed throughout the later Victorian and early Edwardian eras. It encouraged the growing Victorian cult of the celebrity writer, where the reading public endeavoured to discover the minutiae of their favourite writer's life.

In other words, there was the view that a work is best or only understood through the biography of its author. John Ruskin, pre-eminent Victorian art critic, scorned this attitude, but the distinction of objective and subjective became obsolete only when critics came to regard the literary text as something having a life of its own, independent of the animus behind it.

As a young poet-dramatist, Browning quickly came to distrust contemporary literary critics, men who through journals and newspapers held great sway over Victorian taste, and a writer's career could be won or lost in the magisterial columns of the *Athenaeum*, *Blackwood's* and the *Examiner*. Yet, as such they were impossible to discount, especially so for the struggling Browning, who protested to Elizabeth that the literary press frequently made him feel servile, like a farmer taking produce to market, or a merchant 'brought to the Rialto' (letter of 11 March 1845; *Love Letters* I, p. 18). In another letter he likened them to the night-soil men forever emptying their cart on his front door. In fact the renegade Mayor and Corporation in 'The Pied Piper of Hamelin' can be construed as a metaphor for the despised critics who believed it was they who were to call the tune, at the expense of the artist-piper.

In a letter to Ruskin, Browning defended himself against the critics' charge of ambiguity in his poems. It is difficult today to imagine that contemporaries often found them perplexing but he responded fiercely, arguing that a poet's job is neither to inform nor to teach, 'A poet's affair is with God, to whom he is accountable' (letter, 10 December 1855) and he continues,

> Do you think poetry was ever generally understood - or can be? ... do you believe people understand *Hamlet*?

While firmly committed to realism, Browning did regard poetry as having an important mysterious or even mystical dimension, arguing in the same letter, 'all poetry being a putting of the infinite within the finite'. And at heart he thrilled to the idea of duping the critics and subverting expectations – for instance he delighted in the false lead given in the title of Elizabeth's *Sonnets from the Portuguese*, alluding obtusely to a character rather than the language (Browning acknowledged too of the correlation between the author and the confidence trickster).

This goes some way to explain Browning's liking for masks, for himself as well as his characters. The novelist Henry James – and good friend in later years – remarked on the conspicuous difference between his public and private use of language. His poetry is evidence of Browning's fascination with words and in particular the matching of the idiom and register of each monologue to its character so they come to exist as a unity (almost every character in the poems we have examined has a preoccupation with words; for example, 'My Last Duchess' and 'Caliban Upon Setebos'). At the same time, Browning revels in the experiment of fusing the grotesque in subject with the everyday in language, like Shelley's alchemist, then stepping back to observe the chemical explosion.

Even though Browning was essentially bourgeois in his private affairs, mixing with respectable echelons of society, his sympathies lay with the outsider, even the infamous, and his characters naturally enough reflect this. He claimed to be interested in the 'incidents in the development of the human soul' and it is through rummaging in the psychology of these outcasts and recluses, flawed and disappointed, that he was able to explore themes of art, love, religion and time in order to discover what was in fact ordinary about them and extraordinary in his reader.

With regard to Browning's influence on future generations, Thomas Hardy's poetry employs many similar dramatic monologues – he held Browning's techniques in high regard but baulked at his generally optimistic outlook. Ezra Pound fully acknowledged his admiration for and the influence of Browning in terms of his own form and language, while T. S. Eliot probably owes a great deal to Browning's innovations in the dramatic monologue, clearly manifest in, for example his 'The Love Song of J. Alfred Prufrock'. Browning's monologue techniques have clear links too with James Joyce's work, especially in the latter's development of free indirect speech, which Joyce distilled into the stream of consciousness device in interior monologue. Influence is always a ticklish matter to validate, and perhaps the best we can say is that Browning inspires a mainstream of authors whose devotion to psychological forensics puts him in a direct line with the twentieth century via the work of, for instance, Virginia Woolf, D. H. Lawrence and May Sinclair.

7
A Sample of Critical Views

In this chapter we will be looking first and briefly at some Victorian attitudes to literary criticism and then examining in detail some differing critical responses to Browning's verse in five studies of Browning:

G. K. Chesterton, *Robert Browning* (1903)
Robert Langbaum, *The Poetry of Experience* (1957)
Barbara A. Melchiori, *Browning's Poetry of Reticence* (1968)
E. Warwick Slinn, *Browning and the Fictions of Identity* (1982)
Britta Martens, *Browning, Victorian Poets and the Romantic Legacy* (2011)

As a prominent and prolific poet in the nineteenth century, Browning attracted a massive volume of critical attention even in his own time. The purpose of this chapter is to examine the kind of things that critics have looked at in the poetry and to hint at directions in which study of the poetry can be carried forward.

In Chapter 6 we noted Browning's deep sensitivity to the critics and how he felt a great sense of injustice for the scathing treatment of his earlier, especially theatre, work. In a letter of 11 February 1845 he tried to explain to Elizabeth Barrett (whom he had known for only a few weeks) his 'sensitiveness to criticism' as a way of expressing his trust in her. He sides with Keats and Tennyson in the extent to which they too had suffered harsh censure at the hands of reviewers, dismissing critics as 'hucksters'. In the same letter he modestly adds:

> I never wanted a real set of good hearty praisers - and no bad reviewers - I am quite content with my share.

In his early career Browning was never short of encouraging supporters, surprisingly so given his young age and the raw callowness of his output, particularly for the theatre. Family friend William Johnson Fox (journal editor) and actor-manager William Macready had both invested a great deal of support (and hard cash) in their protégé, though more on the basis of potential than consummate attainment.

Even from the occasion of her first letter to him, Elizabeth is among the first to recognise the quality of his writing – and indeed in large measure this is the foundation of what became their mutual attraction. The period of their marriage is also the time of Browning's most commercially successful lyrical output, especially *Men and Women*, which in lots of ways represents the high-water mark of Browning's reputation during his own lifetime. Browning himself was generally bitterly disappointed with the critical response to his writing, appraising one critic's opinion of his work as 'perversity, carelessness and bad taste'. Negative criticism of his published output regularly generated feelings of despondency over his own 'energy wasted and power misspent'.

Nevertheless, the people who really mattered to him, for example the art theorist John Ruskin, editor Leigh Hunt and the political commentator Thomas Carlyle – all big-hitters and highly regarded – saw in the poetry much to be admired:

> Robert Browning is unerring in every sentence he writes of the Middle Ages; always vital, right, and profound ...
> (Ruskin, *Modern Painters*, 1856)

The most common charge, even by well-disposed critics, was of obscurity. Conversely, William Morris defended him against this accusation on the grounds of the 'shallower brains' of his accusers but also that his 'depth of thought and greatness of subject' demanded a more concentrated form of appreciation (*Oxford and Cambridge Magazine*, 1856).

Browning did not reach anything like a peak of critical fame until the reception of what he came to regard as his magnum opus, *The Ring and the Book*, a murder mystery that eventually saw the light of day in the winter of 1868/9, published in four volumes. The work was a resounding success with both the critics and the public. Even formerly hostile critics now feted

Browning, thrusting him into a limelight he was to monopolise from then until his death. This was the crown of his professional life, a period in which he was at last feted by admiring critics and followers, including the universities – who conferred their honorary titles upon a man who had at last become a household name.

Following his death in 1889, the exaltation of his work fostered the first full-length biography of the poet, compiled by one of his closest friends, Alexandra Sutherland Orr (sister of the artist Frederick Leighton) who had met him in Paris during the winter of 1855/6. Soon after its formation in 1881, Mrs Orr joined the Browning Society, by whom she was encouraged to publish *Handbook to the Works of Robert Browning* (1885), a valuable compendium of facts and dates about the poet's life, to a large extent authorised by him and which eventually evolved into her *Life and Letters of Robert Browning*, based on letters supplied by his sister Sarianna.

Such was the fresh adulation afforded to Browning that, paradoxically, in the aftermath to his death in 1889, there developed something of a critical backlash against his work. Among the most conspicuous of this new hostile battalion was George Santayana whose 1900 essay 'The Poetry of Barbarism' savagely denounced Browning's achievement, though chiefly for what he was not, than for what he was:

> For him the crude experience is the only end, the endless struggle the only ideal, and the perturbed 'Soul' the only organ of truth. The arrest of his intelligence at this point, before it has envisaged any rational object, explains the arrest of his dramatic art at soliloquy. (p. 8)

Santayana's argument is that in order to reveal the essence of a character Browning allows it to speak for itself, leaving the outline on the surface instead of going beyond this (as Santayana would regard it) to view it from above. This viewpoint, he believed, would combine the intelligence of the character with the moral slant of the creative poet, as in a Victorian novel. Santayana is really complaining that we do not know Browning's moral attitude towards, say, the Duke of Ferrara or Andrea del Sarto. To which it could be replied that, on the one hand, it never seems to matter that we do not know, for example Shakespeare's attitude to Othello or Richard III and, on the other, that in real life we usually have to make our own minds up about people, without the need of some higher authority.

G. K. Chesterton, *Robert Browning* (1903)

Santayana's critical ambience is an extension of a tradition associated with Matthew Arnold (see Chapter 6), an attitude to art and literature that harked back to classical Greek aesthetics. This expresses the view that for a work to be successful it must conform to certain rationalised principles and the end to which art must aspire under this system is a preconceived ideal. This model is one in which perfection of reason and ethics are stressed and the affective is suppressed as a harmful irrelevance. It is a view largely outmoded today but it does occasionally rear its head, often with political ramifications.

Santayana's attack was the culmination of a general tendency in the last decade of the nineteenth century to discredit Browning's reputation (this tendency also targeted many of Browning's former associates, including Henry James). However, the writer G. K. Chesterton sought to reverse the trend via one of the first full-length analytical studies of the poet, correlating the life with the poetry: *Robert Browning*, published in 1903 in the *English Men Of Letters* series.

Gilbert Keith Chesterton (1874–1936) is best remembered today – if he is remembered at all – as a fashionable comic novelist, most notably for the Father Brown detective stories. A prolific writer of essays, poetry and fiction, he was also a popular critic and literary biographer of Dickens, Thackeray and Chaucer, among others. I have chosen to examine his study of Browning partly because Chesterton was an early voice striving to reverse the drift in the poet's status, but also because his is typical of a style of criticism widespread in the early twentieth century.

Chesterton's biography is fairly breezy, conventionally identifying some of Browning's poetic characters with people in the poet's own life and clearly owes much to Mrs Orr's earlier recollections.

He sets off rather eccentrically by comforting the reader that Browning was neither Jewish nor looked like a 'negro' (p. 4), then his line of argument becomes slightly muddled by deliberating about other racial groups and aristocrats in order to establish how unimportant these actually are:

> ... Browning was a thoroughly typical Englishman of the middle class. He may have had alien blood, and that alien blood ... may have made him more characteristically a native. (p. 9)

Chesterton is at pains to establish that his subject is reassuringly 'one of us' and this is an important characteristic of his package, and one we will return to. The early chapters are a spirited romp through Browning's development, characterised by broad aphoristic generalisations and seasoned with apocryphal episodes from the life, plus frequent kindly asides embodying Chesterton's chiefly reverential response to them and to the texts.

Among the many features that imbue *Robert Browning* with its charm is the author's fondness for colourfully baroque allusions. Discussing *Paracelsus* in Chapter 1, he contends:

> We call the Chinese barbarians, and they call us barbarians ... (p. 24)
> It is not only true that the medieval philosophers never discovered the steam-engine; it is quite equally true that they never even tried. (p. 25)

As he proceeds, Chesterton is also at pains to apologise for Browning's naivety, or to reinforce his reputation by comparison with other, established Victorian writers, such as Meredith, Dickens and even Wordsworth. Moreover, he enlists the support of contemporary admirers – J. S. Mill, Carlyle, Leigh Hunt among them – in order to bolster or remind the reader of the previously solid reputation of his subject.

Chapter I covers Browning's childhood and youth, which are utilised by Chesterton to exonerate him of the abortive early poetry, chiefly *Sordello* and *Paracelsus*. This chapter sets the tone for the rest of book, a eulogy of Browning, and the whole thrust of his thesis attempts to mythologise or consecrate the man and his work. His aim is to put right the snubs of Santayana and his denouncing crew and so raise Browning into Chesterton's pantheon of great authors.

The second chapter takes up the widespread charge of Browning's incomprehensible obscurity, and that this obscurity was rooted in 'intellectual vanity indulged in more and more insolently as his years and fame increased' (p. 35). Chesterton defends Browning by asserting that he was neither vain nor very much an intellectual, but does concede that the early, longer poems assumed a 'whole load of learning' in the reader. In other words, it was all down to youth and a misjudgement of his reader.

The study moves briskly away from this difficulty to acclaim Browning's 1841 collection:

> *Pippa Passes* is the greatest poem ever written, with the exception of one or two by Walt Whitman, to express the sentiment of the pure love of humanity.
> (p. 43)

Such lavish panegyrics are typical of Chesterton (and his whole era), tending to highly glossed paeans in terms of, for instance, the feelings, style or general political tenor of the text.

With indictments of obscurity still ringing in his ear (and a suspicion that he has failed to dispel them) Chesterton takes great pains to show that the strength of *Dramatic Lyrics* lies in its almost total lack of 'intellectual character'. In doing so he pre-empts the possible slur that Browning's verse is sentimental or emotional, contending that these are in fact the most astonishing elements of human reality.

Chesterton frequently navigates by way of paradox, ironically inviting the charge of 'intellectual vanity' himself:

> ... it is the truest of all love poetry, because it does not speak much about love. (p. 49)
> At a supreme crisis in his life he did something unconventional, he lived and died conventional. (p. 77)

There is an unmistakeable air of Chesterton the *poète manqué* yearning to break through the prose – but there is too a prevailing sense that a critical essay should itself be a work of art, aspiring to match the style of its subject.

On the theme of love, the author has some surprising speculations. One is that Browning chanced upon Elizabeth Barrett while actively casting around for a literary mate, another that Elizabeth 'knew that she had grown up in the house of a mad man'. Chapter III is taken up with the heroic courtship of Browning and Barrett offering genteel observations on the perfect aptness of their union in the face of almost universal discouragement and, of course, the 'evil' Mr Barrett lurks as the convenient villain of this melodrama.

Throughout, Elizabeth is a kind of talented appendage to the real star as 'his wife'. She is by his side, supportive, in an Italy where her husband takes a full interest in the romance of rebellion, and excitement in 'the making of a new nation'. Chapter IV gives a flavour of Browning's own liberal politics: 'he was bound to be a Liberal':

> The world was going right he felt ... (p. 86)

Chesterton himself seems comforted that, once again, Browning is one of us.

The writer does not shy clear of the big issues: 'Poetry deals with primal and conventional things' (p. 99). The word 'conventional' occurs time and again throughout this study and once again Chesterton strives to make clear that while Browning broke new ground in his poetry he is essentially of the middle ground ('domesticated', he declares on p. 101). Browning was intellectual but not excessively so: he observed revolution but did not partake, and he tolerated his wife's spiritualism but only as a kind of parlour game:

> This must always be remembered as a general characteristic of Browning, this ardent and headlong conventionality. (p. 100)

Chapter V rounds off the life with a reminder of the crowning glory of recognition, that at last Browning could savour the fruits of a lifetime's struggle and receive the plaudits of a once-frosty critical community.

In chapters VI and VIII Chesterton sets himself the task of drawing literary and philosophical conclusions about the Browning opus. Firstly, he dismisses the notion that Browning was scientific, that is, precise and analytical. This hinges on the contemporary distinction between science and art, such that to describe a writer as 'scientific' was tantamount to a libellous insult, implying cold calculation, in place of the spontaneous outflow of emotion, recollected in tranquillity expected of an inspired, gifted individual.

The question of what Browning believed to be the function of an artist is raised in chapter VI, to which Chesterton responds by saying it is the 'serious use of the grotesque' (143). Another aspect of the artist function is the creation of rugged beauty, through beautiful language and metre, and endeavouring to capture the craggy energy of real, physical nature, whether of the landscape or of mankind. He repeatedly stresses the ruggedness of Browning's poetry as the route into his psychology. By emphasising this, Chesterton seeks to clinch a final rebuttal of Santayana's charge that

Browning's failure is really a failure to go beyond surface and narrative, in order to derive universal meanings.

Chapter VII's brief discussion of *The Ring and the Book* argues that it was Browning's principle here to show all sides of an issue. Chesterton now summarises the observations of his preceding chapters with the final aim of defending the 'philosophy of Browning'. This is not philosophy in the accepted sense but more nearly what Browning adopted as his maxims in art and life. These include the view that man is essentially incomplete and imperfect, the belief that the universe was, above all, optimistic since it emanated from God, and, given these two modules, human 'existence itself is a good thing that sometimes goes wrong' (181).

The further that we read into his final chapter the more we come to realise that the views of Chesterton and Santayana are actually two sides of the same coin – arguing from different premises about the same object. What Santayana regards as a double deficit in Browning – a failure to formulate an idealised metaphysic and a failure to be morally explicit – is actually for Chesterton the strength of the poet since these 'failures' locate him firmly in the experience of actually lived life.

In contrast to Santayana, Chesterton's robust acclamation of Browning accepts the work not as it ought to be but how it actually is. Yet Chesterton also rejects the idealist, neoclassical position of Santayana that sees so much wrong with Browning on these terms.

Chesterton's study has the distinct merit of laying down many of the key themes that have dominated Browning discussion in the twentieth century. On the other hand, the principal limitation of his approach to literary criticism is fairly typical of his era. Judgements on texts and authors are handed down from a superior, 'expert' position with a reassuring voice of certainty and ostensible even-handedness. However, while this kind of critical approach would claim to disavow any hint of a political stance, it invariably emanates from a narrow political consciousness, namely white, male, Christian, upper middle-class.

As I have indicated above, critics in the early twentieth century considered their task as revealing the extent to which the author and text under consideration embraces or incorporates 'conventional' or orthodox moral and political values, understood as 'proper'. In other words, they tend to find or project onto an author a political image of themselves.

Influenced very much by Matthew Arnold (whom he described as an 'intellectual aristocrat'), Chesterton salutes Browning as a liberal humanist, a repository of humane and progressive principles and attitudes even to the point of ascribing to the poet a higher religious profile than was actually the case. He adopts this faith – which is really a projection of his own strong Christian commitment – to bolster the poet's status, an effort that would strike modern critics as wholly unnecessary.

Although Browning is now much less regarded as an obscure or difficult writer in the way that Santayana and Chesterton felt, these critics continue to exert their influence on Browning criticism in the polemical areas of debate that they instigated. Prominent in each man's mind was the extent to which Browning may be admitted to the canon of British authors, such as Shakespeare, Chaucer, Wordsworth and John Donne. It is a kind of elitism recurrent in early twentieth-century literary criticism.

As a result, Browning's stock has fluctuated enormously throughout the intervening period. The 1930s was one of the crucial periods in literary criticism, one that demonstrated the continuing influence of the traditions established by Arnold and Chesterton. It is fair to say that this has had a substantial and continuing influence on the subject (as well as on the 'canon' of English literature). However, for Browning, it was a period of doldrums, in which the most powerful voice of the period, the Cambridge critic F. R. Leavis, dismissed him as essentially irrelevant:

> ... so inferior a mind and spirit as Browning's could not provide the impulse needed to bring back into poetry the adult intelligence.
>
> (Leavis 1932, p. 20)

The chief problem for Leavis was that Browning was too preoccupied with 'emotions and sentiments'. Worse, Leavis's contemporary William Empson discarded Browning as a poet 'with no lyrical inspiration at all' (Empson 1930, p. 20). T. S. Eliot (a student of Santayana at Harvard) banished Browning from his own personal orthodoxy on the grounds that he was 'longwinded', 'not a philosophical or psychological poet', and one

> ... [whose] knowledge of the particular human heart is adulterated by an optimism which has proved offensive to our time.

'Our time' to which Eliot alluded was that of Modernism, an artistic movement that dominated literary writing in the first half of the twentieth century. But then, with the fading of the Modernist 'school', the roller coaster of Browning's reputation has begun again to follow an upward trajectory, starting in the 1950s and increasingly so in later decades.

Robert Langbaum, *The Poetry of Experience: The Dramatic Monologue in Modern Literary Tradition* (1957; second edition 1985)

When this superb study first appeared in 1957, it was hailed as a major contribution to the discussion of a formal genre and to Browning scholarship in particular. It has never lost its currency in literary debates nor its power to arouse strong feelings about its findings.

In reading the early chapters it quickly becomes apparent that Langbaum's thesis will focus heavily on two concepts prominent in his title, namely 'experience' and 'tradition'. The introduction to the book starts by putting out some preliminary feelers about what the phrase 'modern literary tradition' may mean. He quotes statements about nineteenth-century literature that contradict each other over whether it is a literature that breaks with tradition or conforms with it. In particular he considers these differing attitudes in terms of the tradition of Romanticism.

Langbaum hopes to resolve this paradox by suggesting a continuity between them, that both Modern and Romantic traditions derive from the eighteenth century, or Enlightenment, distinction between fact and value (11). Both the Romantics and Enlightenment poets are interested in arriving at fact, but where the latter insist on a classical, objective or scientific route, the former emphasises personal experience as validation. Both are thus empirical attitudes.

There follows two highly skilful analyses of Wordsworth's 'Tintern Abbey' and Coleridge's 'Frost at Midnight' to assert that it is the personal experience of perception in each that gives validity to the statements they make. To sustain this element of validity the poet must try to retain the sense of personal perspective, a vision that will lend authority to the statements being made.

Crucially, then, the poetry of the nineteenth century is a 'poetry of experience' (p. 35). Experience in literature has validity or authority

> ... because it is dramatised as an event which we must accept as having taken place, rather than formulated as an idea with which we must agree or disagree. (p. 43)

This is important in Langbaum's argument because he wants eventually to say that the dramatic monologue is a genre primarily concerned not with eliciting sympathy but judgement.

Wordsworth showed how a lyric poem could be brought to a dramatic climax through a sudden sharpening of the observer's apprehension of the landscape, amounting to 'a revelation of his own sentience in nature' (42). Following the Enlightenment period a conflict surfaced between thought and emotion in art, and the early Romantic poets attempted to 'heal the breach' by evoking a landscape that gave rise at once to thought and emotion.

Langbaum thinks of this process of evoking an experience as one side of a dialogue, and that the 'poetry of experience' is a new kind of genre which

> ... abolishes the distinction between subjective and objective poetry and between the lyrical and dramatic or narrative genres. (p. 54)

Thus, in the poems of Wordsworth and Coleridge referred to above, there are narrative details but these are assimilated with the lyric elements, that is of the observer's description and his response to it.

This 'poetry of experience', as Langbaum terms it, is characterised by epiphanies for the poet-observer, each poem represents a step towards self-discovery or 'soul'. In this manner the romantic lyric or 'poem of experience' becomes both subjective and objective; the poet

> ... talks about himself by talking about an object; and he talks about an object by talking about himself. (p. 53)

As a reaction to hostile criticism of their early poetry, both Browning and Tennyson (independently of each other) brought the lyric form a step closer towards objectivity in their art by cultivating a pre-existing poetic form that combines the freshness of first-hand account with the possibility of detachment of the poet's own voice.

Langbaum regards this 'poetry of experience' as essentially a dramatic monologue because both lyric and dramatic forms merge within as a 'response from the observer' about 'an imitation of experience'. Both are presented empirically, as a fact existing apart from moral judgement, which remains always secondary and problematical.

What makes Browning's dramatic monologue different from Wordsworth's verse is the conspicuous presence in the latter of moral judgement, whereas Langbaum sees the former's poetry as suspending moral judgement. More contentiously for some readers, the author is less interested in the mechanical elements of dramatic monologue than in its literary or philosophical repercussions. Other critics have spent long arguing about whether a dramatic monologue requires an interlocutor or listener, present or implied, and with some interplay between them. However, Langbaum rejects these as too restrictive and in effect a distraction.

When, in Chapter 2, 'The Dramatic Monologue: Sympathy versus Judgement', Langbaum gets down to detailed analysis it is 'My Last Duchess' that attracts his closest attention. He argues that our response to the poem is chiefly not about condemnation of a cruel duke but about or centred on the form of the poem. Moral judgement of the duke is the 'least interesting response'. What interests us more immensely, the writer suggests, is the duke's wickedness, and we actually admire and participate in Ferrara's power and freedom.

According to Langbaum, the brilliance of Browning's poem is that it forces us to suspend judgement of the duke. We try to understand him before we try to be sympathetic or indignant. He contends that the force and power of the dramatic monologue form relies on a tension between sympathy and moral judgement. Meaning is derived less from any external moral code than from the poetic material itself.

As we have seen in our discussion of 'My Last Duchess', this tension between sympathy and judgement also stimulates the possibility of irony. As a speaker's unmediated viewpoint creates sympathy or empathy by letting us into his or her point of view, irony operates to hold us back and allows us to see the reality of the speaker's character.

Langbaum's analysis devotes much of his book to discussion of Browning's verse, but not exclusively so, and the poetry of Wordsworth, Tennyson, W. B. Yeats and T. S. Eliot also comes in for major treatments, chiefly in order to challenge or generalise his findings.

The strength of his treatise lies in its exploring and teasing out formal elements in a dramatic monologue, both in terms of its evolution from Romantic lyric verse and its dual, subjective/objective, nature. But where he commonly falls down is in applying these conclusions to Browning's poetry.

Whether, in reading 'My Last Duchess' or 'Porphyria's Lover', we actually suspend judgement of the speaker is itself highly problematic. We are never quite wholly drawn into either character's mind, at least not sufficiently to allow any sense of sympathy (however we define it), and the fact that the mind or speech is unmediated is just as likely to make us suspect its veracity. Perhaps the word 'sympathy' is also problematic since what Browning actually achieves is not feelings of pity or sorrow but an inside or dramatic view of a character that feels wholly authentic.

More contentiously, on page 208, Langbaum argues, 'The dramatic monologue is essentially a poem of learning, since more is known at the end than at the beginning ...' . It is true that the dramatic view of a character does permit the reader a greater knowledge of him or her, yet there is more to this. Many critics, while accepting that there is data in this kind of poem, would want to argue that poems are not 'essentially' or even primarily concerned with learning, poems are rarely cognitive adventures (and as T. S. Eliot asserted – a poem often works even before it is understood; 'Dante', 1929: *Selected Essays*).

Sixty years on from its first edition, *The Poetry of Experience* still retains a great power to evoke heated debates about the dramatic monologue and the formal elements of a poem, especially as it touches the complex and dynamic relationship between the reader and the text. As one of the most original and stimulating studies of Browning's methods, it also presents its thesis in a remarkably clear, highly accessible style.

Langbaum's is certainly a pioneering work in its polemical observations but, further, in its conspicuous attempt to ground these in rigorous logical argument and rational aesthetics, it also anticipated the ensuing generation of critical approaches, some of which are discussed below.

Barbara Melchiori: *Browning's Poetry of Reticence* (1968)

Written at a time when literary criticism was in transition, Professor Melchiori's study sets out to investigate Browning's use of masks and his motives for adopting them. The book has no introduction and to discover its aim we have to look in the first and final chapters. In chapter I we are told:

> Some of the tension which lends strength to [Browning's] work arises from the conflict between his wish to guard jealously his own thoughts and feelings, and the pressing necessity he was under to reveal them. (p. 1)

and in her final chapter:

> Browning hid himself behind the masks of his characters, which he tried to objectify in order to remain himself impersonal. It seems legitimate to analyse the associations of Browning's poetic images in order to arrive, as he did himself with the characters he created, at his own nature behind the mask assumed for the sake of that prying audience of readers of which he seems so conscious. (p. 191)

And, between these poles of her book, the nucleus of the study seeks to get behind the mask, behind the reticence to reach, less the concealed personality and private life of the artist than to discover the creative forces at work within him or her.

By the 1960s when this book was published, literary studies had moved away from subjective, unmediated judgements based on vague, received notions of morality and beauty, characterised by Chesterton's approach. This eventually came to be replaced by close textual analysis grounded in theories of, for instance, psychology and psychoanalysis, sociology, linguistics and politics (from these have also developed gender studies, black studies and gay studies). In this new generation of criticism, texts were to be seen less as self-contained or isolated but as the product of a context: the author's psychology, social class and gender, his or her culture, prevailing historical attitudes and in reference to other texts contemporary and historical. The general attitude is that criticism is an open activity, texts likewise, rather than entailing any sense of a quest for definitiveness.

Accordingly, Melchiori is not interested in poems as individually separate, nor is she bent on judging the quality of them (in spite of the title of her opening chapter: 'Browning's Poetry – Good or Bad'). Her overall strategy is twofold: to examine the origins and background sources of Browning's poems, and to trace through them recurrent allusions and images (particularly the theme of 'gold') in order to see how they reveal their symbolic importance for the poet. All of the verse under review is correlated through Browning's final major work, *The Ring and Book*.

Each of Melchiori's core chapters takes in turn an examination of six poems, selected (for the best possible reasons) because she 'liked them and felt curious about them' (188): 'The Bishop Orders His Tomb' (chapter II), *The Ring and the Book* (III), 'Red Cotton Night-cap Country' (IV), 'Holy-Cross Day' (V), 'Childe Roland to the Dark Tower Came' (VI), 'Caliban Upon Setebos' (VII) and 'Fifine at the Fair' (VIII). A series of appendixes applies her process in miniature to the sources of three other poems.

Each poem-chapter delves deep into Browning's respective sources; so, in chapter II Melchiori traces the architectural details of 'The Bishop Orders' to an eighteenth-century Dutch treatise on art by Gerard de Lairesse which Browning was known to have researched for some of the landscape horrors of 'Childe Roland'. Melchiori takes up this literary source in order to disclose the extent of Browning's reproachful assault on the Bishop.

Each chapter taps new background influences and analogues in Browning with the intention of revealing the creative mind behind the mask. For example the author sets out to lay bare connections between the diverse Bible resonances in 'Holy-Cross Day' in order to confirm Browning's Congregationist culture. More important, however, Melchiori asserts that the bitter ironies ranged against the 'claptrap of religion' and the radical interrogation of fundamental doctrines actually represent Browning's own doctrinal crises and doubts about the truths of religion.

In another fine example of forensic analysis, Melchiori's careful examination of 'Childe Roland' entails the task of demonstrating the extent to which the journey there represents Browning's latent fears of artistic failure and defeat, based on a speculation that Roland has actually been *misdirected* by the 'hoary cripple' into seeking the dark tower. In this interpretation the work is transformed into a 'poem of hate' in which Browning expresses the fears that he himself habitually fought against and repressed.

Unfortunately, the critic here offers no evidence for this speculation about Roland being misdirected and the poem itself sustains no such wishful thinking. In a more comprehensive reading it could be argued alternatively that this complex epic is as much concerned with heroism and triumphant success – even, ultimately, optimism again – as with failure. The poem is moreover much occupied with the struggle to engage with the quest itself, and emerges more powerfully for this energy than if we see the poem as a comic swindle.

The other major strand of enquiry in Melchior's analysis is a detailed psychoanalytical examination of some of Browning's recurring allusions and imagery, for which her cornerstone is the work of Sigmund Freud (though she eschews detailed Freudian theory or terminology).

From a more global perspective, the psychoanalytical approach has formal advantages too: along with the obvious appeal of delving into corners of Browning's most intimate secrets via Freudian analysis, this lends the book much of its structural unity. With the central thrust of her study focused on imagery of gold and its manifold associates, chapters III and IV introduce detailed examples of Browning's most trenchant symbolism.

Strenuously stalking down all the poet's word-hoard of 'gold' references and its cognates, Melchiori is at last fired up to her task. Almost all of these instances are the springboard for insights on Browning's innermost psychoses (anal-eroticism, for instance; p. 86) with the result that she finds sexual repression in almost every reference to the word. Among its symbolic derivatives, gold as money is a medium of value exchange and by extension sexual pleasure, but also, in classical psychoanalysis, gold is dung; quoting Freud:

> We know that the gold that the devil gives his paramours turns to excrement after his departure. (p. 80)

Elsewhere, at practically every turn, the critic discovers Freudian implications embodied in his characters – Caliban's fear of hubris projects Browning's terror of divine retribution, Andrea del Sarto's nostalgia for the French court unmasks Browning's own secret yearning for fame, while a description to Elizabeth of a lizard losing its tail intimates a castration complex.

The weakness of *Browning's Poetry of Reticence* is partly the weakness of Freud, or at least of Melchiori's sketchy grasp of his theories (later psychoanalytical criticism adopts a much more thoroughgoing foundation in the subject, inducting rereadings from theorists such as Lacan and Julia Kristeva). A more searching analysis of the grotesque in Browning – mentioned teasingly in Chapter 1 – could have been productive in terms of a Freudian investigation. Although the author notes that Browning was himself an outstanding amateur psychologist, this strand is not fully explored

The book's real strengths lie in the research findings relating to Browning's source materials but, frustratingly, these do not go quite as far they promise. Because each chapter generally focuses on a particular, randomly chosen poem, it is easy to feel that the book is an agglomeration of discrete essays, its opening and closing chapters a belated shot at drawing the whole together.

The limited choice of poems – perhaps a necessary limitation – constrains the degree of success of the critic's psychological endeavour so that eventually we are left with two possible conclusions: either that the case is nowhere convincingly answered or, better, that she turns up nugget-sized shards of a very fertile psychoanalytical field of enquiry, perhaps one for others in the future to quarry.

E. Warwick Slinn, *Browning and the Fictions of Identity* (1982)

As I suggested above, Barbara Melchiori's approach is evocative of a revolution in the conduct of humanities and of literary studies especially, characterised by a new paradigm in textual analysis as one element of a broader cultural matrix. This radical reappraisal gave rise to a profusion of cultural, linguistic and political theories and strategies as bases for analysis.

However, E. Warwick Slinn's is one among several voices that has expressed reservations regarding this mid-century revolution. In particular he fears that an overemphasis on critical theorising runs the risk, in the very act of drawing out the multivalence of texts, of misreadings and invalid obscuranticism: or, put colloquially, of throwing out the baby with the critical bathwater.

In the Preface to his exhilarating and innovative *Browning and the Fictions of Identity*, Slinn sets out the book's 'simple aim' of explaining what Browning meant by 'action in character'. Like Melchiori he focuses on the poet as a psychological dramatist, and thus he is concerned with what he describes as the 'histrionic' in the poetry, that is, the ways in which characters engage in verbal utterances that dramatise themselves. As we would expect, this aim has implications for the dramatic monologue form, and the extent to which a character conceptualises himself or herself, which in turn may give rise to internal conflicts and tension. This latter feature also raises implications for notions of subjective reality and, in particular, the function of linguistic strategies in this.

Typically, Browning's people – evidently at the heart of their own construction – are confronted with a dichotomy inherent in this construction: on the one hand, the seemingly multifaceted appearance and potentiality of experience against, on the other, the 'self-determined fiction of a controlled solipsism' (solipsism, the subjectivist view that the 'I' is the sole existent).

Chapter 1 sets out the starting point that Browning's poetry is mimetic in the sense of imitating 'ways of thinking and speaking about the world' (p. 1). Faced with an apparent anxiety in the nature of collectively held beliefs about objective reality, Victorian poetry increasingly shifts its emphasis from *what* is perceived to the *processes* of perception. Given the growing threat to the existence of a common physical world, Browning's characters can be seen to be trying to internalise order and to replicate the former meaning and processes of the world within their internal discourses. However, Browning goes further and, through what Slinn understands as the artifice of language, questions this reality.

For Slinn, the dramatic monologue as it appears, for example in 'My Last Duchess', is a form that is almost always concerned with the nature of personality and perception. So, 'My Last Duchess' focuses the reader less on themes of Renaissance, insecurity and materialism than on character and consciousness. He develops this idea further by suggesting that, since the perceiver/speaker of the dramatic monologue is engaged in an internal process of self-imaging, this is likely to struggle with the process of his or her thinking about the world.

Crucial to Slinn's overall argument is that this gap, operating within the processes of perception, opens up the possibility of disparity between how a character sees itself and the reality of himself or herself as exposed through irony.

Having set up our conceptual stall, subsequent chapters apply this to individual core poems. Chapter 2 takes on irony in *Pippa Passes*, and

Chapter 3 is 'The Drama of Self-Conception', with particular reference to 'My Last Duchess', where Browning moves away from Romantic forms of lyrical expression more reminiscent of the work of Keats and Shelley. Slinn discovers in Browning's embodiment of linguistic contrivances the fusion of poetry and psychology, so language actually becomes potentially a posture.

The Duke of Ferrara is a familiar example of a personality who projects a persona, in staging a show for the envoy. In 'My Last Duchess' the monologue reveals a drive to show how the duke strives relentlessly to maintain scrupulous control over his life and its contexts, and this drive becomes translated into a constant concern with artefacts; as we have seen, when the duchess threatens to destabilise his control she is turned into an object. Slinn sees language as an integral part of this performance of exuding a sense of order as an essential element of imaging the duke's character. There is a perpetual friction in the two movements: a character's rigorous struggling towards stasis, eliminating the contingencies of life, comes up against its perpetual shaping and reshaping of self-image (Slinn describes this as 'ontological dualism').

'Fra Lippo Lippi', 'Andrea del Sarto' and 'Bishop Blougram's Apology' also come under scrutiny to the extent that each of their monologues demonstrate Slinn's thesis, and this is where the study is at its most compelling. The writer offers a close reading of many of Browning's most difficult poems, and not only the familiar short monologues, but he also leads us through the heavyweight mazes of *Fifine at the Fair* and *The Ring and the Book*. As a result, Slinn presents a compelling validation of his core proposal:

> Browning's art reflects man's capacity for histrionic action, action which underlies an individual's perception of himself, articulating self-consciousness, defining a conception of identity, validating that conception through objectifying it. (p. 74)

Slinn reminds us of the fundamental importance of language in both of these functions. Having set the groundwork of his thesis, he moves on to consider how illusion and irony operate within it. In order to illustrate the role of illusion he discusses Browning's 1872 poem *Fifine at the Fair* which is dominated by the vigour of its speaker, the notorious Don Juan of myth. Through his perennial knack of deceiving, Juan learns to master the art of deception, and so perceive the truth in falsehood. Furthermore, he develops an extraordinary capacity for handling appearances.

The quality of *Fifine*'s texture, Slinn asserts, is the quality of Juan's experience and that experience is inseparable from his flirtation with illusion, issuing from the nature of a pageant. The poem, as well as Juan himself, appears to be constantly striving after some enduring sense of truth amid the disintegrating fragments of the external world:

> The result is an uncertain mixture of tangibility and abstraction, where the tangibility of the scene is continually undermined, frequently by some deliberate verbal strategy. (p. 137)

In fact Juan seems to be the very personification of Slinn's thesis because, more than any other of Browning's characters, he is vividly aware of the interweaving of perception and self-conceptualising. Juan is also acutely conscious of his own predilection for illusion, an adjunct to his persistent simulations as an actor in his own pageants, with their foregrounding of the artifice in language.

Experience for Browning's characters then is more than just involvement in a merely sensory event or set of factual incidents. Slinn summarises and clarifies by stating that experience assimilates personal awareness, the interpretation of physical data or the value attached to sensation. Above all, experience, for the speaker of the dramatic monologue, is the awareness that the self interacts with his or her surroundings so that they come to be aware of the change in themselves.

The thesis of *Browning and the Fictions of Identity* is essentially a relatively simple one and its author addresses his exciting proposition in a lucid, non-technical language. That said, by the nature of its central themes – of psychology and epistemology – there will always be the risk of becoming overwhelmed in definitions of the ephemeral – as Slinn appears to do in the final chapter regarding the term 'experience'. But by and large he steers well clear of these traps and in fact his wrestling with the ephemera of mind, transcendent conscious and self-reflexive conceptualisation of character presents thrilling possibilities of a more full-scale treatment of 'action in character'.

In this economic and densely argued study, Slinn never loses sight of his major theme and amply proves his argument. On the other hand, while he presents to us superlative instances of irony in the poetry, Slinn's theory of irony is not quite fully developed, and it would have been a valuable enhancement to learn more of the role of the interlocutor or the imaginary listener, in the understanding of this most essential of Browning techniques.

Britta Martens, *Browning, Victorian Poets and the Romantic Legacy: Challenging the Personal Voice* (2011)

Britta Marten's study of Browning is a subtly nuanced, scholarly work, written in a clear prose style, in which she sets out to prove one thesis by way of (partially) disproving another. Put baldly, she sets out – and largely succeeds – in demonstrating the importance of Browning's lyric poetry in his process of distilling the author out from his work. In the words of the book's preamble:

> Browning deploys varied dramatic methods of self-representation, often critically and ironically exposing the biases and limitations of the seemingly authoritative speaker 'Browning'.

To achieve this aim, she ventures to affirm that while this is a core feature of the dramatic monologues, it is evident (in varying degrees) in the corpus of his other, relatively neglected verse.

Although he sought to erase all traces of his youthful poetic life, the early *published* writing reveals Browning reviewing his early poetics, and attempting to understand what initially attracted him to Romanticism, a process that Martens sees as essentially typical of the Romanticist position. At the same time this review is the start of Browning's attempt to reject the influence of the texts of his youth. To pursue an examination of the tension between these two drives, Martens focuses on Browning's earliest publications, *Pauline* and *Pippa Passes*, which she interprets as transitional texts, part Romantic confession, part dramatic performance.

The book is organised chronologically, and after these early poetic works the author moves on in Chapter 2 to discuss *Sordello*, which she argues has affinities with the much later *The Ring and the Book*. One reason why the earliest surviving works can be considered transitional is what Martens believes is Browning's own explicit decision not to break radically from tradition, on the grounds that his likely readership would reject the radical shifts that he may have been considering. Thus in texts such as *Sordello* there is still a noticeable strand of self-referentiality, even while he is refashioning his younger self behind the mask of a *persona*. And it is this latter feature that is more fully fleshed out in *The Ring and the Book*, the nucleus of Chapter 5.

Martens describes *Sordello* as a 'fictionalised document of the poet's development towards a new poetics' (p. 51). She fleshes out this idea by recognising in this text a syncronicity of three overlapping selves: the hero as Browning's own youngest self, the narrator as the next phase towards an impersonal poetics, the author himself signifying the most advanced phase in this progression. Moreover, she sees this poem as a broadside, announcing Browning's liberation from the pull of Shelley, but also from the persuasive power of Keats and Wordsworth, among others.

Thus, Sordello is a crucial moment for Browning, indicating a repudiation of introspection, the idolatrous 'cult of the self'. Browning's writing post-*Sordello* – published in 1840 – is widely depicted as resolutely impersonal but Martens argues that this is an essential step too in the poet's incorporation of a humanitarian ideal. Ironically, however, this does still necessitate some degree of self-conceptualisation and to a large extent Browning continues to understand the role of the poet as the ultimate origin of literary meaning.

To the extent that Elizabeth Barrett's work displays a close and complex affinity with Romanticist poetics, Browning's meeting with her marks a more implicit encounter with the Romantic tradition that he had striven hard to renounce. Nevertheless, Martens claims that her poetry displays the significant influence of Browning in moving towards the dramatic monologue as an alternative to the authoritative voice of Romantic verse (as manifested in the role of the artist as visionary oracle). At the same time she also argues that Barrett's chief energies were directed onto challenging the male gendering of the Romantic voice. Their professional relationship is characterised as a tension between her preference for subjectivity and his own objectivity, a tension that Browning employed in his renewed struggle to effect self-definition.

Chapter 4 is in some ways the climax of Martens's brilliantly argued and illustrated treatise. In it she articulates the problems facing Browning's difficult struggle towards originality of vision. One of these is the sheer originality of his style – the demands that are placed on the reader made his verse appear obscure and inaccessible. Another is his casting-off of the Romantic role of the poet as societal spokesman. Inevitably connected with these positions is the archetypal poetic form of the Romantics, the lyric, through which a poet appeared to converse directly with the reader.

In her penultimate chapter, deploying examples from *The Ring and the Book*, Martens uncovers Browning's central problem in this text, together with his battery of strategies: a struggle to reconcile readers who had now come to regard literature as essentially fiction with those who still held to the Romantic concept of the poet as oracle, conduit of transcendental truths. Martens concludes that this experimental text is not only an extremely radical leap for Victorian poetry but, with regard to the poem's multi-perspectivism, it even anticipates postmodern theoretics. Like Wilkie Collins's best-selling novels (*The Moonstone* and *The Woman in White*), Browning's best-selling *The Ring and the Book* decentres and effectively subverts ideas of a narrator, the authoritative voice so indicative of the Romantic lyric, and Browning's bugbear.

Martens characterises Victorian poetic taste as consumed with ideals of sincerity, self-expression and accessibility. She sees the 1870s as a period when Browning witnessed the ascendancy of a new generation of poets who either harked back to Romantic models or were intent on taking facets of Romantic poetics to new extremes. At a time of Browning's struggle to diminish the profile of the self-expressive author, she identifies a new challenge for Browning in the rise of the cult of the author. Readers were becoming increasingly interested in their author, and publishers sought to capitalise on this new avenue of marketing.

Although Martens is at pains to reveal how Browning was caught in a maelstrom of competing forces, involving internal and external pressures – stemming from loyalty to both his own poetics and the new dynamics of the marketplace – she paints a picture in which Browning's struggle is one essentially constrained and personal. This is evidenced in the extent to which the nascent generation is heedless of his radical experimentation and instead casts back to Romanticism, but in a perfunctory and desultory emulation of its heroes.

Martens' is a landmark study in at least two directions: it marks – after a hiatus of some years – a renewed academic interest in Browning as a fitting subject for full-length studies, and it also challenges a long-held orthodoxy that the dramatic monologues are fundamentally separate from the rest of the corpus. Focusing on the poems in which Browning speaks in his own voice, and excluding the dramatic monologues, Martens skilfully demonstrates that he adopts a technique quite similar to that of the monologues. In other words, even though adopting the lyric form, Browning pursues the same goal of undermining the special, privileged Romantic role of the poet, a legacy of the subjectivist poets of the Wordsworth and Shelley generations.

Although delivered in a fully accessible discourse, Martens's work acknowledges the complexity of Browning himself and even where she successfully asserts her thesis she recognises the slippery nature of the poet's irony and self-satire, which requires caution in all our readings. As a landmark resurrection of Browning, drawing out his complications and contradictions, avoiding the temptation of reductive readings, Martens's book excites new questions not only in terms of theories of Browning's self-effacement but also in terms of the evolution of Victorian poetics as a whole.

(Fuller publishing details of these and other recommended critical titles can be found in the Further Reading list at the end of the book.)

Glossary of Literary Terms

alliteration This is a technique in which consonants are repeated usually in close proximity (compare assonance).

anthropomorphism Not an exclusively literary term, this is a tendency of a character to attribute human characteristics, personalities or thoughts to animals, gods and even inanimate objects; see 'Caliban Upon Setebos'.

assonance The repetition of vowel sounds usually close together to create certain sound effects, and at the ends of lines of a stanza to create a **rhyme scheme**; Browning often adopts this device to draw attention to key lines and phrases (compare alliteration).

Bildungsroman This German word refers to a poem or other literary work that portrays a young person growing up.

blank verse See metre.

caesura (plural **caesurae**) Short break(s) inserted in a line of poetry, often but not always indicated by punctuation mark (for example a comma or semicolon); Browning commonly employs these in poems where he is trying to emulate the rhythms or non-fluency features of everyday speech.

dialectic This is not an exclusively literary expression, but it refers to a method of reasoning or logical argument. Typically it describes a process in which a proposition is made, that is then countered by another, resulting in a third proposition that is a revised version of the first. Many of Browning's poems and characters employ this process during conversation and interior monologue; for example see 'Fra Lippo Lippi', 'Bishop Blougram's Apology' and 'Caliban Upon Setebos'.

dramatic monologue (see also Chapter 7's notes on Robert Langbaum) This is a poem in the form of direct speech given by a single character usually to a listener present to him or her. In its most fully developed form it is particularly associated with Browning, who took the genre to a new high level of sophistication. While the poet composes the speech, chooses the words and all other formal aspects of the poem, the views and feelings of the poet are not explicitly present in the monologue – unlike in, say, a lyric – and so it is not possible to identify the views of the character with the poet, who may thus use the character as a mask. Although very much in vogue in the Victorian period with Browning and Tennyson, the dramatic monologue has a long pedigree and we could include within its compass Milton's 'Lycidas' and even Chaucer's *The Canterbury Tales*.

end-stopped line A line of poetry with a strong pause at its end.

enjambement In poetry where a sentence, phrase or idea continues without stop from one line to the next or from one stanza to the next.

grotesque In literature this term refers to the use of extravagant, incongruous, ugly, even hideous settings, language, character or plot, often for outrage, satire and comic effects. Browning was very fond of this device and good examples are in 'The Laboratory', 'My Last Duchess' and 'Porphyria's Lover'.

in medias res A method of beginning a narrative in the midst of events that have already begun before a text opens. For instance, the start of 'Childe Roland to the Dark Tower Came' and 'The Patriot'.

litotes This is an understatement used to create emphasis (for example 'Paris is no small city').

metre This refers to the rhythmic patterns of syllables in a line of poetry. Such patterns are arranged in units usually of two or three syllables. An **iambic** unit contains two syllables, one unstressed followed by one stressed, forming a *di-dah, dih-dah* rhythm; for example 'defeat', 'return', 'today'. A **trochaic** unit is the reverse of iambic, being a stressed syllable followed by an unstressed (*dah-di, dah-di*); for example 'listen', 'golden', 'Browning'. A **dactylic** unit consists of three syllables, a stressed one followed by two unstressed (*dah-di-di*) as in 'merrily' 'hopefully', 'Jessica'. An **anapaestic** unit is the reverse of a dactylic, containing two unstressed syllables followed by a stressed (*di-di-dah*), for example 'comprehend', 'manifest', 'Bucharest'. There are technical terms too for the number of units in a line of poetry. For instance, iambic **pentameter** consists of five iambic units in a line, as in the example, 'So petty yet so spiteful! All along' (from 'Childe Roland', line 115). A poem composed in iambic pentameter with lines that do not rhyme is said to be in **blank verse. Tetrameter** refers to a line of poetry with four metrical units in it: 'The rain set early in tonight' ('Porphyria's Lover', line 1) contains four iambic units.

naturalistic fallacy (sometimes referred to as **pathetic fallacy**) This is a device employed in literature (and very common in cinema) in which the natural landscape, weather or animals are arranged to reflect moods or feelings or events in the human sphere. Good examples are found in 'The Patriot' and 'Childe Roland to the Dark Tower Came'.

quatrain A stanza consisting of four lines.

quintet A stanza consisting of five lines; see, for example, 'The Patriot'.

synecdoche This is a figure of speech in which a part of something stands for the whole. For example the 'grey suits' refers to business men or women, 'fifty head' means fifty animals, 'all hands on deck' refers to sailors.

rhyme scheme This term refers to notation applied to the pattern of rhymes in line endings of a stanza. The pattern is normally indicated through alphabetic notation, so in 'The Patriot' the rhyme scheme of the first stanza is ABABA, corresponding to the end words: 'way', 'mad', 'sway', 'had', 'day'; the second stanza has new rhymes and is CDCDC, and so on.

Further Reading

Poetry texts

Browning, Robert, *Men and Women* (Oxford, Oxford University Press, 1911)
Browning, Robert, *Selected Poems*, edited by Daniel Karlin (London, Penguin Books, 2004)
Browning: Selected Poems, edited by John Woolford, Daniel Karlin and Joseph Phelan (Harlow, Longman, 2010)

Biographical

Finlayson, Iain, *Browning, A Private Life* (London, Harper Collins, 2004)
New Letters of Robert Browning, edited by William Clyde DeVane (London, John Murray, 1951)
The Love Letters of Robert Browning and Elizabeth Barrett Browning (London, John Murray, 1899)

Critical works

Armstrong, Isobel (ed), *Robert Browning: Writers and Their Background* (London, G. Bell and Sons, 1974)
Bailey, Suzanne, *Cognitive Style and Perceptual Difference in Browning's Poetry* (London, Routledge, 2010)
Ball, Patricia M., 'Browning's Godot' (*Victorian Poetry*, Volume 3, No 4, Autumn 1965, pp. 245–253)

Bloom, Harold, *The Ringers in the Tower: Studies in Romantic Tradition* (Chicago, IL, University of Chicago Press, 1971)
Bristow, Joseph, *Robert Browning* (London, Harvester Wheatsheaf, 1991)
Chesterton, G. K., *Robert Browning* (London, Macmillan, 1903)
DeVane, William Clyde, *A Browning Handbook* (2nd edition, New York, NY, Appleton-Century-Crofts, 1955)
Flowers, Betty S., *Browning and the Modern Tradition* (London, Macmillan, 1976)
Gridley, Roy, *Browning* (Routledge Author Guides; London, Routledge and Kegan Paul, 1972)
Hawlin, Stefan, *The Complete Critical Guide to Robert Browning* (London, Routledge, 2002)
Jack, Ian, *Browning's Major Poetry* (Oxford, Oxford University Press, 1973)
Karlin, Daniel, *Browning's Hatreds* (Oxford, Oxford University Press, 1993)
Langbaum, Robert, *The Poetry of Experience: The Dramatic Monologue in Modern Literary Tradition* (1957; 2nd edition, Chicago, IL, University of Chicago Press, 1985)
Litzinger, Boyd and Donald Smalley (eds), *Browning: The Critical Heritage* (London, Routledge & Kegan Paul, 1970)
Litzinger, Boyd and K. L. Knickerbocker, *The Browning Critics* (Lexington, KY, University of Kentucky Press, 1965)
Martens, Britta, *Browning, Victorian Poets and the Romantic Legacy* (Farnham, Ashgate Publishing, 2011)
Melchiori, Barbara, *Browning's Poetry of Reticence* (Edinburgh, Oliver & Boyd, 1968)
Miller, J. Hillis, *The Disappearance of God: Five Nineteenth-Century Writers* (Cambridge, MA, Harvard University Press, 1963)
Pollock, Mary Sanders, *Elizabeth Barrett and Robert Browning: A Creative Partnership* (Aldershot, Ashgate, 2003)
Raymond, William O., *The Infinite Moment and Other Essays in Robert Browning* (Toronto, ON, University of Toronto Press, 1950)
Santayana, George, 'The Poetry of Barbarism' (1900; reprinted in Litzinger and Knickerbocker 1965)
Slinn, E. Warwick, *Browning and the Fictions of Identity* (London, Macmillan, 1982)

Slinn, E. Warwick, *The Discourse of Self in Victorian Poetry* (London, Macmillan, 1991)
Wood, Sarah, *Robert Browning: A Literary Life* (Basingstoke, Palgrave, 2001)
Woolford, John (ed), *Robert Browning in Contexts* (Winfield, IL, Wedgestone Press, 1998)
Woolford, John and Daniel Karlin, *Robert Browning* (London, Longman, 1996)

On specific poems

Armstrong, Isobel, 'Browning's "Caliban" and Primitive Language' (in Woolford 1998)
Gray, Erik, '"Out of me, out of me!": Andrea, Ulysses, and Victorian Revisions of Egotistical Lyric' (*Victorian Poetry*, Volume 30, No 4, 1998, pp. 417–430) (reprint in Norton edition)
Houghton, Esther, 'Reviewer of Browning's *Men and Women* Identified' (*Victorian Newsletter*, No 33, Spring 1968, p. 46)

General and background reading

Apuleius, *The Golden Ass* (London, Heinemann, 1915)
Aristotle, *The Poetics*, translated by Malcolm Heath (Harmondsworth, Penguin Books, 1996)
Bristow, Joseph (ed), *The Cambridge Companion to Victorian Poetry* (Cambridge, Cambridge University Press, 2000)
Browning, Elizabeth Barrett, *Aurora Leigh and Other Poems*, edited by Cora Kaplan (London, The Women's Press, 1978)
Desmond, Adrian and James Moore, *Darwin's Sacred Cause: Race, Slavery and the Quest for Human Origins* (Harmondsworth, Penguin Books, 2010)
Eliot, T. S., *Selected Essays* (London, Faber and Faber, 1932; 3rd edition, 1951)
Eliot, T. S., *The Letters of T. S. Eliot Volume One: 1898–1922*, edited by Valerie Eliot (London, Faber and Faber, 2009)
Empson, William, *Seven Types of Ambiguity* (London, Chatto and Windus, 1930)

Flint, Kate, *The Victorians and the Visual Imagination* (Cambridge, MA, Cambridge University Press, 2000)
Hoppen, K. Theodore, *The Mid-Victorian Generation 1846–1886* (Oxford, Oxford University Press, 2003)
Keats, John, *The Complete Poems*, edited by John Barnard (3rd edition, London, Penguin Books 1988)
Leavis, F. R., *New Bearings in English Poetry* (London, Chatto and Windus, 1932)
MacNiece, Louis, *The Dark Tower and Other Broadcast Plays* (London, Faber and Faber, 1967)
Malory, Thomas, *Works* (2nd edition, London, Oxford University Press, 1971)
Vasari, Giorgio, *The Lives of the Artists*, translated by Julia Conaway Bondanella (Oxford, Oxford University Press, 2008)
Watson, J. R. (ed), *Browning: Men and Women and Other Poems: A Casebook* (Basingstoke, Palgrave Macmillan, 1974)
Wordsworth, William and Samuel Taylor Coleridge, *Lyrical Ballads*, edited by R. L. Brett (2nd edition, London, Routledge, 1991)

Interesting websites

www.browningguide.org
www.browningsociety.org
www.victorianweb.org
University of Oxford text archive: www.ota.ox.ac.uk

On YouTube it is possible to listen to a (very) scratchy recording of Browning reciting his own poem 'How they Brought the Good News from Ghent to Aix' (1889 Edison Cylinder).

Literary journals

Studies in Romanticism (Boston University Press)
Victorian Literature and Culture (Cambridge University Press)
Victorian Poetry (West Virginia University)
Victorian Studies (Indiana University Press)

Index

'Andrea del Sarto', 80, 83, 94, 98–117, 118, 127, 129, 130, 139, 140, 142, 151, 181, 197, 211, 216, 232
Aristotle, 82
Armstrong, Isobel, 36, 184
Arnold, Matthew, 164, 203, 206, 208–10, 217, 222
art, 5, 7, 9, 21, 22, 50, 98, 102–3, 144

Bible, The,
　New Testament, The, 54, 75, 79, 84, 89, 92, 124, 147, 148, 166
　Old Testament, The, 148, 161, 166, 170, 175, 177, 178, 182
Blake, William, 83, 159, 201
Barrett, Elizabeth, xiii, 37, 94, 97, 142, 143, 192, 194–9, 203, 210–11, 212–3, 214, 219, 235
Bells and Pomegranates (1841), 194, 219
'Bishop Blougram's Apology', 34, 35, 36, 153–68, 185, 197, 238
'Bishop Orders His Tomb at St Praxed's Church, The', 94, 110, 117, 128, 129, 143–53, 185, 228, 232
Browning, Robert,
　letters, xi, 37, 93, 153, 174, 212, 216
　life 3, 43, 53, 71, 79, 97, 118, 141–2, chapter 5

poetic techniques (*see also* 'dramatic monologue') 7, 20, 21, 23, 26, 28, 29, 30, 32, 36, 48–9, 55, 56, 63, 67, 69, 73, 74, 78, 79, 80, 83, 85, 90, 91, 95–6, 103, 104, 115, 118, 136, 137–9, 144, 148, 152 -3, 155, 157, 185, 215–40 *passim,* 238–40 works, *see* titles of individual works
Byron, George Gordon (Lord), xii, 84, 189, 191, 203
Bunyan, John, 54

'Caliban Upon Setebos', 69, 81, 166, 168, 204, 213, 228, 229, 238
Carlyle, Thomas, 193, 209, 210, 215
Chatterton, Thomas, 210, 211
Chesterton, G. K., 214, 217–23
'Childe Roland to the Dark Tower Came', 53–70, 71, 73, 77, 78, 89, 94, 107, 142, 151, 155, 161, 178, 184, 197, 204, 228, 229, 239, 240
Coleridge, Samuel Taylor, xii, 21, 53, 68, 83, 189, 191, 201, 204, 223, 224
　'Kubla Khan', 53
　Rime of the Ancient Mariner, The, 22, 53, 68

Dante, 54
Darwin, Charles, 168, 174, 179, 183, 184

Da Vinci, Leonardo, 104, 110
Dickens, Charles, 189, 217, 218
Dramatic Lyrics (1842), 23, 194, 219
dramatic monologue, 4, 7, 30–1, 33, 35,
    47, 48–9, 50–1, 52, 58, 59, 69, 76, 84,
    96, 100, 106, 109, 117, 137–8, 146,
    153, 173, 211, 213, 223–6, 239
Dramatis Personae (1864), 168, 198

Eliot, George, 129, 203
Eliot, T.S., 58, 213, 222, 226
'Essay on Shelley', 53, 92, 192, 197, 211–12

Fifine at the Fair, 228, 232–3
Finlayson, Iain, 35, 184
Flowers, Betty S., 62
Flowers, Eliza, 190, 191
Fox, William Johnson, 142, 191, 193,
    210, 215
'Fra Lippo Lippi', 81, 98, 101, 105, 116,
    117–39, 142, 143, 144, 150, 151, 161,
    211, 232, 238
Frew, Jessica, xiii, 239

Golden Ass, The, (Apuleius) 124
grotesque, 17, 32, 37, 40, 50, 61, 178,
    230, 239

Hawlin, Stefan, 35, 181
'Holy Cross Day', 186, 228
'How they Brought the Good News from
    Ghent to Aix', xi, 244
humanism, 127, 128, 131, 132, 134, 150

imagination, 8, 22, 31, 47, 59, 66, 68,
    81, 11, 112, 116, 122, 139, 159, 200,
    201
Italy, 4, 71, 79, 97–9, Chapter 3 *passim*,
    190, 191, 196–7, 206

Jack and the Beanstalk, 54
James, Henry, 213, 217

Jesus Christ, 55, 75, 58, 79, 89, 124, 132,
    147, 151
'Johannes Agricola in Meditation', 23, 25
Joyce, James, 153, 172, 213
Judas Iscariot, 79, 84, 133, 134

Karlin, Daniel, 137, 167
Kenyon, John, 98, 194

'Laboratory, The,' 37–49, 58, 117, 151, 161,
    178, 204, 210, 239
Landor, Walter Savage, 197, 210
Langbaum, Robert, 22, 69, 214,
    223–6
'Lost Leader, The', 54, 82–94, 95, 98, 105
'Love Among the Ruins', 51, 53, 88

Macready, William Charles, 193, 194, 215
Martens, Britta, 214, 234–7
mask, 12, 13, 14, 17, 33, 38, 42, 45, 46,
    48, 67, 77, 86, 121, 126, 152, 213,
    227, 228, 235, 239
materialism, 16, 18, 41, 42, 46, 80, 84, 87,
    93, 115, 117, 128, 129, 131, 144, 148,
    150, 152, 164, 201, 203
Melchiori, Barbara, 117, 165, 214,
    227–30
Men and Women (1855), 4, 88, 97, 98, 109,
    126, 153, 165, 196–7, 198, 215
metre, 27, 45, 50, 68, 78, 80, 86, 152,
    239–40
Michelangelo, 104, 113, 116, 126
Mill, John Stuart, 193, 201, 210, 218
'Mr Sludge, "the Medium",' 94, 168, 197
'My Last Duchess', 4–22, 23, 29, 30, 35,
    42, 48–9, 80, 81, 97, 98, 110, 117,
    143, 151, 153, 162, 181, 213, 216, 225,
    226, 231, 232, 239

nature, 23–4, 25, 59, 61, 62, 67, 78,
    169–83
Newman, John Henry, 143

'Old Pictures in Florence', 97, 105, 140
'One Word More', 97, 126
Orr, Alexandra ('Mrs'), 216, 217
Oxford Movement, The, 143, 154

Paracelsus, 54, 193, 218
'Patriot, The', 70–82, 86, 88, 94, 96, 105, 136, 142, 161, 197, 239, 240
Pauline, 191, 192, 234
'Pied Piper of Hamelin, The', xi, 96, 105, 212
'Pippa Passes', 219, 231, 234
Plato, 128, 150
'Popularity', 97, 105
'Porphyria's Lover', 23–37, 42, 47, 48–9, 109, 111, 142, 151, 178, 226, 239
Pygmalion, 20

Rafael, 104, 110, 116, 126
religion, 34–5, 36, 41, 42, 44, 55, 64, 71, 75, 79, 80, 89, 93, 105, 110, 112, 118, 120–8, 131–8, Chapter 4 *passim*, 190, 192, 201, 206, 208–10, 222
renaissance, 11, 98, Chapter 3 passim, 143, 144, 150, 231–2
Ring and the Book, The, 198, 215, 221, 232, 234, 235, 236
romanticism, xii, 25, 83, 90, 92, 200–4, 223, 226, 232, 235–7
Rossetti, Christina, 203, 206–8
Rousseau, Jean-Jacques, 183, 210
Ruskin, John, 118, 143, 197, 201, 210, 212, 215

Santayana, George, 216, 217, 220, 221, 222
science, 38, 40, 41, 42, 45, 46, 49, 164, 168, 175, 201–2, 206, 209, 211, 220, 223
Shakespeare, William, iv, 44, 53, 79, 107, 156, 164, 169, 210, 216, 222
 Coriolanus, 79
 Hamlet, 107

King Lear, 53, 174
Macbeth, 44
Tempest, The, 168–84 *passim*
Shelley, Mary, 43, 191
 Frankenstein, 43, 191
Shelley, Percy Bysshe, 53, 84, 92, 142, 189, 191–4 *passim*, 197, 203, 210, 213, 231, 235, 237
Slinn, E. Warwick, 214, 230–4
Smart, Christopher, 201, 210
Sordello, 4, 193, 218, 235
Spenser, Edmund, 54
Stigand, William, 17
stornello (folk song), 125, 137
Strauss, David, 154, 169

Tennyson, Alfred, 118, 197, 203, 204–6, 210, 211, 214, 225, 226, 239
time, 9, 25, 26–7, 29, 39, 60, 66, 76, 109, 126, 138, 144–5, 147, 150, 151, 159
Tractarian Movement, The, (*see* Oxford Movement, The)

Vasari, Giorgio, 98, 118
Vernon Lee, 93
Victorian literature, 25, 41, 43, 47, 87, 92, 179, 197, 201, 202–10, 212, 214, 216–23 *passim*

Wilson, John, 36
Wiseman, Nicholas, 153–5 *passim*
women, depiction of, 7, 20, 30, 33, 40, 42, 44–5, 50, 51, 102, 107, 109–11, 115, 117, 123, 138–9, 149
Woolf, Virginia, 153, 195, 213
Woolford, John, 36, 53, 93, 167
Wordsworth, William, xii, 83–4, 87, 89, 90, 91, 93, 94, 159, 182, 189, 201, 208, 218, 222–6 *passim*, 237
 Lyrical Ballads, 83–4

www.ingramcontent.com/pod-product-compliance
Ingram Content Group UK Ltd.
Pitfield, Milton Keynes, MK11 3LW, UK
UKHW021909220326
469204UK00009B/273